D0899213

The Very Narrow Bridge

The Very Narrow Bridge

A Memoir of an Uncertain Passage

Erwin Schild

Adath Israel Congregation/Malcolm Lester

National Library of Canada Cataloguing in Publication Data

Schild, Erwin, 1920–
    The very narrow bridge : a memoir of an uncertain passage

Includes index.
ISBN 0-9696226-1-9

1. Schild, Erwin, 1920– – Childhood and youth. 2. Holocaust, Jewish (1939–
1945) – Germany – Personal narratives. 3. Jews – Germany – Biography. 4.
Holocaust survivors – Canada – Biography. 5. Rabbis – Canada – Biography.
I. Adath Israel Congregation. II. Title

DS135.G5S34 2001   940.53'18'092   C2001-930565-6

Produced for Adath Israel Congregation by Malcolm Lester

BOOK DESIGN: JACK STEINER

Printed and bound in Canada

01 02 03 3 2 1

I dedicate my memoir
to the murdered friends and companions of my youth
who could not cross the very narrow bridge

They answer still
the silent roll call in my grieving heart

"Jacob made himself like a bridge, picking up on one shore and putting down on the other."
(RASHI ON *GENESIS* 32:4)

"The whole world is but a very narrow bridge."
(HASIDIC SAYING ATTRIBUTED TO RABBI NACHMAN OF BRATSLAV)

Contents

Acknowledgements

Whom do I want to thank for *The Very Narrow Bridge?*

First of all, my family: children, grandchildren, nephews, nieces, and cousins. It bothered several members of the younger generation that their knowledge of family origins was hazy and deficient. They wanted to know more about the past and the circumstances that led the Schild family and their relatives from their home in Germany to a new world. I also wrote for my friends who know but scraps of my personal history and whom I wanted to know me better. All deserve my thanks for motivating me.

The gentle urgings of Laura, my patient wife, led me many times back to the computer keyboard when other commitments had forced me to put my memoirs aside for weeks and months. She did not complain when the project stretched over several years and encroached on our time together.

That my memoirs became a full-fledged book I owe to the interest and financial participation of Adath Israel Congregation of Toronto, whom I served as Senior Rabbi from 1947 to 1989, and since then as Rabbi Emeritus. I would like to thank their executive officers and board of governors. Special thanks are due to the two gentlemen who were delegated to the project: Avrom Brown, the synagogue treasurer, faithful, dependable, and generous, and David Feldman, a past president, whose artistic taste and expertise in graphic design provided an extra bonus.

For the efficient production of the book and its beautiful appearance I would like to thank Malcolm Lester, who assumed responsibility and control for its publication from manuscript to the finished book. It was a reassuring privilege for me as author to entrust my work to such competent hands. I would like to thank my editor, Andrea Knight, for applying her literary taste to my manuscript with such gentle understanding and sensitivity. She was thorough, efficient, generous, and kind.

My thanks go to Beatrice Solomon, my loyal and devoted co-worker for so many years. She read the manuscript repeatedly at various stages in its development, helped me with her critique, and reassured me with her enthusiastic comments.

Irene Corbach, in Cologne, and my sister-in-law, Beckie Schild, read the manuscript and enhanced the accuracy of personal names and place names, and of some dates.

Finally, I wish to express my deep gratitude to the Almighty for the gifts of life, strength, and time, and for the blessing of being able to remember, to speak, and to write. He guided me across the very narrow bridge.

Part ONE

Mülheim

Chapter *ONE*

Inauguration

MARCH 9, 1920. IT WAS A GOOD TIME TO BE BORN. The Great War—now called World War I—was over; it had ended just a year and a half before. When I started to ask my father questions about the war, in the manner of little boys who are intrigued by stories of soldiers, guns, wars, and battles, it was still a recent memory for him, though ancient history for me. I was too young to understand or to feel the effects of the "great inflation" that started soon after my birth—a consequence, I was told, of the Peace Treaty of Versailles that had imposed heavy reparations on Germany. I later enjoyed listening to my parents' stories about the time when money became almost worthless—when the price of goods in the afternoon was several times what it had been in the morning and you needed a wheelbarrow full of banknotes to pay for your purchases—until the government stabilized the value of German currency by decree, creating the new German mark and a painful upheaval in the economy. By the time of the Great Depression that followed in the late 1920s and 1930s, I no longer needed to depend on my parents' reminiscences, but had become a young observer of the scene myself.

The Great War of 1914–1918 may have determined the date of my birth. My older brother, Kurt, was born in 1912[1] and the eight-year gap between his birth and mine was probably due to the uncertainties of life in wartime. My father had served in the German army, but a medical condition kept him at a desk job in Bonn until he was discharged in 1916. His older brother, my Uncle Felix, saw active service in the German army. A younger brother, Julius Schild, fell in the war, killed in France in 1917. He was not married. My parents deeply mourned his untimely death. As a child, I was puz-

---

[1]My brother, Kurt, was born on May 27, 1912; my sister, Margot, on April 21,1922.

zled by the depth of their sorrow for an uncle I had never known. It was not until much later in my life, perhaps not until I lost my own brother, that I could appreciate why my mother spoke of him so often, the tears in her eyes displaying a love and a hurt that I could not quite understand. The ironic twists of Jewish fate are illustrated by the fact that the next generation of Schilds, in the second "great war," were American soldiers: my Uncle Felix's son, Joseph, fought the Japanese in the Pacific in World War II and my brother was drafted into the United States army not long after he arrived in America in 1940.

So it is fair to speculate that my conception eight months after the Armistice of November 11, 1918, was my parents' way of celebrating that the war was over and the recovery from its painful losses had begun. My birth may have signified the rebirth of hope for my parents. It was followed just a little more than two years later by the birth of my sister, Margot.

It was a good time to be born. The post-war era saw a burst of fascinating scientific progress. I witnessed the development of radically new technologies that would revolutionize life in the twentieth century. When I am away from home and I use a plastic card to charge long-distance calls directly to my home account without human mediation, I cannot help remembering that a private telephone was still a novelty in my early childhood. One of my earliest memories is of my father standing by the telephone near the back door of the store. Earpiece in hand, he turned the little crank at the side of the box to signal the operator to come on the line and, speaking into the mouthpiece, Father would ask to be connected to the party he wanted to reach. But innovations continued; telephone subscribers were soon given numbers to relay to the operator and, eventually, self-dialing was introduced.

Electric streetcars were commonplace in Cologne long before I was born, but private automobiles were still new, and it took years before trucks displaced the numerous horse-drawn wagons on the streets. I would sometimes watch motorists cranking the car manually to start it, a process often accompanied by appropriate curses on the recalcitrant machine. I remember my first car ride: my father had asked one of the travelling salesmen who often called on my family's shoe store to take the whole family for a ride. It was exciting, especially when the speedometer indicated such breathtaking speeds as 40, 50, and even 60 kilometres an hour. I was probably no more than four years old, but I had learned an appreciation for speed from my older brother, Kurt. It was an unforgettable event. Can members of my children's generation, who were probably picked up from the hospital in the family car after they were born, remember their first car ride?

We never owned a car, but that was probably due more to my parents' conservative lifestyle than to the scarcity of automobiles. Cars became commonplace while I was still a child. My friends and I used to make a game of identifying the different makes: Opel, Ford, Mercedes, Adler, and so on. Identifying license plates, which showed a car's city of registration, also made for an interesting sport, especially when we could spot the occasional car from a foreign country.

The sound of an aircraft would still turn everyone's eyes to the sky, for a plane was a rare sight and regular air travel was still in the future. And I can remember a world in which there were no radios and moving pictures were silent.

How exciting it has been to witness so many breakthroughs and to watch the leading edge of modern technology advance! But my birthdate bestowed more on me than a good seat to watch the electronic, nuclear, space, and computer age unfold in the multi-ring circus of technology. For I was born a Jew in the land where being a Jew became a crime punishable by death. This intersection of time and place made me not only a spectator to, but also a victim of, changing circumstances. I was deeply affected by the catastrophe that consumed six million Jews and millions of other human beings, although it was my good fortune to survive it. I lived through a war far more destructive than the one my parents described to me. And while they perished in the Holocaust, those who, like myself, escaped or survived it were able to watch other great dramas play out on the stage of the twentieth century. I consider myself fortunate to be able to remember the struggle for Zion and the tumultuous birth of the Jewish state while I am still "young" enough to have a reasonable chance of seeing Israel at peace. And, while the Bolshevik revolution happened before my time, I did witness the rise and eventual fall of Communism. Yes, I was to know pain, fear, loss, despair, and sorrow, but, nevertheless, I thank Providence for granting me a unique vantage point by admitting me to this world on March 9,

1920. If the Almighty who controls our destiny wanted it to be my challenge to face the ramifications of being born in Germany, then I do not wish it had been otherwise.

I entered the world in Köln-Mülheim, a suburb of the western German city of Cologne, Köln in German. Mülheim lies on the east side—the right bank, when you face downstream—of the Rhine. Like some other suburbs, Mülheim was originally a separate city under a different political jurisdiction, but it was incorporated into the growing metropolis of Cologne several years before my birth.

Cologne derives its name from the Latin word for colony, *colonia*. It was founded by the ancient Romans on the west bank of the river, and that is where the inner city and its central areas are still located. The Rhine was a very significant feature of my mental geography. The river formed the backdrop to the community, defining my space, a constant presence. Large rivers hold a fascination for me. A river is romantic and mysterious; it is always the same, yet always in flux, forever changing as the water courses through the riverbed, never to return. A river is time and eternity, permanence and motion. Its level rises and falls, it seems to diminish and grow; and, although it sometimes overflows its banks and inundates the city, a week or two later it is the same river again. I loved to walk along the Rhine or across it on the bridge and to watch the water and the boats. As a teenager, I was especially susceptible to its romantic lure. Perhaps it was no coincidence that a century earlier another Jew, Heinrich Heine, had written the famous song about the Lorelei who lures the skipper to his death in the waves. During my many visits to Germany in the last twenty years, I have never failed to walk at least once on the banks of the Rhine and, when the season was right, to take a boat trip on the river that looms so large in my memory. Much as I, as a loyal Torontonian, enjoy Lake Ontario, I am envious of the rivers that grace so many North American and European cities.

People along the Rhine believe what their popular songs say: that Rhinelanders are special, that being born on the river's beautiful banks, or even just living there, confers a unique ability to enjoy life and a disposition for pleasure and geniality. Rhinelanders are laid-back and good-natured, preferring peacefulness to passion.

Some of these environmental attributes may explain circumstances that played a role later in my life. They may have shielded—

for a while—our family and other Jewish people from a few of the ugly experiences to which Jews in other parts of Germany were exposed. However, if I have absorbed any of the qualities that allegedly distinguish the Rhinelander, it must have happened through the mysterious osmosis of nativity and nurture, not through my genes, for neither my mother nor my father were born near the Rhine.

Chapter TWO

Ulmbach

We were in a most unlikely place that summer afternoon. Neither I nor Laura, my wife, had ever heard of it before, and certainly had not planned to be there. It was a very small village in Germany, called Eckardtsroth. We were in an old Jewish cemetery right in the village. There was no evidence of vandalism or wanton destruction, just the signs of decades of neglect. The brick wall surrounding the cemetery was intact and we entered through an open gate. We were looking at tombstones, old and weathered, spread helter-skelter over the field, leaning at crazy angles. Most of them were thin slabs of stone; the lower portions had sunk into the ground and much of the rest was covered by grass and weeds that had not been cut in years.

"I'll start from this side; you start at the other end," Laura had suggested. I was going from stone to stone, moving aside the underbrush with my hand to read the inscriptions. So many of the names were Nussbaum, evidently a prominent clan in this region once upon a time.

Laura was calling out to me. "I think I found it," she shouted. I rushed over to her as fast as the tall grass would allow.

MY FATHER, HERMANN SCHILD,[1] was born on May 10, 1885, in Ulmbach, a small village southeast of Frankfurt, near Fulda, in a part of Germany where nearly all villages and rural towns had

[1]My father was registered at birth under the name Herz, but always used the name Hermann. Although Herz is also the German word for "heart," as a name it is derived from an archaic form of Hirsch, meaning "hart," a male deer. It was used as the German name for men whose Hebrew name is either Tzvi, which means a male deer, or Naftali, Jacob's son who, in his father's blessing, was compared to a fleet deer. My father's Hebrew name was Naftali, which was, coincidentally, also the name of my maternal grandfather, whose German name was Herz as well.

some Jewish inhabitants, ranging in number from a few families to a sizable proportion of the population. As urbanized Jews, we might have looked down on them a little and called them *landsjuden*, or country Jews, lacking in worldly sophistication and having only a rudimentary Jewish education. Yet they held fast to an earthy piety and kept their local traditions faithfully.

My father was only four years old when his father, Judah Schild, died at age thirty-two, leaving his wife, Sarah, with their two sons and pregnant with a third. This sad circumstance must have created much hardship for the family and it curtailed my father's formal education. Judah's brothers did try to help their widowed sister-in-law raise her children and, as soon as my father reached age fourteen and had completed the compulsory eight grades of public school, he was apprenticed to his uncle Max Schild's shoe and clothing business in Bonn. This move eventually established our branch of the Schild family in Cologne, only a short distance from Bonn.

Felix, Sarah Schild's oldest son, remained in Ulmbach to help his mother. It was probably expected that, as the oldest son, he would take over his father's estate—a house, a few fields, and a little business. Felix married Bertha Schuster, and their only child, Joseph, nicknamed Seppel, is my only first cousin on my father's side. Cousin Joe, as we call him, still lives in New York and has been a true and devoted member of the family. He managed to save his parents from the Holocaust and was instrumental in bringing my brother to America.

The third son, born after his father's death,[2] was Julius. As I mentioned, he fell in World War I, in 1917, as a soldier in the German army. His name is on the warriors' monument in Ulmbach.

During summer holidays, our family sometimes travelled to visit Uncle Felix, Tante Bertha, and Seppel. Since the village of Ulmbach was far from a main railway line, we usually had to take two or three trains, which made the journey more adventurous for my sister and me. The most exciting part of the trip came at the end, when we were picked up from the nearest railway station, in the neighbouring town of Steinau, by a horse and cart.

[2]This explains why his Hebrew name was Judah, like his father's. Among Ashkenazi Jews, a child is named after a parent only if the parent has died.

My father's ancestral home was a typical village house. The street was unpaved and the house was set back behind a farmyard. A compost heap near the road produced the healthy country smell that is firmly associated, in my memories of childhood, with the village where my father was born. The little village synagogue was across the street.

My family maintained a connection with Ulmbach. When my parents needed help in the house—my mother being very involved in the business—they turned to Ulmbach. A young woman of about eighteen, Lina Röder, was happy to come to the big city of Cologne to work in the household of a family from her own village. She felt very much at home with the Schild family and, after a few years, married the son of our upstairs tenants.

The last visit to Ulmbach that I remember was for Seppel's bar mitzvah in 1931, when I was eleven. A photograph that I have of Seppel, Margot, and me playing in the yard in a miniature hay-wagon may come from this visit.

I lived in Toronto for thirty years before I set foot on German soil again. The reason for the long interval does not lie entirely in my negative feelings for the land of my birth. True, in the first few years after the war, I could not even think of going back for a visit, but, eventually, curiosity and a wish to confirm memories that seemed increasingly unreal mitigated my reluctance to expose myself to the painful experience of a visit to Germany. However, the opportunity for extended travel did not arise until 1972. By then, our children were adults and my congregation had grown large enough to engage an associate rabbi. That year Laura and I made our first trip to continental Europe. Our itinerary started in Switzerland and it was delightful to explore that beautiful country in our rented car. Our vacation was to end in Holland, where we would visit family and drop off our car before flying back to Canada.

The route from Switzerland to Holland leads through Germany.

Going back to Germany was as emotionally difficult as I had expected. However, I was eager to show Laura the geography of my childhood and her company helped me negotiate my inner conflicts. At the Swiss-German border I proudly presented my Canadian passport, hoping that the official would make a comment on my German birthplace. I was disappointed that he did not even look at the document. Germany was no longer the bureaucratic nation of my youth.

We had a few days to spare before we were booked into our Amsterdam hotel, so we were not in a hurry. Our plan was to visit Cologne, where I would show Laura the places that held so many of my memories and, possibly, we would visit the Jewish cemetery in Mülheim. I knew that my grandmother, Sarah Schild, was buried there and not with her husband in Ulmbach. She had died two months before I was born, while visiting my parents; she had come to help my pregnant mother.

As we were driving north along the Rhine valley, I had a sudden impulse to make a detour from our projected route. Distances in Germany are small compared to our Canadian spaces. I suddenly wanted to see Ulmbach again. Would I find the house? Would anyone remember the Schild family? Unbearable anti-Semitic harassment at the hands of their village neighbours had driven out my uncle and aunt in 1935.

Guided by my maps and driving through towns and villages whose names sounded so familiar, I found Ulmbach. It no longer looked as I had remembered it. The streets were all paved and automobiles had replaced the horse-drawn vehicles. We walked up and down. I knew we had passed the house I was looking for, but I could not recognize it. Then I saw a very old lady on the street; she looked ancient enough to remember. I approached her. Did she remember a Schild family? "Of course!" I introduced myself. In an instant, she remembered the Cologne branch of the Schild family. "Lina Röder, who worked for your family, was here a week ago. Her husband has just died, so she came to visit her relatives." I was stunned. I had stayed in touch with our former tenant family, whose son Lina had married, since the end of the war and we had hoped to see Lina during our stay in Cologne. The death of her husband was unexpected news.

I asked the lady to direct me to the old family house, and then another thought struck me. "Listen," I said to her. "If a Jewish man had died in Ulmbach around 1890, where would he be buried?" She looked at me with some surprise, as if I should have known the answer myself. "In Eckardtsroth, naturally!" And where was Eckardtsroth? She assured me that it was only a few kilometres away and that the Jewish cemetery still existed. She gave me directions to find it.

First we went to see the house. It must have been renovated more than once since I had last seen it, for it bore little resemblance to the image in my memory. To rest a while and refresh ourselves, we entered a nearby pub where I had a beer. The proprietor claimed to have been a friend of my cousin, Joseph. Then we drove to Eckardtsroth to search for my grandfather's grave in the Jewish cemetery. Laura found it. "Judah Schild," read the faint inscription, "from Ulmbach." The date agreed with what my father had told me.

Here I stood, with deep emotions sweeping over me. "A grandson has found your resting place, almost a hundred years after your death. Your little four-year-old boy, your son Hermann, became my father. Where he is buried, I will never know, and his grave, if he has one, I will never be able to visit. But he spoke to me about you. He told me how you came to Ulmbach from your native village, Völkersleier, to marry Sarah Nussbaum and to live in Ulmbach with her family. I see that her kinfolk lie buried in this holy place with you. In a day or two I may see her grave, too, if I can find it in Mülheim. Alas, you had to leave her too soon, but it all worked out. See, here am I, your son's son, from distant Canada, a country you may have never heard of. Far away, spread over many countries, your seed lives on: grandchildren, great-grandchildren, and even great-great-grandchildren, whose number will grow and grow, with the merciful help of the Almighty."

I said the Hebrew memorial prayer. I could not help wondering when the words had last been said in this place.

Two days later, at the Jewish community building in Cologne, I picked up the key to the Jewish cemetery of Köln-Mülheim. Guided by my memory, I had little difficulty finding the cemetery and the tombstone of my grandmother, Sarah Schild.

❖

What a hard and sad life this woman endured! She was only thirty-three years old when her husband died, less than six months after she had lost her mother. Her father had died ten years earlier. Her husband's death left her with two young sons and pregnant. Her parents-in-law lived in a different village. She must have suffered terrible material and emotional hardships and despair. Can we imagine the day in 1917 when she received the news that her youngest son, named after the father he had never seen, had fallen in the war?

Sarah Schild left Ulmbach in 1919 to help her son and pregnant daughter-in-law in Köln-Mülheim. Again, fate was not kind to her. She died soon after she arrived, in January 1920. It must have been a sad blow for my parents. To make matters worse, she died while the Rhine was on the rampage. Flood waters had risen over the low lying parts of Mülheim and inundated our street. Her coffin was carried on a little boat from our house to higher ground. My parents told me the story often. It sounded exciting to my young ears and only much later was I able to see my grandmother's life in perspective. When my sister, Margot, was born, she was given the Hebrew name Sarah after our grandmother. Several girls born in the Schild family after Margot's death in 1991 carry on the name.

Thus, when I was born in March 1920, only one of my grandparents was still alive: my mother's father, Herz Neugarten, whose wife had died four years earlier.

Chapter THREE

My Parents

When my brother, Kurt, first met his wife, he said that her eyes looked just like our mother's eyes.

Kurt met Beckie while serving in the United States army, when he was stationed at Camp Wheeler, near Macon, Georgia. The local Jewish girls had invited the Jewish servicemen from the camp to a social at the synagogue. There was a wide gap between their respective backgrounds, between Kurt Schild, the recent immigrant who spoke imperfect English with a distinct German accent, and Beckie Michael, the Southern belle with a patrician pedigree and a Georgia drawl, as American as one could be. But she looked like Mother and Kurt fell in love. Beckie was drawn to the handsome, suave stranger and his charming manner, his gift for interesting conversation, and his consummate piano playing.

They were married in Macon on January 25, 1942. I was unable to attend the wedding, but when I first met Beckie six months later in the summer of 1942, I could see that she did, indeed, resemble our mother, especially around the eyes. I see the same likeness in some of my granddaughters. I am glad they look a little like the great-grandmother they never knew. That Beckie had similar features was a fortuitous coincidence—or was it a device of Providence to help Kurt find his true mate?

A FOCAL POINT IN THE LIVING ROOM of our home in Mülheim was a gold-framed portrait of my mother as a young woman. It was a picture of a beautiful young woman, about twenty years old, her full bosom accentuated by a tightly cinched waist. A high, lace collar surrounded her neck, and her fine face was surmounted by a bouffant hairstyle. My mother was still very beautiful when I was old enough to store her image in my memory, but she had become a little plump compared to her picture, having already begun her battle against weight-gain and the emergence of a double chin. Even though she was an active business woman with little time to spare for vanity, she was always well-groomed and looked after her appearance carefully. I feel anguish when I think of her being worked to death in a German labour camp.

My mother was born Hetti Neugarten on October 9, 1887, in Herdecke, a town in Westphalia. Her ancestors, both on her mother's and her father's sides, were modest business people who lived mostly in small towns along the Rhine. In one of these towns, Bad Breisig, the local synagogue was in the house of one of my forebears.

My maternal grandfather, Herz Neugarten, had moved to Cologne. He lived in a suburb quite close to Mülheim, Cologne-Kalk, in a big house that he shared, at least for a time, with his son Gustav. He seemed a stern person to me, not like a doting grandfather, but my memory may not be fair to him. What I remember best is playing with Margot on the thick Persian carpet in his living room and climbing over the elaborately carved woodwork that supported an enormous dining room table. I also remember, a few years later, when I was about ten years old, my parents, uncles, and aunts voicing their worries about him in hushed tones during his lengthy final illness and grieving at his death, but I do not remember feeling a personal loss.

My mother was thirty-three years old when I was born. It sounds maudlin, but in the deepest layers of my memory, I can feel her love surrounding me with a cocoon of warm, womb-like security. I can almost see myself falling asleep to Brahms' "Lullaby," the words of which I still remember. I also remember the intensity with which, as a little child, I loved my mother. I often pondered whether I loved my mother or my father more—and arrived at the conclusion that I loved them both equally. Looking back, though, I realize that my love for my father was more cerebral, less visceral than my overwhelming feelings for my mother. I admired my father. I can recall playing on his knees, putting my tiny hands into his, awed by their size, fascinated by the deep lines etched into leathery skin that he used to soothe with a glycerin lotion. As I grew older, my love deepened in response to his personality, his knowledge and wisdom, his conscientiousness and warmth.

As a child, I was absolutely certain that special good fortune had granted me the most marvellous parents. I still believe it. I owe them so much. It is no wonder that even after many years, when I introduced my wife, Laura, to a cousin of mine, he said, "If you had only known Erwin's parents!" What a pity that my children would never know them.

In retrospect, I remember my mother as an active, self-reliant person, with a great deal of initiative. She was a full working partner with my father in our retail shoe business. At the same time, she organized and supervised the household and the upbringing of her children. We lived in a big house, with tenants upstairs, a sales staff of two to four people in the store, and a household staff of two. My mother knew how to integrate the areas of her responsibility into one harmonious, well-run operation. Even now, meals sometimes evoke memories of my mother's kitchen, and I am often reminded especially of one annual organizational highlight: the day set aside for pickling and preserving. I disliked it, not only because the whole house was in an upheaval, with normal operations suspended, but also because of the horrible smell of the burning sulfur that was used to sterilize the jars. Salesgirls, tenants, our *Kindermädchen*, or nanny, relatives, and friends—everyone was pressed into service on the assembly line that started with bushels of produce on one end and ended with rows upon rows of jars holding cucumbers, onions, jams, and fruit preserves on the other.

My mother had a friendly and happy disposition. She was fun-loving and enjoyed going out to concerts, theatres, and clubs, as well as to get-togethers with family and friends. She gave life, colour, and a special ambiance to our home and our lives. Unfortunately, just as she reached the years that should have brought her the greatest happiness from her family, her spirit was dampened by the terrible dangers and troubles threatening all of us.

My father had one very conspicuous physical characteristic: he was totally bald. He had lost all his hair as a very young man, as my parents' beautiful engagement picture, taken in a Cologne studio in 1911, shows. I remember, as a very young child, sitting on my father's lap stroking the perfectly smooth skin of his bare pate admiringly. He only grew a little hair above his ears and over his neck. I enjoyed his trick of wrinkling his forehead, creating a row of perfectly formed ridges. It gave him a funny look that made me squeal with laughter.

While my father's formal education had been limited to eight years in the elementary village school in Ulmbach, he was, nevertheless, an educated person. He read extensively; he knew history, geography, and politics. He taught himself French by subscribing to a self-study correspondence course—the Langenscheidt method—and carefully collected the printed lessons in proper binders as they arrived in the mail. Thus, he learned to read and speak French quite well, quoting French sayings, proverbs, and rhymes of political or historical significance that he always explained to me. My father's knowledge of French was to stand me in good stead when I was studying French in school, although I always criticized his pronunciation, rather unfairly and thoughtlessly, considering that he had never had the benefit of listening to a teacher.

My father was also very good in practical mathematics, book-keeping, and many other business skills. Most importantly, he was a person of great integrity, trusted by his customers and others in the community. He was the person to whom family members turned when they were in trouble. His wisdom and impartiality were also appreciated in our small Jewish community. He tried, with some success, to keep the congregation together when factional divisiveness and personal politics—a terrible propensity of small-town Jews—threatened to tear it apart.

I find it so frustrating that I know so little of my parents "pre-history," that is, of their lives before my birth. I wish I had asked more questions or remembered more of what they told me. How and where did they meet? Why did my mother's family move to Cologne?

Visits to California many years later gave me the opportunity to ask some questions of the last surviving family member of my father's generation, his first cousin Alice. Her father, Max Schild, was the brother of my grandfather Judah. Uncle Max was the merchant in Bonn who had brought my father—his late brother Judah's son—from Ulmbach to apprentice in his store, so Alice had known her cousin well. Nor were Alice and I strangers when we met again in California. Bonn is not far from Cologne, and we occasionally took the radial train—the *Rheinuferbahn*, or Rhine Bank Railway—to visit Uncle Max, Aunt Sophie, and their three daughters. Alice, Olga, and Else were very friendly and attentive to my sister and me, and we became quite close despite the age gap.

Kinship was not the only reason for our frequent visits. As Uncle Max aged and could no longer manage his business, my father took it over. He considered it his duty to help his Uncle Max in return for his having brought my father from Ulmbach when he was a fatherless lad and taking him into his business. I think that Uncle Max had also helped my parents set up their own store in Köln-Mülheim after they married.

Uncle Max died in Cologne after he retired. Alice emigrated with her husband, Fred Lämle, to the United States and eventually settled in Los Angeles. Her sister Else Lederman also made it to the United States. Aunt Sophie and her daughter Olga survived the Holocaust in the Theresienstadt camp, and I met them again on one of my first visits to New York. By this time, Aunt Sophie was a very old lady. I cannot recall seeing her and Olga again. Else did not live in New York and, unfortunately, she died before my circumstances permitted extensive travel.

When we visited cousin Alice and Fred in California, Alice was the only surviving member of her family. In contrast to her ailing husband, she was robust and healthy. We were with them several times, spending our first enjoyable visit together when Laura and I met them in Carmel, and other visits a few years later in Palm Springs and at their home in Los Angeles. I fully expected to see Alice again—she promised to visit us in Toronto—but she died suddenly, predeceasing her husband, and took her knowledge of my parents as young people to her grave. I had asked her quite a few questions when we met, but they were mainly about members of the family I had never known; I did not ask her enough about my parents.

Alice's husband outlived her by at least five years. We visited him once in his retirement home. They had no children, and when he died he left me a little bequest from their estate, the only inheritance I ever received from a relative. I would have preferred to have Alice's photo collection, but, unfortunately, Fred became almost incapacitated after her sudden death and was not able to save it for me when her personal effects were disposed of. Fortunately, Alice had already sent me a few photographs, including some portraits of her grandparents—my great-grandparents, the parents of the unfortunate Judah who died so young that they survived him.

Alice did tell us one surprising item on our last visit: my parents' courtship had been very ardent and romantic. I was surprised because I had never thought of my parents as romantic friends or lovers—their love for each other was obvious to me as a child. It was constant and even, not something dynamic or explosive, a state of perfect balance, as natural as the sun and as dependable as the alternation of day and night. They simply belonged together. There was never a flare-up of temper; they never appeared angry with each other; I never heard a word of blame or reproach. Even as a child, I saw that they were totally devoted to each other. When I was old enough to have discovered romantic love and foolish enough to think I knew all about it, I relegated my parents' love for each other, deep but quiet and unexciting, to a different category. I was already a grandfather, yet it was a deliciously shocking surprise when Alice told us how my father had fallen in love with the beautiful Hetti and became an impetuous suitor. He pursued my mother with gifts and flowers and entertained her lavishly. Fortunately for me, he won her heart and her hand. They were married in Cologne on August 15, 1911. Their wedding, I have been told by relatives, was a major social event.

Chapter FOUR

My Brother and Sister

When Laura and I drafted our wedding invitations, we chose a conventional text. It indicated that our parents—mine as well as Laura's—were the hosts of our nuptial celebration. Regrettably, short of a miracle, my parents would have no knowledge of their son's marriage, even if they were still alive. We could not even guess where they and my sister, Margot, were on our wedding day. Thus I derived great comfort, strength, and courage from the presence of my brother, Kurt, and his wife, Beckie. Kurt, resplendent in his United States army uniform, handsome as ever at age 32, represented my family. That Kurt was fully aware of his role and his responsibility was obvious to me, as it must have been to any discerning observer. In loco parentis is the legal phrase for a parental surrogate, and that is what Kurt had become for me. His presence conferred on me status and respect. It proclaimed that I was not a homeless refugee, a rootless tumbleweed that might be blown by shifting winds to another nowhere. I was connected, my brother's presence said, I had roots in a family where relations by blood and marriage were taken seriously. Family is where you belong; family bonds impose obligations and create commitments, building structures of love and duty, of companionship, dependence, and dependability.

I DO NOT REMEMBER that my parents ever lectured me or my siblings on the meaning of family, its obligations and its benefits. We learned what family means, as we did so many other values, from our parents' example, from the experiences of our life with them.

My first awareness of my brother, eight years my senior, must have been part of the same early learning process that familiarized me with my mother and father. I do not remember Kurt playing with me as an infant, and the difference in our ages precluded our being pals during my childhood, but he certainly appears in the role of a good brother in so many of my early memories. Later in life, after the passage of time had wiped out the age difference, our brotherly love became very strong, surmounting serious differences in our outlook, lifestyle, and religious orientation. As a child, though, I had never been able to catch up with Kurt. When I entered elementary school, he was already in high school; when I entered high school, he was already working.

We had quite different personalities, inclinations, and interests. I was the little scholar, somewhat shy with individual people, though at ease in front of a class or an audience. Kurt was an indifferent student, but an outgoing, socially skilled, popular, and polished young man of the world. He played tennis, was a natural musician, an accomplished pianist, and had lots of girlfriends. School simply did not interest him, to my father's chagrin. I remember our father, driven to exasperation by something Kurt had done or not done in school, giving him a sound whipping. I do not know whether it had any effect on Kurt, but it certainly had on me. Though I experienced a gentle slap on the behind as an occasional expression of parental disapproval, I cannot remember another instance in which my father was so vehement. Fortunately, in the course of time and events, my father realized that Kurt had developed the strong sense of family responsibility, informed by the principles of honour and integrity, that were so characteristic of our parents.

Kurt's bar mitzvah in 1925 was a big event. Since he had a good voice, Lehrer[1] Leopold Vogel, who was the religious teacher and cantor of the congregation, had no problem teaching him to recite the *haftarah*. While I have no recollection of the synagogue service, I clearly recall the dinner that had been prepared by a host of busy helpers under my mother's direction. The kitchen and other areas of the house teemed with the household and business staff, several aunts, and of course, Frau Roggendorf from upstairs. I remember especially Tante Bertha, who with Uncle Felix and Seppel, had come from Ulmbach for the festivities. It was said that she was an expert cook. We sat down at long tables set up in our living room and dining room. At dinner, I was the first to taste that a major calamity

---

[1] The German word for teacher. It was the title of the religious official in smaller Jewish communities who performed the functions of cantor, religious instructor, and religious school teacher.

had occurred: the soup had turned sour and had to be thrown out. But it was still a memorable feast for numerous relatives and friends.

Kurt, older and so wise in the ways of the world, initiated me into many mysterious and wonderful things. It was Kurt who introduced me to the recently invented radio. I was six years old, I believe, when he took me into a large room in the back of a store on the Buchheimer Strasse. We each received a set of headphones and joined other people who were similarly equipped, and my brother plugged the headphones into a receptacle on a long table. With a sense of wonder and awe, I heard my first radio broadcast. I knew, of course, and was duly impressed, that the broadcast emanated miraculously from a transmitter miles away without the benefit of wires, unlike a telephone. I had an inkling at that moment of how great and revolutionary the invention of radio was. A short time later, Kurt acquired his own crystal radio set and became adept at coaxing the signals of the few radio stations then existing into the earphones that he allowed me to put on. A little later, we acquired our first radio set with vacuum tubes, powered by large wet batteries that required careful attention, and, still later, our first plug-in radio with a loudspeaker that replaced the uncomfortable earphones. Kurt was the chief radio engineer of the house; my parents were a little distrustful of this invention. At first, they were reluctant to become familiar with it—so much like the elders of today whose children teach them about computers, VCRs, and other similar innovations. It was Kurt who hung the simple antenna—a coil of copper wire— through the hall or the living room; he connected the separate parts of the apparatus—a receiver, an amplifier, and a speaker—and he became quite adept at it. He even learned the trick of converting a speaker into a microphone. He once used his technique to "broadcast" his own messages into the living room while my mother was entertaining friends—they were startled when the "radio announcer" suddenly commented on Mrs. Levenbach's new hat! I'll never forget the hilarious scene.

Despite our age difference, Kurt often allowed me to accompany him when he met his friends. I remember him taking me to the tennis court, where I enjoyed retrieving the balls—a convenience for Kurt and his partners. I have a photo taken on a tennis court where I am the mascot-like centrepiece in a group consisting of Kurt and his tennis-playing girlfriends. I remember a few of their names: Lore

Stern, Alice Levenbach, Else Schubach. Else's older sister, Hanna, eventually became our first cousin when she married Arthur Kracko.

The differences between Kurt and myself were illustrated soon after his bar mitzvah. Among his gifts was a hefty book on astronomy, entitled *From Distant Worlds*, that showed the sun, the planets, the moon, and the galaxies, how parallaxes and spectral analysis worked, galaxies, how astronomical distances were measured, and so on. Though I never attended nursery school or kindergarten—or, rather, because I never did—I had learned to read long before I entered grade one. I must have been less than seven years old when I devoured the astronomy book, reading it several times, becoming an expert on the science of the heavenly bodies, and firmly resolving to become a professional astronomer when I grew up. Kurt never opened the book and did not mind at all that I incorporated it into my growing library.

When he was only about three years old, according to my parents, Kurt would go to the piano in our living room—a respectable middle-class house had to have a piano—and play tunes that he knew. Naturally, our parents were thrilled with his talent and provided piano lessons. He could have become a concert pianist. For a while, our father dreaded the possibility that Kurt might choose a musical career. *Brotlose Kunst*, he used to call it: art through which you could not earn your daily bread. Kurt had perfect pitch and learned music easily, but he did not have the patience and self-discipline that a musical career requires. He loved opera and had a wide knowledge of music. He enjoyed playing by ear, improvising arrangements of light classical and contemporary music, and enchanting us with his renditions of music from operettas and popular hits. Sometimes, he sang the music as he played. He was equally brilliant at playing the accordion. For Kurt, the piano was a tremendous social asset. His talents made him very popular at parties and when he emigrated to America, he earned his first dollars by playing the piano in cafes and bars. He could play practically any piece on demand.

When I was young, I watched my brother play and listened to him with fascination. I owe him, among many other things, my appreciation of music and some knowledge of the various composers and their work. When I was about eleven years, I took piano lessons for nearly two years with only moderate success. However, eventually I learned to imitate a little of Kurt's style of improvisation, which explains why the piano many years later played a decisive role at a crucial moment in my life.

Before the conditions for Jews in Germany deteriorated, Kurt was able to enjoy some travel. He visited the North Sea, Scheveningen in Holland, and, as the highlight, he went to Paris, where he could see his beloved operas by Jacques Offenbach performed. Since he was not interested in finishing high school, however, Kurt had to find a position in business, first in Cologne, then later out of town. He was a charmer and a born salesman. Even after 1933, when the Nazis were in power and employment was difficult to find for a young Jewish man, Kurt managed to get along well, thanks to his skills and personality. He worked in Offenbach, the city for which the composer's father had been named, and in Giessen in the mid 1930s.

Before 1933, Kurt was involved in Jewish organizations, especially those which, like B'nai Brith, tried to combat the growth of anti-Semitism. Kurt was proudly Jewish, but not in a religious or nationalistic sense. He was fervently German, believing—along with the majority of German Jews—that being German and Jewish was a valid, viable, and, perhaps, ideal combination: Jewish by faith, German by nationality. The success of the Nazi party, he once concluded in an address to a meeting of his organization, would turn out to be but a "ludicrous intermezzo" in German history. I have a suspicion that Kurt never recovered spiritually from the shock of seeing his cherished beliefs so thoroughly refuted by events. He later focused an even more fervent, sincerely patriotic love on the United States, grateful to his adopted country for having offered him a second home.

My sister, Margot, was born when I was two years old. I have always believed that I can remember this event, and I also have a clear image in my mind of one nightly scene in my parents' bedroom— my father in a nightshirt stepping over the bed to get to the crib. Margot turned out to be a great blessing—generous, kind, unselfish, and loving—but in our childhood, she often reduced me to furious tears and blinding frustration. She would distort the truth—from my point of view—about our sibling quarrels, and my parents, so it seemed to me, always believed her version, always sided with her, and hurt me to the core. As we got older, however, we became close companions and spent a great deal of time together in our shared circle of friends. When we entered our teenage years, the conditions under which we lived in Nazi Germany bonded us very closely. Margot and I shared important developments in our religious evolution that were of the greatest consequence. The story of her childhood and early youth is firmly entwined with my own.

Chapter FIVE

Home! Wallstrasse 43

My Uncle Willi survived the Nazi occupation of Holland hidden in a basement by Gentile neighbours. In the summer of 1945, a few months after the end of the war, he sent me an eerie photograph he had taken on his first post-war visit to Cologne, his former home city. Cologne had been virtually flattened in repeated bombing raids by the Allied air forces—just, if only partial, retribution for the atrocities the Germans had committed. Nevertheless, I was shocked to see in the picture the ruins of my parents' house. A jumble of beams, masonry, and rubble was all that remained of Wallstrasse 43, the solid house that had been my home for the first eighteen years of my life. Here, under the comfort of this collapsed roof, I had learned the meaning of family, love, and home; I had learned to crawl on the carpets, the linoleum, and the parquet that once covered these crumbled floors; within these fallen walls, I had read my first book.

In the summer of 1972, when I revisited Cologne for the first time, I saw that the ruins had been replaced by a typical early-post-war-style apartment house: squat, plain, drab—an ugly intruder that had invaded a sacred space in my memory; a mocking blasphemy of a remembered shrine. Ah, it had been such a big, beautiful house, filled with mysterious places that my imagination invested with the secrets and sweet terrors of beloved fairy tales. If only I had a photograph to corroborate the images in my mind!

Then, something miraculous happened. A former high school classmate brought me a precious gift to a class reunion held in my honour during one of my visits to Cologne in the 1980's: an old picture postcard, captioned "Greetings from Mülheim." Right in the middle of the card, framed by a decorative border, was a view of our house, at the corner of the Wallstrasse and the Bachstrasse, then the business centre of town. The photo had been taken long before my time, probably even before my parents had bought the house, but it showed the exterior of our home very much as I remember it.

❖

*T*HE ELEGANT ENTRANCE TO OUR SHOE STORE had greatly impressed me as a child. We always referred to it as "the portal," to distinguish it from the more commonplace private entrance to our home. The portal was a neat architectural solution to the problem of providing equal access from the two streets that met at this intersection. A round pillar at the very corner of the building supported two entrance arches set at right angles to each other, one on the Wallstrasse, the other on the Bachstrasse. People approaching the store from either side would step up to a terrazzo platform and enter through a door set at a 45-degree angle to the two arches. The portal was flanked by large store windows, displaying the merchandise arranged with a professional decorator's touch to pedestrians on both streets.

The partly glazed front door opened into the store's large sales area. Beyond that was the stockroom, where hundreds of shoe boxes were stored neatly on the shelves that lined all the walls. On the sales floor stood groupings of comfortable chairs with try-on benches. When there were no customers, my sister and I used the slanting surfaces of the benches as miniature slides. There was a large, solid counter with drawers and storage space underneath and a cash register to ring up the sales on top. Also mounted on the countertop was a sturdy wood-and-metal contraption that dispensed grey-white wrapping paper from a huge roll, always assuring me of a generous supply of paper large enough for drawing maps. I would stand there sometimes and watch the salesperson or cash register operator, frequently my father or mother, tear off a piece of the paper to size on the cutting edge of the contraption and then, through a series of educated folds, neatly wrap the shoe box in a tidy package. The store was always entertaining, with our sales staff, the customers, the window washer, the mailman, travelling salesmen, and others dropping in. I have never felt a desire to become a merchant, but I learned a lot from the conversations—sometimes things that I was not supposed to know about. Even if I did not quite understand what was being said at first, I was usually able to figure it out eventually. The banter between the window washer and some of the salesgirls was especially interesting and informative. I even remember his name: Peter Monschau.

Houses in old European towns do not stand by themselves, but are attached to the neighbouring houses. Thus, a corner house like ours, with frontage on two streets and large display windows, enjoyed a great advantage as a business location. During business hours, we usually entered the house through the "portal," but there was a second private entrance as well, on the Wallstrasse where our building joined the neighbouring house. A solid door opened onto a long corridor that ran the entire length of the house. The corridor was wide enough to accommodate additional shelving for merchandise along part of the wall. The terrazzo floor provided a good place for playing ball, riding a scooter or other toy vehicles, or playing with wheeled toys that worked best on a hard surface. Sometimes, I remember, my sister's baby carriage was in the way. Halfway down the corridor was an entrance to the store from the house. At this point, the long corridor jogged left in order to accommodate the staircase leading up to the next floor.

Further along the corridor was the door to the stairs down to the cellar, which was always dank and damp owing to the proximity of the Rhine and the frequent floods that often inundated cellars in the neighbourhood. The river waters would rise mysteriously within the cellar, seeping through the walls, even before the flood waters reached the streets outside. A few light bulbs hung down from the ceiling beams and dimly lit an eerie place to which I would descend only in the company of an adult. Some of the walls were lined with shelves stacked with jars of pickled cucumbers, small onions, fruit, and preserves.

Behind the last door, near the end of the corridor, was the water closet, or toilet, where a long pull chain with a porcelain grip at the end hung down from the water tank mounted high on the wall. The flush toilet was probably a recent addition to our house; indoor sanitary plumbing was fairly new and not yet universal—I remember the evil-smelling trucks that pumped out the holding tanks from the less modern homes. Fortunately, we did have that luxury, though for a time there was only one toilet in the house. Chamber pots, neatly hidden in commodes or night tables were still essential furnishings in every bedroom and only gradually fell into disuse. I would prefer to skip this subject, but for the sake of honesty, and in fairness to the psychoanalytically inclined reader, I cannot suppress one of my clearest and most awkward memories. I must have been three or four years old at the time. Whenever I had used the toilet for serious business, I had to call for assistance in performing the required cleansing operation. My loudly shouted announcement that I was finished summoned one of the salesgirls, Katherinchen or Fräulein Schlehbusch or one of the younger girls, who had to come from the store and do what was necessary to qualify me to rejoin the clean, civilized society. I wish I could forget the whole thing! I hated it even then. But I insisted on pulling the chain myself.

The corridor ended at a door which led outside to the small, dark, backyard storage area for garbage bins and other items not fit to keep indoors. The yard was surrounded by walls and houses that were too high to admit sunlight. One of my early memory makes it even darker. My parents and our nursemaid had been trying to wean me off the pacifier that prevailing custom allowed me to use during infancy. Several times I had consented to quit the habit, but I had insisted that my beloved pacifier be not thrown out. Of course, I promptly relapsed each time. When I was finally ready to renounce my addiction for good—when I was about four years old—I made the heroic decision to dispose of my pacifier myself. I marched into the backyard and flung it into a garbage can where it came to rest on top of some very unappetizing filth. That did the trick. I remember the episode so clearly, with all its attending emotions and heroics.

My memory is less clear when I try to recall the living areas of our home. This lack of clarity may be due to a major renovation that took place during my childhood and has jumbled my recollections. Originally, our living quarters were on the first floor above the store, and included a living room, dining room, kitchen, and bedrooms. Our tenants, the Roggendorf family, lived on the top floor, where they had been living when my parents bought the house. At some point, the store had to be expanded and our growing family needed more space, as well. My sister—as the youngest child—was still sleeping in my parents' bedroom and Lina, our household helper, needed a room.

The solution was to add a large part of the second floor to the store area and connect it with the ground floor by means of a new internal staircase. I marvelled at the large opening that was made in our floor to accommodate the stairs. We now had a new living room and dining room and a modern second bathroom. The top floor was enlarged and the attic rooms were rebuilt to give the Roggendorf family more space. My brother and I still had to share a bedroom, but my sister got a room of her own, as did Lina. Gas lines were drawn into the house. The coal stove in the kitchen was replaced with a gas range and the bathroom now had a real tub with plumbing and a gas water heater. What luxury! Yet I still remember those earlier bath nights—Thursday evenings—when Margot and I were given a bath in a portable tub filled with water that had been heated on the kitchen stove. I even remember the celluloid ducks floating in our bath water to keep us entertained.

Once Lina had a room of her own, I had to learn a child's lesson about privacy the hard way. I wandered into Lina's room early one morning and asked her—or perhaps my mother—about the bloodstains I saw on the sheets of her unmade bed. Instead of an answer, I got reprimanded for going into her room unannounced and uninvited, and was warned never to do that again. I could only conclude that there was some deep, dark, adult secret that I was not supposed to learn. Yet I must also have sensed the adults' embarrassment and felt some alluring suspicion that would fix this insignificant incident so firmly in my memory.

All in all, our house was quite up-to-date for the time and very comfortable. From large windows, I could watch the goings-on in the street. On a landing between floors, we had a large icebox from which water had to be drained every day. There were cupboards for our many toys and games. There was room to play and space to read and, in later years, to do our homework. However, the house had no central heating—a feature of newer and more elaborate homes than ours. There was a huge enclosed fireplace with a lot of marble and intricate metalwork in our living room and heating stoves in some of the other rooms. Keeping the house well heated in winter took a lot of coal briquettes and a lot of work.

The location of our store was excellent for business. The Wallstrasse was a central commercial street and the Bachstrasse, where it met the Wallstrasse at our house, formed a wide square that was the site of a busy farmers' market on certain days of the week. At one time, there had been a water-driven mill near the end of the Bachstrasse, as I knew from old pictures. Perhaps the waterwheel was still there when I was a little boy. Certainly the name of the street indicated the presence of a creek—*Bach* in German—that provided power for the mill. The Bachstrasse led to the Freiheitstrasse, a busy traffic artery, beyond which lay the bank of the Rhine. I suppose that the proximity to the Mülheim's harbour and several industrial plants was also a commercial asset of the area.

It did not occur to me to ask my father why he opened a branch store, or, if he needed it to increase the volume of business, why the new store was only a few short blocks up the street. I assumed it was a matter of convenience. Father could walk back and forth in minutes and had time, after we had eaten our main meal about one o'clock, to sleep for a few minutes on the living room couch. Only much later did I begin to understand the urban changes that must have given my parents cause for grave concern when I was five or six years old.

Mülheim was connected to the centre of Cologne, which was located on the opposite bank of the Rhine, by means of a bridge. A few kilometres upriver, in the downtown section, there were several modern bridges, but Mülheim had an old-fashioned, picturesque, pontoon bridge. Platforms constructed of heavy wooden planks formed a bridge resting on metal pontoons that floated on the river, solidly anchored to the shores and to the riverbed. Pedestrian and vehicular traffic crossed the bridge close to water level. I can still hear the rattling of the planks under the wheels of horse-drawn wagons, cars, and trucks.

The Rhine is a busy river, a marine highway crowded with passenger ships, long narrow freighters, and tugboats pulling freight barges, so the centre sections of the bridge were removable. Whenever the river traffic made it necessary, a marine steam engine pulled or pushed the hinged centre sections of the bridge aside, allowing the river boats to pass, while bridge traffic waited. It was a very picturesque scene—the subject of hundreds of paintings, sketches, and photographs—but an intolerable obstacle in a modern urban environment. Thus, in the 1920s, work began on the construction of a suspension bridge across the Rhine. Its design incorporated the latest technological advances in bridge construction, making it possible to do away with pylon supports in the middle of the waterway. The bridge spanned the river in one gracefully curved arc from shore to shore, elegantly suspended from a pair of towers on each bank.

The wide, elevated approach to the bridge intruded far into the heart of Mülheim, cutting a wide swath through an area of old residences and stores. For several years, the bridge construction had severed the lower part of the Wallstrasse, our location, from the busy upper part where it met the Buchheimer Strasse. When the construction was finished, our house was only one short block—on the "wrong" side—away from the massive concrete overpass that carried the approach road over the Wallstrasse. The open-air market had long since disappeared. The new bridge had shifted business life permanently in a new direction.

My father did the right thing. While retaining the original store, he leased a second store on the Buchheimer Strasse, only two blocks away. Very soon, this store became the busier of the two. My mother, an expert business person, had always played an important part in running the store, but her role became even more crucial when the second store opened. While my father was in the new store, Mother took charge of the original store, so that she could also keep an eye on our home and family. To make my mother's dual role possible, she needed help with the children and, as her responsibilities grew, a housekeeper.

I cannot think of my childhood without Anna and Lina.

Chapter SIX

Significant Others

"A Rabbi Speaks of his Ecumenical Experiences" was the title of a lecture I gave in Düsseldorf in October 1996. German Christians are interested in a Canadian rabbi's interaction with Christians. What had been the nature of his contact with Christians? When and where do these interfaith contacts occur in Canada? Who are the participants? How do these interfaith activities relate to the general responsibilities of a rabbi? The nuance that was particularly relevant to my audience was that this rabbi, Erwin Schild, was born in Germany and entered Christian-Jewish dialogue burdened with his own experiences of persecution at the hands of Germans who were, at least nominally, Christian.

I had a great deal of material to share with my audience. I described my experiences in the B'nai Brith's League for Human Rights, whose first director, an ordained Anglican priest, had drafted me to chair a task force to address problems encountered by the Italian community in Toronto. I described the mission of the Canadian Council of Christians and Jews and the Christian-Jewish Dialogue of Toronto. I mentioned the dialogue programs held jointly by Jewish and Christian congregations, the annual ecumenical Holocaust Education Week, the regular visits by students of public and denominational schools to my synagogue, my work as a guest lecturer in Christian churches, and above all, the joint involvement of Christian and Jewish clergy in the innumerable causes that affect the general welfare of the community.

However, I prefaced my comments on my ecumenical experiences as a Canadian rabbi with an account of my interfaith experiences in early childhood. My German listeners were intrigued when I recalled my close, daily contacts with the Catholic family who were tenants in our home, the Roggendorf family. It is especially difficult for younger Germans, who are conditioned to think of Jews as a separate self-contained community, to imagine so close and harmonious a symbiosis of Christians and Jews. How could they know that such a relationship was quite ordinary before Nazi Germany ghettoized and demonized the Jews?

IT WAS CHRISTMAS EVE. My sister, Margot, and I had been put to bed, but expectancy drove sleep away. We were waiting for the son and daughter of the Roggendorfs, our tenants. The house was quiet. Finally Hermann and Kathrinchen appeared, lifted us out of our beds and carried us upstairs, clad in our pajamas, to see their Christmas tree. It was lit with real candles and adorned with beautiful ornaments, shiny baubles, coloured globules, metal-foil chains, and white angel hair. Under the tree were gifts, toys, and delicious sweets, waiting for us to enjoy.

I was too young to be afraid that my participation in the Roggendorfs' Christmas, or in the search for the coloured Easter eggs at Easter, might compromise my religious loyalties, nor were my parents bothered by such a fear. We simply shared the joy of our neighbours' celebration just as they shared ours when they attended our lighting of the Hanukkah menorah or when they ate our matzo and tasted the Passover delicacies my mother produced.

The Roggendorf family lived upstairs from us, on the fourth floor. Their residence was not partitioned from ours, and they used the open staircase that passed through the floors we occupied. I am sure that, as an infant, I became aware of them at the same time I became aware of my own family. They were like relatives—devoted, loyal, and close— and Frau Roggendorf often helped my mother in the household. The old man, Johann Roggendorf, was a hard-drinking working man, a bit rowdy and rough, but he was always respectful of my parents, who would sometimes intervene in his frequent drunken spats with his wife, Lena. And he was playful with Margot and me—he would lie on the floor and let us climb all over him, punching him and pulling his hair, while he raised us high on his feet or, standing up again, lifted us to the ceiling with his strong arms. I think that he was employed for some time as a night watchman. He had a truck garden on the other side of the Rhine where he grew vegetables and raised rabbits. He often shared the little shack on his plot of land with his lady friend, much to the relief of his wife. We—at least the children—visited him there occasionally and he once showed me how to kill a rabbit with one single stroke of a gridiron across the back of its neck.

Käthe Roggendorf, whom we called by her German diminutive, Kathrinchen, started work as a salesperson in our store as soon as she had completed school. She continued to work for my father as long as our business existed and grew to be his most trusted, experienced, and reliable employee. She remained true and faithful to my parents even after the Nazis expropriated our store. Disregarding the danger to herself, she collected outstanding accounts to relieve my parents' dire financial situation. During the war, when Jews were on starvation rations and my parents had been forced to move to a "Jewish house" in Cologne, she supplied them with necessities as best she could, until my parents were deported to Riga in 1942. After the war, she was the key witness in the judicial proceedings through which we were awarded some compensation for the business taken away from my parents.

Kathrinchen married late in life and had no children. After the war, she moved away from Cologne to a small town, Ehringshausen, where her husband's family had some property. My wife and I visited her regularly on our trips to Germany and so did my brother. She was with me in 1982 when I visited Mülheim at the invitation of Christian churches, both Catholic and Protestant. On one occasion during this visit, I addressed a women's church group in Mülheim. I will never forget the challenging, passionate speech she made during the discussion period, after some of my listeners had boasted how friendly and loyal they had been to my parents. Kathrinchen pointedly and forcefully deflated some of their self-serving remarks. What had they really done for the remaining Jews of Mülheim? she asked.

Kathrinchen's husband died a few years ago; she herself is now well past ninety and suffering from Alzheimer's disease. She spends her days in a private nursing daycare for seniors, where we last visited her in October 1996. Her short-term memory is completely gone, but she recognized me and talked in the present tense about the distant past when our families had lived together. She remembered the names of all the salespeople in our store. For her, it was only yesterday. Her parents and mine were still alive...

In order to allow my mother time to devote to the business—and in keeping with the style of middle-class families—my parents engaged a *Kindermädchen* soon after Margot's birth. *Kindermädchen* is a nanny or governess—but neither word fits our Anna Winterschladen. Many years later, when I visited Anna on my trips to Germany, it dawned on me that Anna must have been a young girl, in her late teens or early twenties, when she started working for us. To me, she was the epitome of an elderly spinster—fussy, correct, pedantic, squeamish, square, cautious, prudish, modest, and a very devout Catholic. To think of her in a bathing suit or with a man was impossible. Her clothes were outrageously old-fashioned and she always wore a bell-shaped hat. Anna did not live in, although she accompanied us on family vacations, yet she became part of the family. She was thoroughly involved in bringing up my sister and me and was utterly devoted to us. She would have run through fire for us. I cannot think of my childhood without her.

Public preschool facilities did not exist in Germany in those years, so neither my sister nor I started school until we were six. Many of my vivid memories of Anna come from the four years between the time she entered our household and the time I started school, but in the relative perspective of a childish memory, it was a long, long time. School hours only occupied the morning, so even after I had entered elementary school, Anna spent plenty of time with us.

Despite Anna's idiosyncrasies and her intellectual limitations— as a bright child I soon became very much aware of them—I owe much of my moral and social upbringing—good manners, virtues such as honesty, cleanliness, and a sense of propriety—to her. Anna taught us sayings and songs that I still occasionally sing to myself when I am alone; she made sure our ears were clean, our necks were washed, and that we wore the proper clothes. Every day, unless it rained too hard, she took us for a walk, usually to the Stadtgarten, a municipal park where she met another *Kindermädchen*. Therese looked after the Mohl children, who became our closest friends.

Once in while, Anna took us to her home, where she lived with her mother. Her house seemed a little spooky to us, a place right out of fairy tales. It did not have a flush toilet yet, and I found it not only uncomfortable, but scary, to use the facilities. It was a long walk to get there, for it was away from the Rhine and close to the railway tracks that circled the city. On my first return visit to Germany in

1972, Laura and I walked there. I found it without difficulty, though I had forgotten the number, and I was surprised to find that Anna's house was not nearly as far from our house as I had imagined. It was so strange: the house, untouched by the war, looked and even smelled exactly as I remembered. The same pictures of Jesus and the saints that had so intrigued me as a child still adorned the walls. And Anna herself looked almost unchanged! The visit was a surprise for her, though we had written her that we might stop in Cologne on our way from Switzerland to the Netherlands. She was overjoyed and could hardly believe her eyes: Erwin, standing before her! The passage of time had not dimmed her love and loyalty. Her face beamed; she could not do enough to express her feelings. She readily agreed to take a sentimental walk with us to the park—after first putting on her hat. Alas, the bench where we had met the Mohl children almost fifty years before was no longer there, but, for a moment, I felt like the child in Anna's care again.

We visited Anna several times over the next fifteen years, whenever I visited Germany. The last time came after ill health had forced her to seek care in a nursing home. After she died, about two years later, I was deeply moved by evidence of her loyalty that came to light. Her nephew—her closest surviving relative—sent me two items that were found among her personal effects. The first was a letter of recommendation that my father had written for her when we could no longer employ her. To my shock and surprise, it showed that she had only been in our household for ten years. That was a long time for a Kindermädchen, *but I had thought of her as being with us—forever! Her letter of reference was typed on my father's business letterhead, the only copy of this letterhead now in existence. The second item was a postcard that I had written to Anna on January 26, 1939, seven years after Anna had left her position with us, and on the very day that I hurriedly left Germany. I wrote that I was sorry I could not say a proper goodbye to her in person and that the card would be the last piece of mail I would write and mail in Germany. Anna treasured the postcard for over fifty years, until her death, keeping it together with my father's letter.*

Not long after Anna entered our household, my parents decided to engage a housekeeper in order to relieve my mother from domestic chores that interfered with her responsibilities in the store. To find a suitable person, my father turned to his native village, Ulmbach. Country girls often looked for positions in large cities where they had better prospects. Lina Röder, of Ulmbach, was offered the job and joined our family, probably around 1924.

Lina had less of a direct influence on my upbringing than Anna. Nevertheless, like Anna, she became an integral part of the household. She cooked our food, washed our clothes, and kept house. Unlike Anna, she lived in, so her relationship with us was very close. She was fairly and respectfully treated and came to sincerely love our family; she was especially fond of me. Lina married Hermann, the Roggendorfs' son, around 1935. That was the year that the notorious Nuremberg Laws were enacted by the Nazi government. It became unlawful for Jews to have "Aryan" household employees, so Lina had to leave us. How she felt became evident when her only child, a son, was born and she named him Erwin in my honour.[1]

Laura and I visited Lina on our first trip to Cologne and on nearly every subsequent visit. I saw her for the last time in April 1993. She had retreated into herself while enduring several years of severe illness. She rarely spoke any longer and seemed to be in a world of her own. However, she reacted with a show of excitement when told that I was about to visit her, got herself dressed, and willingly left her nursing home to meet me at her son's home in a suburb of Cologne. She was silent during most of the visit, but never took her eyes off me for a moment while I was there. She died two weeks later.

I continue to maintain contact with her son, Erwin, and his wife, Inge. Erwin worked as an archivist for the city of Cologne until he opted for early retirement a few years ago. In

---

[1] The reader may recall that when Laura and I, on our first European visit in 1972, stopped in Ulmbach to see my ancestral home, the lady who directed us to my grandfather's grave mentioned Lina as soon as I introduced myself.

this capacity, he used to send me interesting material published by the archives that related to the Nazi period in Cologne and the fate of the Jewish community. Erwin and Inge usually come to hear me lecture in Cologne. They enrolled in a three-week course on Jewish festivals that I taught at the Catholic Karl Rahner Academy in Cologne. Erwin's mother, Lina, who had become thoroughly familiar with Jewish festivals when she looked after our home, would have been very pleased.

Chapter SEVEN

The Relatives

*In a child's developing definition of identity, being a descendant is
a given. The first thing I knew about myself was that I was my
parents' child. It took a long time before I could project my image
into a future and think of myself as a potential ancestor. Today,
being an ancestor lies close to the core of my self-definition. Laura
and I have three children, Daniel, Judith, and Naomi, who have
enriched us with eleven grandchildren. Together with their spouses,
and a growing number of great-grandchildren, they certainly
qualify us for the title ancestor. My place is now in the upper half
of the six generations of my family that are bracketed by my life.*

*It may sound odd, but the tautological observation that all my
descendants are related to one another always gives me a jolt. My
children are uncles, aunts, and siblings-in-law; my grandchildren
are cousins, and my youngest child is a grandmother! A network
of relationships woven by Laura and me knits all of us together—
a wondrous fact to contemplate when an occasion brings us all
together. Whenever that happens, I also feel a tinge of regret. It
seems to me that my descendants are not as close to one another as I
was to the members of the family circle to which I belonged in my
childhood and youth. But then again, my children's and grandchildren's lives are so vastly different from my life and the lives of
my contemporaries when we were their age.*

A S FAR BACK AS I CAN REMEMBER, I learned that, besides the
familiar figures of father, mother, brother and sister, there were
people whom I was to call *Tante* or *Onkel*. I cannot recall the precise
moment it dawned on me that my aunts and uncles were related to
my parents as I was to Kurt and Margot. At some time, I must have
noticed that my family—as the generic term that included everyone
who was related to me by blood or by marriage—was lopsided: there

were many branches on my mother's side of the family tree, but only Onkel Felix and Tante Bertha Schild were related to me through my father, and their only child, Joseph, called Seppel in the local dialect, was my only cousin on my father's side.

My education in family relations started with the Kracko family. They lived only a few minutes' walk from our house in Mülheim, so we saw them more often than other relatives. Aunt Nettchen was my mother's oldest sister, a woman with a wonderful disposition, resourceful and friendly. My mother must have often relied on her experienced advice and help in domestic matters. Her husband, Onkel Emil Kracko, had a butcher shop. Onkel Emil and Tante Nettchen lived above the shop in a house that seemed very dark to me, perhaps because it was located on a narrow street and built of dark brown bricks.

Tante Nettchen and Onkel Emil had four children. They were my cousins, I learned, but were all much older than I. Only ten years separate my oldest grandchild from my youngest; my cousins' age spectrum was much wider. Hertha, the first-born Kracko child and the oldest of my many cousins, was a very chic young lady, beautiful, elegant, and vivacious. She established herself as a couturier and opened her own studio in which she employed a number of seamstresses. Although I loved exuberant, affectionate Hertha, I was utterly bored when my mother took me to Hertha's workshop to order or try on a new outfit.

Arthur, the eldest son in the Kracko family, was as short in stature as he was short-tempered, but he was also lively, competent, and interesting. He loved sports, both as a fan and as a player. When the Nazis excluded Jews from participating in sports with Aryans, Arthur became active in the Jewish sports organization, Makkabi. He was a specialist in marine diesel engines and worked for the giant Deutz Motoren Company, who got around the embarrassment of employing a Jew by posting him to England where he supervised the installation of their marine engines in British ships. Arthur remained in England and eventually prospered in his own marine engine business.

When we were little children, Erich Kracko was the cousin that my sister and I liked best, for he often visited us and demonstrated his physical strength by boosting us up to the ceiling by our ankles, as we kept our bodies stiff. He was a plumber by trade and came to our house whenever plumbing work was required. His tool box was very impressive.

The Krackos had another son who was about the same age as Kurt and quite close to him. Unfortunately, Walter became a victim of the Nazis while he was still in his twenties. He was arrested for a violation of racial laws—*Rassenschande*, desecrating the racial purity of the German people—and convicted of having relations with an Aryan girl. He may have been innocent, but he was jailed and, after completing his sentence, he was taken to a concentration camp and murdered.

My parents were also very close to another uncle and aunt who lived in Cologne, Tante Frieda and Onkel Gustav Baum. Frieda, my mother's sister and close to her in age, was a very beautiful woman, not as robust as Tante Nettchen. I remember how devastated our entire family was when Tante Frieda developed cancer and died quite young, around 1935. Frieda and Gustav had one daughter, Hilde, a very sophisticated young lady whom I greatly admired. She seemed intriguing and mysterious, and held a good position in a business office. Hilde was a little older than my brother, Kurt, but she was very friendly with him; he very likely benefited from her social expertise and worldly wisdom. My sister was quite attached to cousin Hilde, who, in turn, took a great interest in Margot.

Since my mother had three sisters and three brothers, there were more uncles, aunts, and cousins. I eventually became acquainted with all of them, but because my mother was the second youngest in her family, most of my cousins were much older. They also lived farther away, which made it more difficult to have a close relationship.

Another aunt on my mother's side was Tante Selma. She and her husband, Onkel Louis Moses, lived in a more distant suburb of Cologne. Although we often spent Sunday afternoons together, I did not feel very close to them. Selma was a nervous type; Onkel Louis was a little gruff on the surface, and did not bother much with us kids. Their two children, Edith and Kurt, about my brother's age, emigrated to Paraguay in 1936.

My mother's eldest brother was Gustav Neugarten, whose wife Johanna had died too early for me to remember her. My grandfather Herz Neugarten lived with him, or vice versa, in Cologne-Kalk. Gustav's only child was Walter. Both Onkel Gustav and cousin

Walter managed to emigrate to South Africa, where they prospered as clothing manufacturers.

Next was Onkel Salli and his wife, Ida, but my memories of them are very vague. Their only child, Ilse, lived in Belgium.

Onkel Willi Neugarten, the youngest of the Neugartens, and Tante Else were close to us, although they did not live in Cologne. I remember how hard they struggled to make a living in a small town called Dinslaken, not far from the Dutch border. They left Germany for Holland, soon after Hitler came to power. My aunt, a good seamstress, sewed skirts and my uncle sold them from house to house. Out of these humble beginnings they built a substantial clothing manufacturing business. Their daughter, Hannerl, just a few years older than I, was exceptionally beautiful. She had all the features of the handsome Neugarten family that I still perceive in some of my grandchildren. Unfortunately, Hannerl did not survive the Holocaust. Onkel Willi and Tante Else also had a son, Hank, my only cousin who was younger than I. Hank still lives in Amsterdam and we keep in regular contact.

Sunday was usually a family day for us, with visits and family get-togethers. While the ladies talked and the men played cards, the children played and enjoyed refreshments. When the weather permitted, the family spent Sunday afternoons in the countryside, wandering along a forest path from the suburban railway station to one of the many idyllic rustic restaurants that had a large playground for the kids and outdoor tables for the older generation to play cards and drink beer or coffee. The children often brought friends along and played soccer or other games. At other times, our parents took us into the city on Sunday afternoons to enjoy the fabulous pastries at a city cafe or to wander in the magnificent Stadtwald, the city forest. The Cologne Zoo, a major animal park, was also a frequent Sunday destination, but we had annual subscription tickets and often visited it on weekdays with Anna. I knew the zoo and its inhabitants very well. Next to the zoo was the Flora, a wonderful botanical garden with many kinds of horticultural exhibits, where we often walked with our parents. Although the zoo and the Flora were on the opposite bank of the Rhine, they were not very far from Mülheim.

❖

When Laura and I were in Cologne in 1993, we went for a walk in the Flora, along the paths that were still familiar to me. We visited the tropical hothouse, that has been improved and enlarged, but is in the same location. Laura admired the park, but my heart was heavy with a memory that clung to the Flora.

On a Shabbat afternoon in 1938, when I was eighteen years old, I walked in the Flora with a deeply unhappy girl. The tragedy of being young and Jewish in Nazi Germany cascaded down on us. It was an end time, a time to reveal feelings that had never been confessed before. I was trying to comfort her, but we knew that our world was about to dissolve. We walked for hours and talked, and we were choking inside with the knowledge that we would never walk together and talk like this again. And so it was.

However, that scene was unforeseeable and its circumstances unimaginable at the time when I was learning about my place in my world among the people who lived in it.

Chapter EIGHT

Finding God in Mülheim

THE READER OF MY STORY may well begin to wonder.
"Rabbi, your adult life has been dedicated to the Jewish religion. You became the rabbi of a congregation, a servant of God, so to speak. You have told us how you became aware of your environment, of your parents, your brother, your sister; how other people entered your young life: your neighbours, Anna, Lina, your uncles, aunts, and cousins. How and when did God enter your life?"

Good question. God did not enter my childish mind with a flash of sudden illumination. I cannot recall a dramatic instant of conversion or revelation. God has no beginning, say our theologians, and God had no beginning in my consciousness. According to a fanciful rabbinic suggestion, were not the souls of all Israelites yet to be born gathered at Mount Sinai to partake of the original Revelation? Wait! Souls! That was what it was like for me. When I was a child, I was taught to say a little prayer each morning upon waking up: "I thank you, o living and eternal King, for giving me back my soul in merciful kindness; great is your faithfulness!" I understood that every night, when I went to bed—as I never wanted, but inevitably had to—I gave up my soul as I fell asleep. Something flew away and left me less than I had been, but was returned the next morning, when my eyes opened again. As far back as I can remember, I understood that it was God who looked after my soul while I slept, and not only my soul, but also my sister's. And Mother's and Father's and the souls of everybody else who went to sleep, and that is why people sometimes invoked God's name, saying, thank God! if God wills; with God's help. Or why people prayed to God.

My parents never talked to me directly about God. I did not learn until much later, from my more religious friends, that God is really called Hashem,[1] but as a child I began to understand the idea of a Supreme Being and it grew with me. God was the sum total of everything and everyone I had to obey: my parents, policemen, Anna. But God was good and he wanted everyone to be good and to be thankful to him. We said a long prayer after we ate, to thank God for the food. I learned to say some of it by heart. It was in a different language, but when the prayer was finished, everybody said, "*Mahlzeit*!" In German! Kurt used to say it especially loudly. And I said it before I could say the other words, although I didn't know why we said it. *Mahlzeit* only means meal, or mealtime. Eventually I found out that it was really short for *gesegnete Mahlzeit*, blessed meal, but people had forgotten that and just said *Mahlzeit*, without knowing what it meant, just to make sure that everyone knew that the prayer after the meal was finished. Much later, when I was no longer living among German Jews, I asked myself why *Mahlzeit* was not said before the meal, rather than after. The answer occurred to me after I had observed the Christian practice of saying grace before the meal, not after, as we do. It makes sense to say, A blessed meal! after grace, if grace precedes the meal, just as one starts eating. But German Jews evidently wanted to copy Christian custom, and so they said it after their own grace, too.

Anna, our nursemaid, talked to us about God sometimes. I must give her credit—devout Catholic that she was—for never trying to subvert our Jewish faith by telling us about Jesus and the saints in which she so deeply believed. But she did make it clear that God would love us more if we were good and clean and obedient.

So God entered my life and my consciousness gradually. His presence in my rational mind was reinforced through religious practices and experiences. Among these was the mysterious sensation of sitting beside my father in the synagogue, the emotional lift of Shabbat, the kiddush on Friday night, and listening to conversation around the Shabbat table, especially when we had a learned guest. The exciting Passover seder, an occasion for staying up late and learning unique melodies, involved me in the mystery of God. I knew intuitively that synagogue and prayer and the Torah scrolls all had to do with God. Not scribbling or painting on Shabbat had

[1]Literally "the Name"; a traditional usage to avoid referring to God by using his actual name.

something to do with God. And so had waiting three hours after eating meat before I was allowed to eat a piece of milk chocolate— a serious problem when you eat the main meal at one o'clock in the afternoon! And I began to understand that if I wanted something really badly I could ask God for it. I could pray. And I did pray, mostly that nothing bad should ever happen to my parents and that they should always be with me.

Strange, really, that later on, when I thought more profoundly about God, his immanence and transcendence, and about pantheism, nature, and creation, when I read Marcus Aurelius and Angelus Silesius, when I discussed God with my peers, or debated atheists in our Jewish high school and irreligious Zionists in the youth movement, I never asked myself when and how God had entered my life. Perhaps he really was there from the beginning. Or perhaps my life was taking place within him. Does a fish have awareness of the ocean?

That I was Jewish, I understood quite soon. Because our tenants were not, and Anna was not. They were Christians. And when I started school, it was a Christian school and I did not pray with my fellow students and something within me warned me that certain stories the teacher told were not meant for me. It did not disturb me; on the contrary, it made me feel special. Superior, even? Of course, soon after entering school, I also started religious school in the synagogue.

The Jewish community of Mülheim was small, but it had a synagogue, a communal structure, and a long history. It ought to have been a peaceful community, but a political controversy threatened to pull it apart in the late 1920s. I remember how my father tried to bridge the ugly partisanship of a divided community. At issue was the question of whether the Jews of Mülheim, a few hundred in number, should join the Jewish community of Cologne, which numbered about 17,000 souls. The city of Mülheim-on-the-Rhine no longer existed. It had become Cologne-Mülheim, incorporated as a suburb of Cologne a few years before my birth. Thus it would have become anomalous for the Jewish community to retain its independence. It is important to remember that the official religious bodies were part of the German political structure; the Church had always been intimately linked with the state. The Reformation — the split within the Church of Rome—had resulted in a cruel and long-lasting war that almost devastated Europe. Since the emancipation of the Jews, a similar linkage to governmental authority was extended to Judaism. Jewish communities and their institutions were recognized, regulated, and supported by the state. The state collected a religion tax from all who confessed a religious denomination, and the proceeds were then available to the recognized administration of that religious community. Members of the Jewish clergy were officials of the state. Representatives elected from the members of the community advised the government and, in turn, were charged with the responsibility for the proper functioning of synagogues and other communal institutions.

The move to deprive Jewish Mülheim of its independence and join it to Cologne was probably logical and, I suppose, mandated by the government. However, it gave rise to political wrangling and dissension within the community. The politics can only be understood against the background of internal Jewish tensions.

The major Jewish communities recognized by the state were "unity communities," which created and supported facilities for worship and education for both Orthodox and Liberal Jews. Cologne had a major Orthodox synagogue on the Glockengasse, today the site of the new opera house, and a Reform, or Liberal, temple on the Roonstrasse. The latter was rebuilt after Word War II and has functioned ever since as the only synagogue in Cologne. However, in addition to the large, Jewish unity community of Cologne, there was also a smaller, independent, and separatist Orthodox community founded by Orthodox Jews whose religious conscience did not permit them to belong to, and support with their taxes, a community that fostered Reform Judaism, an anathema to the Orthodox. After a long and bitter struggle for state recognition in the nineteenth century, led by the Frankfurt *Austrittsgemeinde*, or secessionist community, under leadership of the famous Rabbi Samson Raphael Hirsch, the government had to relent and accord recognition to the separate Orthodox community. The same status had been achieved by the Adass Jeschurun Congregation in Cologne. Similar battles for recognition had been fought and won in many other major cities.

The threat of secession now hung over our community as well. Some of the more Orthodox families, among them our friends the

Mohls, did not want to be swallowed by the large unity community of Cologne that they considered to be beyond the pale because it included Reform Judaism. I may not have realized it at the time, but there were also personal considerations involved, as well as a few hidden agendas.

From my perspective, the quarrel swirled around the professional leader of the Mülheim synagogue in the person of Lehrer Leopold Vogel. As I have mentioned before, the German word *Lehrer* does not merely denote a teacher, but also serves as a title. Just as a medical doctor was addressed as Herr Doktor and a rabbi as Herr Rabbiner, a teacher was Herr Lehrer. If a synagogue under the jurisdiction of the official community was not large enough to have its own rabbi, a *Lehrer* was assigned to serve their spiritual and ritual needs. Such a *Lehrer*, as our Lehrer Vogel, was a graduate of an accredited seminary, trained as a religious teacher and as cantor. These religious functionaries often had an excellent academic background in Jewish and general subjects, but were not ordained. Their religious functions were supervised by the *Oberrabbiner*—chief rabbi—of the larger community with which the synagogue was affiliated, or by the *Landesrabbiner*, the government-appointed district or provincial rabbi.

Lehrer Leopold Vogel was really a very fine, learned, and talented gentleman of quiet and refined temperament. His duties in the synagogue were to lead the services and take care of everything that pertained to them, as well as serving as the religious teacher who taught the boys and girls of the community several hours a week. He was a bachelor, a slight handicap in his professional life, and lived in an attractive little villa on the outskirts of Mülheim, under the care of a housekeeper. I cannot say whether this circumstance had anything to do with the controversy that enveloped him. My parents liked Lehrer Vogel and frequently invited him for dinner. He enjoyed the calm atmosphere of our home. He had a very fine voice and played the violin, and Kurt would often accompany him on the piano. When he was our guest on Friday nights he would lead us in the singing of Psalm 126, "Shir Hama'alot," singing a tune which I still use at home sometimes. He was also with us for Passover seders, and I am sure I learned a great deal from him.

However, Lehrer Vogel was not Orthodox enough to satisfy the Mohl family. He was a graduate of a proper seminary but he was inclined towards a modern interpretation of Judaism and adhered, no doubt, to the *Wissenschaft des Judentums* school, the enlightened proponents of an academic study of Jewish heritage. Those teachings were acceptable for the leaders of the inclusive unity community— the *Grossgemeinde*, as it was called—but not for some of the more extreme Orthodox families of Mülheim. I am not sure exactly how this controversy related to the absorption of the Mülheim synagogue into the Cologne community, but looking back at that turbulent drama, played out while the Nazi party was gaining strength in German politics, I realized that it left Mülheim temporarily in political limbo. Lehrer Vogel resigned his post; I doubt he was old enough to be pensioned. I do not know what happened to him afterwards. The controversy affected but did not destroy our friendship with the Mohl and Speier-Holstein families, but the children re-enacted in our teasing way the antagonism that had split the adult community. My sister and I were branded as *Vogeltiere* by our friends, a verbal compound difficult to render in English. *Vogel*, the teacher's name, is German for bird; *Tier* is an animal, and a *Vogeltier*—or "bird-animal"—was simply a somewhat derogatory name for supporters of Lehrer Vogel.

There was no real replacement for Lehrer Vogel. His office as cantor and Torah reader was taken over by Herr Israel Janowski, an immigrant from Poland, who had the requisite skills, although his eastern European manners and accents were abrasive to many congregants. However, his religious credentials were beyond question, and he really was a nice man. As children we used to make fun of him because of his faulty German—he was a Yiddish-speaker originally—and several of his habitual or occasional linguistic slips became part of the secret code words which we, just about to become teenagers, used in our private verbal communications. Poor Mr. Janowski never caught on to what was so funny, or—more likely— he was smart enough to pretend he didn't. Incidentally, he was also licensed as shochet, a ritual cattle and fowl slaughterer, a useful qualification for the Mohl family, who were in the meat business, wholesale and retail.

Although Mr. Janowski was very learned in the traditional Jewish law and lore, he did not possess the formal educational and pedagogical qualifications of a Jewish religious teacher. Actually, my friends and I learned a great deal from him in informal teaching sessions and from personal interaction. He never stinted in sharing his wide knowledge. He encouraged us to learn how to read the Torah and had us read for the congregation on Shabbat afternoons. The effects of his efforts in this direction are still evident in my ability to recite by heart the first section of many weekly Torah portions.

Formal religious school had to be conducted by officially approved teachers. By coincidence or design, or most likely by making some political deals behind the scenes, a relative of the Mohls became our religious teacher, a gentleman by the name of Oskar Simons. He was a Hebrew teacher in Cologne, identified with the secessionist community. He was a brother of Rosalie Mohl, mother of my closest childhood friends. He was also an excellent and forceful teacher. Eloquent and persuasive, he articulated very strong Orthodox views, and exerted a decisive influence on my spiritual growth. However, after a while he was succeeded by his brother, Rabbiner Dr. Julius Simons. The two brothers were not on the best of terms and differed in temperament and Jewish philosophy. Rabbiner Dr. Simons was one of the rabbis serving the main Cologne unity congregation. Thus he was bound to be more tolerant of differing interpretations of Judaism. He represented a more enlightened Orthodoxy that contained a healthy dose of pragmatism and flexibility. The synagogue he served was in Cologne-Deutz, a suburb on the same side of the Rhine as Mülheim, but closer to the city. Mülheim was now placed under his rabbinic umbrella and he took charge of the children's Jewish education. He was also a good teacher, a fine role model for Jewish living. I continue to acknowledge my indebtedness to Dr. Simons for the religious direction my life took in the course of time. But he was too pragmatic, too cautious, and too sober to excite the inquisitive, searching minds of teenagers. As I outgrew my childhood chums, however, I became very close friends with two of his children: his son Ernst, still my friend in Cologne and Jerusalem, and his daughter Martha, in San Francisco, a very dear friend to this day. The rabbi's wife, Mrs. Veronika Simons, was a sister of the Mohl brothers, while Dr. Simons was a brother of Mrs. Rosalie Mohl—a case of a sister and brother marrying another pair of siblings. I spent a great deal of time, including many Friday nights, in Dr. Simons's spacious apartment above the synagogue in Deutz. The synagogue is no longer standing, but a street is now named after him: the Dr. Julius Simons Strasse.

At the time, the political implications of the designation of the two Simons brothers were not clear to me. In retrospect, I speculate that Oskar's appointment was a temporary move in the direction of a separate community—or perhaps a private arrangement financed by the Mohl family. The emergence of Dr. Julius Simons, on the other hand, probably sealed the entry of Mülheim into the Cologne unity *Grossgemeinde*. It is, however, only my interpretation of events.

Long before I understood the complicated congregational politics, our synagogue had become part of my childish world. It was typical of small-town synagogues built in the early nineteenth century, at a time when it was still common to hide a synagogue from public view, since the sight of a Jewish house of worship was considered offensive to the eyes of good Christians. The building stood at the back of an interior courtyard, far behind the street line. The street frontage was occupied by the community house, indistinguishable from adjoining houses, which contained classrooms and meeting rooms, as well as the apartment of the *Synagogendiener*, or sexton. The entrance to the modest, but handsome, synagogue, already old and venerable when I was a child was across the courtyard, accessible through an arched passage way. I loved to pull myself up by the braided rope that served as banister on the narrow spiral staircase that led to the ladies' gallery. Of course, newer synagogue buildings erected in a more enlightened age—that is, roughly after 1850—were handsome and impressive edifices built right on the street, proclaiming to all both the acceptance of Jews as citizens of Germany and the righteous tolerance of an enlightened Christian majority. Who would have expected that they all would burn to the ground on the night of November 9, 1938, *Kristallnacht*.

As a young child, my father took me to synagogue every Shabbat morning. I learned some of the ritual, and came to know some of the venerable personalities. Herr Spiegel, an old gentleman and one of the pillars of the community; and Herr Wolff, a learned elder, related to some very famous rabbis and scholars. Herr Wolff frequently took a turn in conducting the synagogue prayers and rituals, such as the sounding of the shofar on Rosh Hashanah. My father was one of the honourary officers and stood beside the Torah scroll during the reading of the weekly portion. I can remember the cover and heft of his Chumash, his Hebrew-German copy of the Pentateuch, from which he used to follow the Torah reading, thus learning a good deal of Hebrew. The volume had two narrow columns on each page, Hebrew on one side, German on the other; and it had a typical old-book smell. The smell was similar to that of my father's tallit, which I liked to drape around myself. This vignette, etched in my memory—sitting on the bench next to my father, his tallit drawn over my head and shoulders—probably only represents a very brief period of my childhood, but it epitomizes the eternity of being a child.

Chapter NINE

So Many Toys,
So Many Books

"*T*IME WARP" IS A CONCEPT that the entertainment industry has borrowed from modern science. In some contemporary motion pictures, past, present and future crazily intersect. Members of generations yet unborn intervene in the lives of people who are destined to become their ancestors. We go back to the future or forward to the past.

A kind of time warp bends my childhood memories. I remember a mass of vivid details and vignettes from my early years. I can retrieve places and things: toys, games, books, tools, construction and chemistry sets; I can recall songs and verses, and snatches of stories and fables. But I cannot fit all these items sequentially into the very limited number of years of my life to which they belong!

The jigsaw puzzle has too many pieces. The scenes, objects, and events that crowd my memory seem to overflow the time frame of my childhood. How can so much fit into so short a period of time? When could I have played with all the toys I remember? Germany was renowned for its toy industry and I had a generous sampling of its production: wind-up toys, wooden and metal building sets of progressive levels of complexity, loop-the-loop cars, mechanical horse racing sets, electric trains, model air planes, and kites. I remember a little metal car on a looping track—at a certain point the car's momentum hurled it on an airborne trajectory—which at the end of its downward course triggered an elevator which raised it back up to the starting level. There were board games and card games, as well as collecting cards of different types, some of which came from cigarette packs. In retrospect, it seems as if I were busy for months with a set of different types of ships, complete with harbour installations, that I had cut out from a cardboard construction set and pasted together. Probably I manipulated the little ships, the dry-dock, and the cranes, for only a few days. Was I five years old then, or seven? Or ten?

I am also puzzled when I try to recreate a time sequence for other activities. Was it before or after I had started school that I played all those games in the park with my friends, the Mohl children, on our daily outing in the park with Anna? *"König, wie viel Schritte schenkst du mir?"* (King, how many steps do you grant me?)—"Two giant steps." We played games with balls, with hoops, and with ropes, we raced one another on the wide paths and played hide-and-seek among the trees and benches...

When did all the incidents and projects that I remember so vividly take place? When did I invent the perpetual calendar?

Yes, I invented and built a perpetual calendar. The idea struck me one day and I made the calendar with material from the shoe store. I cut three long strips from the huge roll of wrapping paper. On one strip, I wrote the numbers from 1 to 31, on the second, the days of the week, and on the third, the months of the year. Using a shoe box, I constructed a little box with strategically placed slots through which I threaded the three strips, and rolled them on little wooden rods that I inserted into the sides of the little box before I pasted it all together. By turning the protruding ends of the rods, the day of the week and month of the year would appear on the outside of the calendar box. The idea was ingenious for a little boy, I think, but the execution was sloppy: the sides of the box kept coming apart because I had not glued them properly. That was typical: I was good at the concept but lacked the mechanical skill, or the desire, to do it properly. I was never skilled at sawing, hammering, or fastening. A little carpentry set that I was given was one of my least favourite toys. However, I was proud of the calendar—and very disappointed when I discovered that my invention was not as original as I had thought.

Like many fortunate children, I was exposed to literature very early in my childhood. I have clear memories of my parents—both my mother and my father—telling me stories or reading to me. Anna, our *Kindermädchen*, read to me as well. She also loved to quote sayings and proverbs, often in rhyme, and to sing sad romantic songs of love and death, of flowers and graves. I can remember some of them even now.

Long before I started school, months before my fourth birthday, my parents helped me learn to read. Reading was easy for me and I enjoyed it. I had loved listening to the fairy tales by the Grimm

Brothers and Hans Christian Andersen, but I enjoyed them even more when I could read them myself and repeat my favourite passages over and over again. I can still feel the pleasure! I liked especially the more gruesome and eerie stories, with blood-curdling ghosts and spooky monsters, hardly correct by modern standards of children's literature.

But, again, I cannot fit all the books I read and liked into the relevant time frame. I did read very fast, so fast, indeed, that my parents would not believe sometimes that I was finished with a book or a story. They tested me, and I remember how proud they were when I could recite the stories practically verbatim. I had the same good short-term memory then that stood me in such good stead, many years later, in my university exams!

In the skewed perspective of childish memory, it seems that I must have spent years reading my favourite fairy tales; in reality, it was probably a lot less. I must have enjoyed several books at the same time. I remember wonderful illustrated books with rhymed morality tales, intended to impart a moral or practical lesson: *Suppenkaspar—Casper of the Soup*—graphically conveyed the lesson that you must eat your soup; the horrible example of *Struwelpeter— Peter the Unkempt*—warned that you must have your finger nails cut, your neck and ears washed, and your hair combed. The verses were quality literature: funny, sometimes cruel, and often frightening, and fragments of them still stick in my memory. My reading included the exciting rhymed adventures of two daring but naughty boys, Max and Moritz, who came to a sad end—in a meat grinder, if I remember correctly—a fate that was intended to amuse and to deter. I was surprised and thrilled when on a visit to Cologne last year, I found many of these books in a book store. My discovery dispelled the air of unreality that sometimes shrouds childhood memories that have not been corroborated. At least I knew I had not been dreaming!

How old was I when I read all those books that left so deep an impression on my mind? Lina and Anna, and some of my friends and relatives, with a mixture of admiration and ridicule, called me a bookworm, but not my parents. They probably foresaw that the printed word was to play an important part in my future and were happy to watch me devouring books from an early age. I was indeed a bookworm, spending many hours reading and exercising my imagination.

I progressed from children's tales to sagas of the age of chivalry. I read many versions of the lives and battles of the medieval heroes, the circles of knights and the royal courts, the myths of the Germanic deities and demigods, Siegfried and the Nibelungs. At one point I became so fascinated by Greek mythology, by the Homeric epics, by Hercules, Hector, and Achilles and by that whole wonderful ancient world that also introduced me to Demosthenes and Socrates and other famous historical figures. And when did I read *Gulliver's Travels*, and the fantastic tales of Jules Verne, about exciting explorations of the ocean deep and of outer space? I had already become an "expert astronomer" by reading Kurt's astronomy book, *From Distant Worlds*. At age seven, I could knowledgeably explain spectral analysis and parallaxes. More down to earth were my books on animals. It was easy for me to whip quickly through a text-book on zoology. While the text was dry, it had wonderful illustrations, and made our regular visits to the zoo so much more meaningful and interesting. Then there were the fascinating *Boys' Annuals* that not only contained stories, but also reviewed new technological developments. I remember reading in one of them about the problems of rocket propulsion, and deep-sea diving, and about experiments to revive the obsolete idea of wind power for ships by means of rotating cylinders. I read history, as well. I can still see and even smell one hefty tome, bound in red leather, with stories from the ancient past. I read historical fiction and nationalistic propaganda, such as the tales of heroism and suffering during the time when Germany chafed under French occupation in the Napoleonic period.

Reading made a deep impact on my intellectual and emotional development. I was moved to tears by such classic animal books as *Maya the Bee*, who, after a beautiful life of sunshine, flowers, gentle meadows, and shady woods, came to tragic end in the web of a spider. I must have read the last sad chapter a dozen times! I also enjoyed humorous boys' books such as *The Flying Classroom* and *The Thirty-first of February*. I also read—clandestinely, of course—the "girls' books" that my sister and her friends read, which I haughtily disdained as inferior literary fare.

At the age of eleven or twelve, I discovered adventure books. During the next few years of my life, I devoured practically all the books by Karl May, a popular German author. His adventures were set in the American West and in the Arab Middle East. I thus became acquainted with the worlds of the American Indians and the Bedouins of Arabia. At the same time, I also appreciated the adventure books of Jack London and similar authors; I had discovered James Fenimore Cooper at an earlier stage of my literary journey. Amundsen's quest for the pole, the epics of world travellers, from Magellan to Marco Polo, adventurers and explorers who travelled to the sources of the Orinoco river and the mountains of Afghanistan— I read everything. The world opened up to me: I travelled with Jules Verne in *Around the World in Eighty Days*, thus learning all about America, India, and time zones.

Looking back from the vantage point of my present age, I am impressed by the wealth of books that I read as a child. It seems strange to me now that, in later years, I thought I had wasted so much time on second-class literature. I felt embarrassed that it had taken me so long to discover "real" literature, by which I meant the "serious" books that I read and discussed in my middle and late teens: the poets and novelists of the early twentieth century, and the classical and romantic literature of earlier periods. Only much later did I realize that I may owe the modest language skills I possess, and above all my creative imagination, to the writers who nourished me in childhood. I did not just read—I lived the adventures, the defeats and triumphs, the pain and the joy of those literary characters.

Somewhere down the road, however, came a turning point. It may have been teachers or other influential guides, or the beginning of an inner maturation, that transformed me into a questing soul and led me into the world of ideas, of intellectual speculation, and the romantic search for meaning, wisdom, truth, and, above all, for the mystique of the world within. The maze of the human soul became so much more intriguing, and its exploration so much more alluring, than the adventures of the explorers of the physical universe. I remained interested in history, but my earlier fascination with the epics of heroes, kings, generals and conquerors gave way to an appreciation of the great movements and developments that lie beneath the surface of events; developments that had to do with faith, religion, enlightenment, discovery, and with the growth of knowledge and ideas that proved more powerful than the conventional instruments that had been assumed to control human behaviour, individual and collective.

At that point, the precocious, inquisitive child had grown into a thoughtful and emotional young man. There must have been a fork in the road. The road I followed took me away from some of my childhood friends, perhaps even from my family. Intellectually, it took me away from Mülheim, from the atmosphere of a small town and its good burghers, preoccupied with the mundane. The boring details of their humdrum lives were no longer for me. I needed to know, to dream, to muse, to feel, to experience, to roam, to live in the world of art, of philosophy, of striving, of being consumed, of mystical union with the transcendental. I needed like-minded companions to share my journey. Or to follow me.

The story of this young man will have to wait a little longer. The mature septuagenarian who is writing it is just beginning to understand. He can look at the young man dispassionately, as if he was someone else. Yet he can still regress and taste how life felt then. But he is not finished with the child yet.

Chapter TEN

Golden Years

A SENSE OF CALM AND SECURITY blankets the memories of my early childhood. My life was simple, carefree, and warm. I was too young to perceive any of the effects that the economic cycles had on my parents' business and, inevitably, on my parents' disposition. Their strength guaranteed my well-being; no shadows fell over my life; there was nothing to fear.

By the time I had outgrown this childish perspective—say, by about age five—times were indeed good. The great inflation had been stanched and my parents began to prosper moderately. The mid 1920s must have been kind to our family. My parents worked hard during the week, but they also enjoyed home and family. Life was stable. Sundays were enjoyable family days. I mentioned the frequent family excursions in the countryside, which in the cooler seasons were replaced by fancy pastry and coffee in downtown Cologne or visits to relatives.

During the week, my sister and I were in Anna's loving care. My brother, Kurt, was somewhat remote, on the periphery of our space. Anna came early in the morning and looked after us while my parents worked in the store. Anna washed, dressed, and fed us, and supervised our play at home or took us for walks. Her routine varied, but as I have said earlier, when the weather was right, she most often took us to the Mülheim Municipal Gardens—the Stadtgarten—where we met our friends the Mohl children, with their *Kindermädchen*, Therese. Sometimes the Mohls' cousins, Jojo Mohl and the Speier-Holstein girls, joined us.

The main meal of the day, usually including soup and a meat course, was served at midday. When we were quite little, Anna had usually finished feeding us at a separate table before the grown-ups sat down to eat. The grown-ups were my parents, Kurt, our housekeeper, Lina, and Anna. On occasion, I would hear my mother instruct Anna, "Let the children eat with us today." I soon learned to protest against our segregation and everyone thought it was funny when, after having been fed by Anna, I demanded, "I want to eat again with us!" My parents did not mind, but, of course, I was no longer hungry and merely lingered for a few minutes over a few morsels on my plate. It did not take too long, I guess, before we were allowed to eat with the adults. We practiced our best table manners so as not to forfeit this privilege.

Food was ample and good in our home. Breakfast usually consisted of rolls, butter, cheese, and jam, with milk for the children and coffee for the grown-ups, or barley coffee for all. My father often returned home for a mid-morning snack. Dinner was at about 1:30 in the afternoon. School was from 8 a.m. to 1 p.m. or, once we were in high school, 1:30 p.m. My dad would usually lie down on the sofa for a 15-minute nap after the midday meal. Around 4:30 p.m. was time for another snack, usually a piece of cake and a drink. Supper, served around 7 p.m., was a light meal, often a cold platter or omelets. Although Lina was our housekeeper, my mother maintained control over the kitchen. We did not eat "Jewish" food, except for a few specialties. My mother, and Lina, too, prepared wholesome, tasty dishes in the regional German style. In fact, the joys of the table rank high among my memories. I actually remember how certain foods tasted. My mother made delicious hot soups—especially white asparagus soup—and, in summer, luscious cold soups: fruit soups, wine soups, and beer soups, usually with fluffs of meringue floating like ice floes on top. She cooked a variety of mouth-watering meats, made wonderful blueberry pancakes, and a deliriously fantastic chocolate mousse.

After Margot and I had graduated to the grown-up table, the family ate always together, with rare exceptions. Mealtimes were important, not only for nourishment, but also for conversation. My parents would ask about our day in school, and then we would discuss the news or current events. Our parents were pretty strict about regular bedtime, but after supper, before being put to bed, we always had some time with our parents. We played board games or read books of rhymes and stories. Naturally, my sister and I often begged to be allowed to stay up longer. I remember that once our parents allowed us to stay up as late as we wanted. Margot and I fought off sleep for a good few hours, finally crawling into bed long after our parents had gone to sleep. As we grew older, there was more time after supper for family togetherness or for doing our homework, until gradually my reading and social or school activities eroded my nightly time with the family. All the same, I can still evoke the atmosphere of our living room—and it truly was a living room. I can see my father smoking his cigarillo; my mother reading a magazine or helping my sister dress a doll; Kurt playing the piano while I read a book in one of the easy chairs. In winter, there was a fire in the *Kamin*, the big iron, brass, and marble hearth.

Occasionally, during the summer months, our Sunday excursions would take us to places beyond the forest cafe in the woods to the north-east of Mülheim, to the Cologne Stadtwald, the municipal forest, where we would wander on the pathways, and row a boat on the lakes and through the canals. One of the exciting highlights of the summer season was our annual steamer excursion on the Rhine. As the steamer took us upstream, past Bonn and other towns, I learned the meaning of navigational signals and markers on the shore and on the river. My instructor was Kurt. The busy river traffic, the boats and barges plying the Rhine up and downstream, was an absorbing spectacle, especially when names and flags indicated a Dutch, Belgian, French, or other foreign registry. Soon I knew every ship in the fleet of the Cologne-Düsseldorf Steamship Line, which offered the most popular cruises. The docking manoeuvres at each stop were also terrific to watch. The Rhine cruise would not be complete for me without a fascinating visit to the engine room, deep in the bowels of the ship. Through an observation window, I watched the huge steam engines turning and listened as the captain gave the signals from the bridge that would command the giant metal pistons and rods to accelerate, slow down, or reverse. Our destination was usually Siebengebirge—the Seven Mountains—where, by incline railway, by donkey, or on foot, we made our way to the castle ruins on Drachenfels—Dragon's Rock—and retold or listened to the ancient tales connected with it. Sometimes we cruised further and admired the many medieval castles, mostly in ruins, on the mountains along the course of the Rhine, and the picturesque towns and vineyards. After we disembarked, we usually visited one of the popular outdoor restaurants perched on a mountainside or in the town.

The mid 1920s were good times. A sweet misty aura surrounds memories of summer vacations with my parents and Anna, who came along to help. One of my earliest memories is of our stay in

Bad Ems, walking along the river with my father as he explained the functions of a canal and the locks required to raise and lower the boats to the changing water levels. A year or two later we vacationed at a kosher hotel in Bad Königstein, in the scenic Taunus mountains. I remember a long trail leading to a look-out. For several years, we enjoyed *sommerfrische* in Bad Neuenahr, where we stayed at a kosher hotel, owned by the Gottschalk family. The Gottschalks were also vintners and wine merchants—the Ahr valley is one of Germany's main wine-producing regions. Bad Neuenahr was and still is a beautiful clean town on the Ahr river, a small tributary of the Rhine, not very far south of Cologne. It is a health spa, with a handsome therapy centre, a casino, and therapeutic mineral springs, surrounded by a lovely park where a band played on a bandstand. We often walked among the men and women drinking the foul-tasting but health-giving waters, sat on the chairs in front of the bandstand and listened to the beautiful music, or wandered on paths along the picturesque river or leading up the mountains and through the vineyards. The casino itself was out of bounds for children, of course.

On our first trip to Europe in 1972, Laura and I also drove to Bad Neuenahr, to escape from the emotionally difficult atmosphere of Cologne. The town was exactly as I remembered it. A walk up to the mountain evoked some magic memories. We stayed longer than we had planned and turned up one day late for our reservation in Amsterdam.

From my childish perspective, these idyllic times seemed to last forever. Time stood still, or moved imperceptibly. In hindsight, this happy time must have been of short duration, probably only lasting a few years in the mid 1920s. Altogether there were less than fifteen years between the end of World War I in November 1918 and the beginning of the Nazi regime in January 1933. Only fifteen years! And the early 1920s were a period of severe economic distress. By the time the decade was over, the Great Depression had begun, producing the turbulent politics and near-chaos out of which the Nazi party rose to power. Business took a painful downturn. My father's worried looks and his hushed discussions with my mother about falling sales, financial pressures, trouble with the bank, and problems with mortgage payments belong to that period of time.

The good years that I so remember vividly can only have lasted from about 1925, when I turned five years old, to 1929. In my childish imaginings, I endowed my parents with nearly divine wisdom and providential power. Sometimes I entertained the notion that they had created my surroundings for my benefit, protection, and pleasure; that as God had done for Adam and Eve, my parents had placed me in a world of their own making and that all the men and women, the river, the park, the lawns, and the houses were only stage props set up at my parents' bidding to create an illusion for my enjoyment. In due course, I accepted the objective reality of the world, at least until I studied the philosophers who made me doubt it again.

I still feel very sad when I recall my beaming father and happy mother and contrast that image with the one that later events forced me to visualize: my poor parents reduced to slaves, to helpless victims of a fate that robbed them of dignity, of happiness, and, eventually, of life itself.

Chapter ELEVEN

Friends

Parched is our heart, bone-dry is our core;
O Dew of Friendship, moisten us that we may bloom once more!
—*MOSES IBN EZRA*

This poem captivated my imagination when I came across it in an anthology. I found it in the original Hebrew and was struck by the elegance of the language. It is an exquisite distich, merely two lines, separated provocatively at a point that coincided neither with the caesura nor with the break between clauses. The Scriptural allusions are obvious, but the meaning of the poem in the context of the life of the medieval author, a distinguished savant and poet, is an intriguing mystery. Rendering it into English while preserving its flavour and elegance was an enjoyable challenge.

    Quite likely, the poem intrigued me because it reflected my own appreciation of friendship. It came to my attention at a time when I was especially grateful for my friends. I was observing the fiftieth anniversary of my election as rabbi of Adath Israel Congregation. Friends, old and new, surrounded and sustained me. Friends and friendships have always been important in my life. A hunter may organize tales of his safaris around a showing of his trophies. A tourist may relive his travels by looking at the souvenirs he brought back. An archaeologist reconstructs the history of a site from potsherds and coins found in the strata of his excavation. I could anchor my biography on the roster of my friends. Each stratum of my life has left its record on the lengthening list of my friendships. It is a long list, not because of the number of names it holds, but because it stretches around the globe. It begins in Cologne-Mülheim with my playmates. After a long detour, it extends to Toronto, where one special friendship led to marriage. It circles to Australia and Israel. It rewinds to Germany where my involvement in the last two decades has added new names to the list.

"Acquire a friend!" [1]*—a basic need in life. The meaning and the nature of friendship were subjects which my teenaged friends and I often discussed. One conclusion we reached was that friends, if wisely chosen, help us develop the best within us. I was fortunate in that Laura shares my old friends with the same affection and enthusiasm that marked her adoption of my relatives as her own. As a result, we have friends in many places and stemming from all stages of my life.*

Old friends are unique. An aura of sweet nostalgia surrounds them both in my memory and whenever I meet one again. The impossible "what ifs" of life and love cling to some of them. Not all friendships survive. Some dissolve as a result of changes in geography or in the orientation of the heart. It hurts to lose a friend. Friends may die, with increasing frequency as we grow older. My dead friends sometimes visit in my dreams.

The passage of time usually heals the hurt of loss. We receive comfort. But the opposite is true of me and, I suspect, of many others who grew up in Europe before the Holocaust. The more time goes on and presents me with the increasingly rich harvest of years, the more I mourn the tragic fate of childhood friends, who were murdered while still on the threshold of life. Of life's varied menu, they tasted little but despair, pain, fury, and death.

I have dedicated this chapter of my memoir to them. They have no burial places, no gravestones, no monuments. So complete was their extermination that only a few people remained who know that they ever lived and died. These pages will probably be the most elaborate account they leave behind: only the names and birth dates of some of them are found in the lists of victims that the Nazis left as a record. I ask my reader, therefore, to read what I have written about my friends. It will be an act of redemption if you will take note of the little that there is to tell. You will, for a moment at least, raise them from the tomb of obliteration.

THE FIRST CIRCLE of our childhood friends—my sister's and mine—was formed by five children from the Mohl family, or as one would say in German, *die Familie Mohl*. It also included their

---

[1]Pirqei Avot 1:6

cousins, the three daughters of the Speier-Holstein family. The Mohl family was a prominent part of the Mülheim Jewish community, in terms of numbers and wealth. Three brothers—out of a total of seven siblings—formed the backbone of the family: Markus, Abraham, and Joseph, the latter who was usually called by the German-Yiddish form of his name, Juppemann. These three brothers managed and controlled the substantial family business. The titular head of the family, though, was their mother, the matriarch, *die alte* Frau Mohl, as she was respectfully known— old lady Mohl. Her given name was Elisabeth.

Frau Mohl lived on the Bachstrasse, not more than a hundred yards from our home, in a little house that contained both a small meat store and their living quarters. She had been a widow for as long as I had known her, and was a corpulent elderly lady, her face deeply furrowed and crowned by a head of thin, snow-white hair. Her short stature was accentuated by a stiff back and her forward-leaning posture, and she was only able to walk slowly, with halting steps. Still, she exuded authority and was awe-inspiring to me as a child. She looked like one of the characters out of the German fairy tales who populated my imagination.

Frau Mohl shared the little house with the oldest son, a bachelor named Moses, who also seemed ancient to me. He had a long beard—beards being quite rare at that time—and a hoarse, rasping voice. I have one strong, clear image of him, in a scene that was repeated on many Saturday nights at the end of Shabbat: I am with my friends, Moses's nephews Jojo, Heinz, and Walter. We have spent the afternoon together and now we are listening as Moses Mohl performs Havdalah, the ceremony that concludes the Sabbath with a flickering torch-like candle, an ornate, turret-shaped, silver spice-box, and a small glass of very strong, clear brandy— Treister—that is more fiery than the candle flame that is extinguished in a little puddle of spilled brandy on a plate at the end of the ceremony; after the candle had been dipped into it, the brandy continues to burn impressively for a few seconds. Moses Mohl sings Havdalah according to an old German rite that begins with a lovely poetic prayer in the old Jewish-German dialect, a prayer for our well-being in the week to come. To finish the ceremony, we sing "Ha-mavdil," a traditional Hebrew hymn that we all know by heart. Then, in later years, when we are teenagers, my friends and I leave to play table-tennis or other game or activity that we have planned.

The Mohl family business, managed by brothers Markus, Abraham, and Juppeman, was meat—trading cattle, slaughtering, wholesale distribution, and the small retail store on the Bachstrasse where we bought our kosher meat. They also employed some of their relatives: Dieter Stern and Otto Plaut came from Büdingen, a town in southern Germany—the hometown of Bertha Mohl, Markus's wife and Jojo's mother—to join the firm.

The house on the Bachstrasse was the front of a complex of buildings that stretched through the entire block to the next street, the Stöckerstrasse. A small open courtyard led to a centre building that housed a large stable for cattle on the ground level, in addition to offices and residential space on the upper floors. I remember gradually overcoming my fear of walking through the stable on my own until, eventually, I enjoyed the excitement of seeing and smelling real, live cows.

Coming from the Bachstrasse, I had to cross the stable to get to another interior courtyard and Markus Mohl's house, where Jojo lived. Of course, one could also enter from the Stöckerstrasse, where a large gate opened to allow the truck to park in the interior vaulted driveway that led from the street, through the house, to the yard and the stables. There was also a smokehouse from which Markus Mohl, a jovial, earthy man, would occasionally produce some delicious smoked meat or similar delicacies for us.

Joseph, or Juppemann, the brother in charge of the financial end of the business, was a bachelor, at least technically. It was rumoured—and I suppose the adult members of the community knew it as fact—that he had a non-Jewish lady friend. The Mohls were a strictly Orthodox family, so intermarriage was unthinkable. During *Kristallnacht*, Juppeman was arrested and taken to Dachau. He was eventually released and made his way to Buenos Aires where he lived for several decades. Of the four brothers and three sisters of the Mohl family, only he and his sister, Billa, survived the Holocaust.

Friedchen Mohl, Jojo's older sister, was about eighteen when my friends and I were teenagers. She was always willing to give us advice in affairs of the heart—and seemed to enjoy it. She had an unhappy love affair with Otto Plaut, her first cousin on her mother's side, who came to work in the business as bookkeeper. I once inadvertently caught them in an embarrassing situation in the office—at least I found it embarrassing. They were passionately kissing in the hallway. Her parents, Markus and Bertha Mohl, made a tragic mistake in not allowing the two of them to get married because they were cousins. Friedchen eventually also managed to escape to Buenos Aires, where her Uncle Juppeman tried to help her through difficult times. She married a non-Jewish Argentinean and had a child, but was later divorced. She died a few years ago; she had a sad life.

At first, my sister and I were closest to the four children of Rosalie and Abraham Mohl: Heinz (who was a year younger than I), Walter, Hannah (who was one year younger than my sister), and Martha, the youngest. They were the children with whom we played almost daily in the park, under the watchful eyes of Anna and Therese. Their cousin Jojo, who had no *Kindermädchen*, often came with them.

Mohl's family lived in a modest but beautiful house—with no store on the ground floor—just around the corner from us on the Formesstrasse. We were always welcome and spent many hours of every week there. We shared the adventures of growing up with them and were constant companions until our paths diverged as we grew older.

All four children perished in the Holocaust.

Abraham Mohl had the means to send his children abroad to safety, but he refused to believe that the Jews of Germany were in mortal danger. Although he was a strictly Orthodox Jew, he was also a German patriot and proud of his army service in the Great War of 1914–18. He was confident that the Hitler regime would soon collapse and so he waited—until it was too late.

Lena, a sister of the four Mohl brothers, was married to Dr. Victor Speier-Holstein, and they were the parents of Ruth, Edith, and Susi. The three girls were also part of our circle, though as young boys Heinz, Walter, Jojo and I had little use for girls. At one of Susi's birthday parties, on June 28, that my sister and I attended along with all the Mohl cousins, the boys formed a club for boys only and named it *Amicitia*, the Latin word for friendship. The club existed for quite a while—weeks? months?—though it had only one purpose: to tease the girls and make them jealous.

Ruth, the oldest daughter, was my age, only a month older, and became my close friend. Edith, two years younger, also played a part in my growing up. Susi was the youngest of the Speier-Holstein girls. I remember one scene that took place on the street in front of our store when I was six. Susi's nanny, Bertha, was passing by with the high-wheeled baby carriage and stopped to let us see the new baby. Even on my tip-toes, I could not raise myself high enough to see what was under the covers. "It's a joke," I declared. "There is no baby in the carriage." But I was wrong. Susi would become the only surviving link to that early ring of childhood friendship.

Dr. Speier-Holstein was a great physician, sensitive, compassionate, and deeply involved in the welfare of his patients, Jews and Gentiles alike. His contemporaries described him as an angel of mercy. He used to make his rounds on a bicycle—doctors still made house calls in those days! Being an Orthodox Jew, he did not schedule office hours on the Sabbath, but he would always walk to attend any seriously ill person when he was called. He never accepted any fee for medical services he rendered on the Sabbath.

The doctor was a disciple of the great German Orthodox rabbi and theologian, Samson Raphael Hirsch of Frankfurt. When I was older, Dr. Speier-Holstein introduced me to the teachings of this influential rabbi on many occasions. In religious conflicts within the community, the doctor would invariably, without compromising his integrity and Torah-true position, plead for peaceable approaches and reasonable solutions to avoid hurting anybody's feelings. He did his best to temper the impetuous, uncompromising approaches of his brothers-in-law, the Mohls.

Dr. Speier-Holstein was an adherent of the Agudas Yisrael, an international Orthodox organization that opposed political Zionism as a heresy. Still a powerful party in Israel today, the Agudah differed from the Orthodox Zionist Mizrachi organization in holding it to be contrary to Torah Judaism to join in any ideological enterprise with non-Orthodox Jews.

I was always happy to go—even as a patient—to the doctor's home, Regentenstrasse 19, where he had his office on the main floor. It was not just because of the three girls. The house was magnificent. It had central heating—an unusual feature then for older houses—and a beautiful garden, where we had often played as younger children. I remember best of all the luxurious *sukkah* that we visited on every Sukkot festival, which had beautiful painted scenes from Jewish history on the wooden walls and carpets covering the floor. An electric heater provided comfort on cold days.

One day, during the first weeks of 1939, while I was waiting to leave Germany for Britain on an expected student visa, Dr. Speier-Holstein took me aside. A few days before, Susi had been accepted by a British refugee agency. She would join a number of Jewish children who had been granted entry to Britain—without their parents, of course. Susi was then about thirteen years old and her parents were worried about sending her alone. "Please, Erwin," the doctor asked me, "look after Susi." I promised I would and I kept my promise as far as it was in my power to do so.

Susi now lives in Fairlawn, New Jersey, with her husband, Johnny Berber. We have remained close friends, talking regularly on the phone and enjoying frequent visits. Her home is about half-way between the home of my nephew, Herbert Schuster—my sister's son—in Monsey, NY, and that of my nephew David Schild—my brother's son—in Bergenfield, NJ. Although the location of the three homes is coincidental, it symbolizes how closely our old friendship joins Susi and Johnny to the Schild family.

Susi's mother died in 1942, when the family was still living in Mülheim. I visit her grave whenever I go to the Jewish cemetery there. She was spared the gruesome and violent death that her husband, together with Edith, were soon to suffer at the hands of the Nazis. Ruth managed to emigrate to Holland before the war. After Germany invaded Holland in May 1940, I received one Red Cross message from her, but after that, I never heard from her again.[2]

In 1998, the city of Cologne finally agreed to name a street in Mülheim after Dr. Victor Speier-Holstein. On our recent visit to Cologne, we visited the new street and took a few photographs. It was a deeply moving moment.

---

[2]Nazi records that came to my attention later indicate that, after being interned in Westerbork, Ruth was deported to Sobibor on March 2, 1943, and was killed three days later.

At the Mohl home, I also met and befriended their other cousins, the children of Rabbi Dr. Julius Simons. The Mohl and Simons children were cousins twice over, since the rabbi married Veronika Mohl and Abraham Mohl married the rabbi's sister, Rosalie Simons. My relations to the Simons family, and that of my sister, grew into a close, lasting friendship, and Rabbi Simons played an important part in my religious education.

The entire Simons family was able to emigrate to Holland, which, unfortunately, was not far enough. After the Germans conquered the Netherlands, the family was in the clutches of the Nazis again. The rabbi and his wife were deported to the east and murdered, as was their oldest son, Hermann. Their second son, Kurt, despite chronic heart disease, survived the concentration camp, only to die in a car accident after his liberation. As a rabbi's son, he was asked to help the Allied army chaplains to reinstitute religious services for Jewish survivors. The crash happened while they were travelling to find a Torah scroll.

The three other Simons children, Ernst, Martha, and Ruth, who were among my close friends during my teenage years, survived; their experiences could fill another book.

Ernst and I renew our friendship whenever I visit Cologne, where he lives part of the year. Martha lives in San Francisco; Ruth in Amsterdam. My sister, Margot, and Ruth were good friends, especially during the years that Ruth lived in Riverdale, New York. Both Ruth and Martha, together with their cousin Susi, came to Toronto to help Laura and me celebrate our fiftieth wedding anniversary.

Margot and Edith Speier-Holstein had another friend in Mülheim, Ilse Moses, who was able to leave Germany before the war broke out. On one of my first trips to New York, we arranged to meet and shared an afternoon of reminiscing. Ilse and her husband, Ernst Marx, also live in New Jersey, not far from Susi. Laura and I usually meet them at Susi's home when we visit.

Chapter TWELVE

School Days

I NEVER WENT TO KINDERGARTEN. Though the word kindergarten for a pre-school obviously points to a German origin, it was not an option that my parents chose for their children. My sister and I had Anna to look after us while our mother spent time working in our family business. Nonetheless, I was well prepared for school. My parents had nourished my curiosity and I grew up in a home where learning was important. I could read fluently before I started school.

I could hardly wait for school to begin. In Germany, the school year starts after Easter. It was Anna's job to take me to school every morning, but on the first day, in the spring of 1926, my mother accompanied me, as well. It was a happy and exciting experience.

My school was the Evangelische Volksschule, the Protestant elementary school on the Fichtestrasse. Our teacher was Fräulein Elfriede Dickgräve. She knew our family well—she had probably been a customer of our shoe store—and made me a teacher's pet right away. Of course, I was no trouble. I was well behaved, followed her instructions without question, folded my hands on the desk when the class was asked to, and I already knew what she was teaching us: the alphabet, reading, printing, and sums. I was always the pupil she sent out to read the time from the large clock towering over the school yard, because I could tell time! While most of the pupils tried agonizingly to read by putting letters together, the words seemed to simply fly off the pages of my primer.

In the Fall of 1988 I visited Cologne in order to give a number of lectures and to address the annual Protestant church rally. My host and patron was Dr. Paul Gerhard Aring, a Protestant theologian and educator who had become a close friend. A few weeks before my visit, Dr. Aring mentioned that a lady who claimed to have gone to school with me in Mülheim was anxious to see me during my stay in Cologne. Dr. Aring could only remember her

first name, Bernardine. But I needed no further identification: it could only be Bernardine Weisshaupt. I had never forgotten her name and the way she looked when I last saw her.

At age six or seven, I did not know what sex meant, but I felt an erotic attraction to a few of the girls in my class. My secret favourite—secret in that I never told any of them or made any display of affection—was Lotte Weber. Together with her cousin Mathilde Weber—names etched in my memory—Lotte was at the social centre of the class. The Weber family was prominent in the marine shipping industry. Lotte, I thought, was the picture of perfect feminine beauty. Next in my affection came Bernardine, a slim, lithe girl, elfin and of dark complexion. Lotte and Bernardine stimulated my romantic imagination and appeared in my innocent childish fantasies.

After I had finished one of my lectures in Cologne, a simply dressed elderly lady introduced herself to me. It was Bernardine. I would not have recognized her; she bore no resemblance to the girl I remembered. She told me briefly the story of her life and said that she had a little gift for me, a souvenir that she wanted me to have. It was our class picture, taken in 1927, when we were in second grade. The students are seated on the wide steps leading from the school yard into the school. And there was Miss Dickgräve, standing beside her class. She was unmistakable, but instead of the middle-aged schoolmarm of my memory, she was a nice-looking young teacher! And Lotte Weber? How different she was from my remembered image! In the photo she appears as a rather plain, baby-plump seven-year old. Mathilde was prettier than I had thought. Bernardine looked elfin and cute, exactly as I remembered. Jojo Mohl was in the front row. I sat a little farther back, with the characteristic curly wave falling on my forehead. I am ashamed that I remember my smug vanity that the curl made me look handsome, and that my high forehead was an indication of my superior intelligence. What a conceited snob I was!

In our class picture, I am dressed in a sailor suit, as I am in several other boyhood photos. In summer, I wore a white sailor suit with navy blue stripes and piping; the rest of the year, the suit was navy blue with white accents. Of course, I wore the customary short pants, with long stockings to keep me warm in winter. In the Germany of the 1920s, the long pants that are standard wear for North American boys, were reserved for "big boys," and were worn with pride as a mark of growing up. When that time came for me, I had long discarded sailor suits, which I had grown to detest, and wore sweaters and other less formal clothes. Actually, wide knicker-bockers had become very popular by the time I was twelve or so, and they became my preferred style of trousers. I had at least one suit that came with two pair of pants, knickers and regular pants.

I did not realize it at the time, but the sailor suits were really a social statement on the part of my parents, indicating their standing in the community as solid members of the German middle-class. The sailor suit was almost like a uniform for middle-class children; several other boys, including Jojo, are similarly dressed in the class photo. Working-class children generally did not wear sailor suits.

When I was a child, clothes were bought with an almost ritual regularity. At certain times of the year, I was outfitted in a new suit, which became the "good suit," while the previous good suit was downgraded to the status of everyday suit. Old suits were given to people who could not afford new clothes. To this day, I feel glad when I walk through discount stores, such as K-Mart or Wal-Mart, and see warm winter jackets and other clothes for sale at prices that even low income earners can afford. For me that epitomizes the prac-tical democracy of the New World! During my childhood in Germany, especially in the depression years, many people depended on hand-me-downs.

Why did I attend a Christian school? The German elementary school system was denominational. This should not seem strange to Canadians, where some provinces have only recently abolished an inherited system of denominational schools. In Köln-Mülheim, there were only Catholic and Protestant elementary schools, and Jewish children, by some arrangement or tradition, attended the Protestant schools, where, perhaps, the religious indoctrination was less intense. There was a Jewish elementary school in Cologne, but it was much too far from Mülheim to make attendance feasible.

Besides, I doubt that my parents were in favour of a separate education for Jewish children.

Of course, Jewish pupils were excused from the religious exercises that were part of the school routine and from religious instruction. Miss Dickgräve, our teacher, was extremely conscientious in this respect. She must have considered it her personal responsibility to make sure that nothing in her class would compromise the religious integrity of her two Jewish students or make us feel uncomfortable.

During the first week of elementary school, Miss Dickgräve told the class a fascinating story, about a man named Jacob and his sons. One of his sons, Joseph, his father's favourite, was sold as a slave into Egypt by his jealous and cruel brothers. Dramatic adventures followed. I had no idea that our teacher was telling us a Bible story, which leads me to conclude that, as a six-year old, I had learned little or nothing about the Torah. This gap in my education puzzles me, in retrospect. Why did I know most of Grimm's fairy tales, but was so ignorant of Bible stories?

When I entered second grade, however, my formal Jewish religious instruction began. My Christian classmates were receiving religious instruction, from which Jojo Mohl and I were excused, so we did not mind the fact that from now on we had to attend religious school at the synagogue. A number of rooms in the congregational house were used for religious instruction, where Lehrer Vogel was the only teacher for about fifteen boys and girls ranging in age from seven to about fifteen. He somehow managed to teach us all at our own level, even though we met at the same time. We learned to read the Hebrew alphabet from a primer and were soon practicing our skills by reading from the prayer book. Then we graduated to a more advanced stage and began translating the words into German. This was the traditional method of teaching Jewish texts to children.

By the time my own children entered Hebrew Day School, this method had fallen into disrepute among modern Jewish educators. The modern method is *"Ivrit b'Ivrit,"* Hebrew in Hebrew. While the modern method boasts ideological purity, eliminating the use of the vernacular and immersing children in the Hebrew language from the very beginning, it is very time consuming because the teacher has to explain the meaning of each new word in Hebrew to students who only know a few words of the language. Ideological purity also comes at the price of an imprecise understanding of Hebrew words, since the meaning is conveyed by paraphrase.

Be that as it may, using the translation method, I soon acquired a growing Hebrew vocabulary. We learned to find the roots of words and gradually learned basic Hebrew grammar inductively. From prayer book translation we proceeded to selected texts from the Torah. We also learned to write Hebrew in the cursive script.

Nevertheless, our religious school was a rather marginal form of Jewish education, limited to only a few hours a week. Fortunately, my Jewish education was reinforced at home and by my friends. I had become familiar with Jewish practice by growing up in a household where religious rules were observed. We ate only kosher food. I knew early on that one must wait three hours—the German *minhag*, or custom—after eating meat before eating dairy. Yet my parents were not Orthodox. We observed the basic rules of Shabbat, such as not to write, ride, cook, switch on lights, and so forth, but some of the finer points of Shabbat restrictions were unknown to me. The Mohl children were different. Not only had they been raised to be strictly observant, but they had also absorbed the rather militant and scornful attitudes of their parents regarding those who were less observant. Heinz and Walter wasted no time in castigating Margot and me as religious inferiors. "*Posheh, posheh!*"—the German-Jewish word for sinner—they would shout, whenever they saw me or Margot doing anything that was not in accordance with the rules. However, their influence became very beneficial. In time, we grew more conscientious in matters of observance, such as not carrying anything on Shabbat or touching money; we became more careful to recite the blessings before eating and for other occasions and became accustomed to saying the Minchah prayer in the afternoon. Perhaps even more effective than the pressure of the direct example and exhortation of the Mohls was the gentler and more intelligent influence of Dr. Victor Speier-Holstein, our family physician. This influence grew more effective as time went by.

My parents did not mind that Margot and I adopted gradually a stricter religious practice. They were quite pleased, I believe, if a little amused, by our childish seriousness. Kurt was not affected by the growth of our religious commitment. He was in high school and struggling with his studies. He was secure in his own social circle and enjoyed his popularity. Soon he would be entering the working world. The direction of his life might have continued to take him further away from his Jewish roots, but he was soon affected by the threatening shift of political events in the last years of the 1920s and the early years of the 1930s.

Elementary school hours ended in the early afternoon, so there was still a good part of the day to be filled with other activities. I had my books, my toys, and my friends. Anna still supervised my sister and me. Margot started school when I entered third grade. Our daily routine began to change, reflecting the stages of our growing up.

Anna left our household in 1930. That was the year I entered high school, at age ten. The two events were certainly connected. Anna was no longer needed as much and the economic recession was affecting our business. However, Anna remained attached to us, and we to her, even in the years when the Nazi rule made such a relationship risky and potentially harmful. Storm clouds had been gathering on the horizon. My parents struggled in business more than I realized at the time. Politically, the depressed economic conditions gave rise to extremist parties: the Communists on the left and even more ominously, the National Socialist Party —the Nazis—on the right. Nazi propaganda blamed the Jews for every disaster and misfortune. My adult mentors, including my parents, refused to read the writing on the wall. Even more surprisingly, in retrospect, is that they did not read the writing in the history books, German as well as Jewish.

I read the newspapers regularly and observed the turbulent political scene. Yet I did not realize that the violent currents in public life might eventually affect me personally. I was growing up, happy, sheltered, and favoured. When I turned ten years old I had the whole world in my hands—or so it seemed.

Chapter *TWELVE*
77

Chapter THIRTEEN

The Procession

Are Jews in the Western world completely open and honest in our relationship with Christians? Do we not have some discreet reservations in the back of our minds, reservations that, difficult to explain and defend, we would prefer be kept under a wrap of polite silence?

There are some delicate issues that require a little tactful ignoring.

In Christian-Jewish dialogue we treat each other as equals. It is one of the axiomatic conditions of interfaith dialogue. We are equal partners in dialogue; we relate to each other as equals. We want Jews and Christians to meet, to get to know each other better. We arrange public dialogues between churches and synagogues. Yet, as a rabbi who believes in dialogue, I would be alarmed and hurt if a dialogue that I arranged, led to intermarriage. So I have my reservations, my limits, my fences.

Despite all the good will, the two sides are not evenly balanced. They may be equal, but they are not equiponderant—of the same weight. It is the old story of the mouse sleeping with the elephant. The elephant just wants to turn over, but the poor mouse gets squashed.

The Christian church, through the ages, was victorious, triumphant, all-powerful. The Jew and his synagogue survived marginally. Under the best of circumstances, the Christian attitude was one of tolerance, a benign condescension, thinking, perhaps the Jew will come to his senses and join the right side, the winning side; stubborn as the Jew is, in the warmth of our tolerance his obstinacy is bound to melt; and, if not, there are always other, less benign means of persuasion...

In this atmosphere, any response of mutuality, any gesture of neighbourly acceptance on the part of the Jew was open to dangerous misinterpretation. It could be seen as the signal of weakening, as the white flag of surrender that the adherents of the triumphant faith were waiting for. An innocuous visit to a church—to seek shelter in a storm, to see a famous piece of art or to enjoy the archi-tecture—could be taken as an act of homage to the Christian faith, a portent of impending capitulation. Even among the Jews themselves, an openness to Christian custom and a willingness to extend de facto recognition to the Church became regarded as sus-pect: a hint of betraying those who had suffered so much for their steadfast rejection of Christian missionary overtures.

As a result of this history, and of the defensive taboos it engen-dered, a great many Jews will not enter a church, at least not the sanctuary, under any circumstances. Others will be more lenient and discriminating. They may permit themselves and others to visit a church, as long as it cannot be misconstrued as a religious act, such as worship. They will visit a church as part of sight-seeing, when on a tour. Still more liberal minds will not even object to attending a Christian wedding or funeral at a church. I know of Jewish people who like to attend midnight mass on Christmas as an artistic or cultural experience.

In the last decades, my own position on this spectrum of practice has shifted toward the more liberal end. Primarily in Germany, I have given addresses and lectures to Christian congre-gations in their church. I even have delivered sermons—Jewish sermons, to be sure—at Christian services. Occasionally, the organizers of a function at which I am to teach or speak will, in deference to my sensitivities, modify a religious assembly so that it cannot be considered worship, but I do not insist on it. The point at which I draw the line is participation in worship: I make it clear and evident that I will not participate.

My rationale for making light of the traditional restrictions is that the relationship between Christianity and Jews on the level of theology and spiritual values can no longer be compared to the elephant-and-the-mouse dilemma. True, I am opposed to a relax-ation of restraint in the area of social relationships. Young unmar-ried people have to find prospective mates. The demographic odds and the inherent vulnerability of a numerically small minority put Jewish survival in jeopardy. Selectivity, restriction, and risk avoidance are, therefore, mandatory. However, the playing field of interfaith dialogue has already been levelled to a large extent. Precautionary restrictions to allay the fear of mutual exposure seem

obsolete. Being a spectator at Christian worship or bringing a
Jewish message to a worshipping Christian congregation does not
compromise me nor does it corrupt my religious integrity.

In the arena of theological dialogue, we may be more self-
assured. In the post-Holocaust world, Judaism as faith, as reli-
gion, is not an endangered species. A Jewish teacher is respected by
a majority of Christians. He is respected as a member of a spiri-
tual nobility, of the original and everlastingly covenanted commu-
nity that modern Christians believe they have joined, but not
replaced. Sometimes, when I stand before my audiences, I am
reminded that our ancient teachers anticipated a time when the
scholars of the Law would teach Torah in the theatres and colise-
ums of the Romans.

A few years ago, while getting ready for a visit to Cologne, I
received an invitation that strained even the liberal guidelines I
had adopted for my participation in Christian events. To anyone
like me, who grew up in Mülheim as a Jewish boy, the invitation
would seem utterly fantastic. It was an incredible chance! What
would my parents have thought! They could not have imagined it.

Father Joseph Metternich, the Catholic priest of the Liebfrauen
Congregation in Mülheim, invited my wife and me to be his guests
on the main ship of the famous annual Catholic Gottestracht, *the*
sacred procession on the Rhine. The same invitation was also
extended to my friend, Dieter Corbach—then, before his recent
death, the co-ordinator of Jewish-Christian relations for the
Protestant Church. He was almost as shocked by the invitation as
I. A non-Catholic guest at the most solemn religious spectacle of
the year! With a Jewish couple! I have to take the reader back to
my childhood to understand the reason for our shock and surprise.

CHILDREN IN MÜLHEIM looked forward to the annual fair that was
held on the large, dusty fairgrounds not very far from our home.
Of course, the centre of attraction for us was the midway, with its
carousels and other thrilling rides, such as the roller coaster, the
Great Whip, electric bumper cars, and rows of amusement booths
and side shows. Some of the rides were considered too dangerous for
children but we were allowed on others; even just to watch the dare-
devil amusements was fascinating.

The fair was called the *Kirmes*. Only many years later did it occur to me that the etymology of the word points to its Christian religious origin. As a child, I never asked why—it never seemed really important—the fair opened each year as a sequel to a splendiferous Catholic ceremonial, the Procession. It was a huge annual parade, for which Mülheim was specially renowned and which attracted tourists, as well as religious pilgrims, from far and wide. My sister, my friends, and I were awed by this annual spectacle, long before I learned that it commemorated a reported miracle that had occurred on the Rhine river several hundred years before. Some churlish burglars broke into the church and stole its precious sacred treasures. They fled with their spoils by boat, but their boat miraculously stuck in midstream, immovably detained by a strange power, thwarting their escape.

Naturally the procession was a great civic event for all the citizens of Mülheim, not only Catholics. Thousands of the faithful marched with great pomp and circumstance, reciting strange sounding prayers during pauses in the religious music played by the marching bands, bearing icons, altars, and sacred ceremonial objects. Homes and businesses, especially those lining the route of the procession—including ours—were decked out with flags and bunting. Catholic houses might also display additional religious decorations, pictures of the saints, floral tributes, and so forth.

The other children and I, together with our parents and the sales staff from the store watched the procession from our windows on the second floor. I knew intuitively that we were somehow excluded. I envied the young altar boys who accompanied the parade, waving the golden censers from which the smell of burning incense wafted up into our nostrils. I was impressed by the ranks of nuns and seminarians reciting their Hail Marys and paternosters, and awed by the sight of the elaborately attired priests and dignitaries of the Church, the icons, chalices, monstrances, and maces, and other precious ritual objects carried under brocaded canopies, and the sheer number of participants in the procession.

We watched with a mixture of excitement and secret fear. Even as children we understood that, despite our show of respect by flying a flag on the flagpole that angled out from one of our windows into the street—as we were accustomed to do on other national holidays—this procession was definitely not ours, and that somehow, its pomp and circumstance and majestic proportion were a threat to our little synagogue and to the much more modest observances of our faith.

After the procession had passed, the store reopened and the adults returned to their work, while the children waited for the opening of the *Kirmes* later in the afternoon. We knew that there was a gap of a few hours between the end of the procession and the opening of the fair, but until we were a little older, we had no idea about the spectacle that was staged after the procession had passed by. The march ended at the bank of the Rhine, where one of the biggest Rhine cruisers waited, adorned with beautiful decorations and bunting, while throngs of onlookers crowded the shore. The dignitaries walking beneath the canopies, the participants in the religious ceremonies to be held on board, then boarded the ship, with all the treasures, altars, monstrances, and icons, followed by those of the faithful who had admission tickets. Other participants boarded additional waiting steamers and soon the convoy moved off, escorted by hundreds of smaller ships and boats of all descriptions, decked with flags and floral tributes.

The huge fleet slowly proceeded upstream toward Cologne, while the crowds watched from the shore. Mortars and cannons fired in tribute as the fleet advanced up the Rhine; at home, we listened—a little frightened—to the distant thunderous reverberations. Of course, Jews would not be among the crowds. I cannot remember ever seeing the main event, the procession on the Rhine, for which the march through the city was the prelude. Even when I was older, it would never have occurred to me that this was a place for me to go.

And now, sixty years or so later, I was invited to be on the main ship as an honoured guest! Somehow, I was again the little awe-struck Jewish boy watching the procession. It seemed so incredible that I, a Jew, could be on the ship. Yet here were the admission tickets in the envelope. Notwithstanding my liberal attitudes, I had some qualms. Could my presence be interpreted as a religious exercise? But how could I refuse such a chance?

It was a warm, brilliantly sunny day. We did not see the Procession on land, but went directly to the boat. The crowd parted respectfully as Laura and I waved our special tickets and boarded the ship, with our camera, looking for Dieter Corbach. We watched the escort fleet assemble—fabulous yachts, commercial ships, ferries, and lowly motor boats. We waited for the arrival of the procession. To my utter amazement, it was exactly as I remembered it: the gold canopies, the splendiferous garments, the shepherd's crooks of the bishops, the monstrances and other glittering ceremonial objects, the religious orders and lay organizations with their colourful banners and standards. It was an extraordinary experience: the boat ride, the choirs, the litany, psalm recitations, and liturgical renditions. My host, Father Metternich, proudly came to greet us, pleased by our presence. He invited me to read a Hebrew psalm or the Blessing of Aaron over the public address system. But here I drew the line; I thanked him and refused.

All the time I kept thinking of my parents: would they ever have believed that some day a child of theirs would sail as an honoured guest on the procession boat? How Kurt would have relished listening to my tale of this adventure! He and Margot would have understood what I felt: the wonder, the amazement, the irony, and—as a bit of added spice—a pinch of triumphalism.

Chapter FOURTEEN

Gymnasium

*I*N ONE OF MY *BOYS' ANNUALS* I read that the tenth birthday is a turning-point. "From now on, your age has two digits!" the writer pointed out. I waited impatiently to pass over this threshold. Aside from the double digits, age ten also meant that I would go to the *Gymnasium*, the German term for high school.

The German educational system has undergone significant changes since my youth, reflecting both political upheavals and social evolution. When I was a child, six-year old boys and girls in Cologne entered a denominational elementary school for four years. It was called a *Volkschule*, or public school, a designation that was later changed to *Grundschule*, or foundation school. After the fourth grade, the boys destined for high school entered the *Gymnasium*; the girls the *Lyzeum*. The Latin terms were indicative of the classical roots of education.

Not all students would go to high school. Admission depended not only on academic qualifications, but also on financial ability. Elementary school was free, but parents had to pay a tuition fee for high school, which eliminated the children of low-paid industrial or commercial wage earners. Children who remained in the free elementary stream continued on for another compulsory four years. By then, they were either ready for a job in commerce or industry, or for an apprenticeship in a trade. Some attended a technical or trade school. Academically gifted children had an opportunity, after eight years of elementary school, to continue their education in a middle school. Obviously, the school system perpetuated a class structure inherited from the old social order. It was difficult for working class children to aspire to careers in the professions or in business.

In larger cities, there were different types of high schools to choose from. The humanistic *Gymnasium* featured a classical curriculum based on Latin, Greek and the humanities, while the *Realgymnasium* offered a more liberal and practical education that favoured modern languages and the sciences.

There were two *Gymnasium*s in Mülheim. I was lucky that my parents made the right choice for me. Even though I might have preferred the classics, my parents opted for the *Realgymnasium*. As a result, I began to study French at age ten and English at age thirteen, while Latin waited until I was fifteen. I shudder to think what would have happened to me in later life if I had been allowed to follow my own inclinations. My parents must have realized that modern languages were especially important for Jews. Owing to their foresighted choice, it was possible for me to flourish in a Canadian university and to have a career in a field in which it is very difficult to attain success without linguistic proficiency.

I was also fortunate in that my teachers stressed proper pronunciation. Some sounds in the English language are notoriously difficult for German speakers. Our teachers drilled us relentlessly until at least some of their students were able to pronounce the "th" sound in both its soft and hard varieties, to shade their pronunciation of vowels and diphthongs in the Anglo-Saxon manner, and to produce the various nasal vowels required for French.

To be in high school was a special distinction; one was proud to be a *gymnasiast*. Grades were no longer designated by number— first, second, third—as in elementary school, but by beautiful-sounding Latin names, which I could rattle off by heart long before I had crossed the portal of the gymnasium: *Sexta, Quinta, Quarta, Untertertia, Obertertia, Untersekunda, Obersekunda, Unterprima, Oberprima.* I later realized that these high-sounding names were only made up from Latin ordinal numerals in reverse order, but that did not matter. I envied my older brother's high school paraphernalia. As I have said, though, Kurt did not enjoy school and was an indifferent student. He had quit high school for a job in the business world while I was still in elementary school.

So, after waiting impatiently and enviously, I became a *Sextaner* at last. I wore the distinctive high-school cap whose shape, colour, and ribbon indicated the school and the year to which a student belonged. Each year, depending on the rules of the school, a new cap or a new ribbon was bought and proudly worn. However, I never got the chance to wear the distinctive white cap of the *Primaner*, the upper-class scholar. When the Nazi authorities took over the educational system, they abolished the students' caps as an egalitarian boost for the working class that had helped the Nazis gain power.

German boys were now expected to join the Nazi youth movement, the Hitler Jugend, and to wear the brown uniforms with belt, shoulder strap, swastika armband, and caps adorned with the Nazi insignia. Jewish students looked with dread at the uniforms, particularly at the dagger which completed the outfit of the older boys. The Nazis also shortened high school by reducing the *Prima* from two years to one, so as to accelerate the young men's entrance into military service and officers' training in the German armed forces or the Nazi militias.

But that was still in the future when I proudly entered the *Sexta*, the first year of the *Gymnasium*.

High school was different in other significant ways. Elementary schools were denominational and co-educational. Catholics and Protestants went to different schools, but boys and girls were together. The high schools were non-denominational, but boys and girls were separated. A wide boulevard, the Clevischer Ring, divided the *Realgymnasium* Köln-Mülheim from the *Lyzeum* where my feminine peers, and, two years later, also my sister, attended school.

The change that impressed me most as a new high school student was that we had different teachers for different subjects. One of our teachers was the class teacher, charged with the administrative work for our class, but several other teachers, each with his own personal views, habits, and idiosyncrasies—and nickname, of course— taught the different subjects on our curriculum. Some teachers taught more than one subject; our mathematics teacher in the *Sexta* also taught us biology, for instance. In the higher grades, however, most of the teachers were specialists who held various academic degrees. All of the teachers were male. Students were not called by their first names, as was the custom in the elementary grades, but by their family names, in an almost military fashion. "Schild, what's the genitive plural of *le cheval*?" And at some point in the higher grades, teachers stopped using the familiar *du* when addressing students, but had to respect the students' adult status by addressing them more deferentially as *Sie*.

If I can be grateful to the Germany of my youth for anything, it is for the no-nonsense education I received. The high school curriculum was demanding, even in the lower grades. There were no optional subjects; one could not get through high school without

My parents' formal engagement picture, 1911. The groom, Hermann Schild, is 26 years old; the bride, Hetti Neugarten, is two years younger.

My uncle Julius, the youngest of the Schild brothers, who fell in World War I.

My uncle Felix, oldest of the Schild brothers, who served in the artillery during World War I.

A former schoolmate of mine who is a collector of picture postcards gave me this precious card showing our family home and store in the city of Mülheim, now a suburb of Cologne. This picture was taken circa 1910.

Annual Rhine steamboat excursions to the Seven Mountains were *de rigueur* for middle-class families in Cologne, as was the conventional photo taken near the ascent to Drachenfels, a famous castle ruin. My sister's absence from the portrait suggests that it is from 1923, when Margot was only a year old and could be left at home with our nanny.

Intended as a surprise birthday present for Father, this photo was to remain a secret till May 10, 1925. But I fell for Father's ruse to worm the secret out of me when he asked how we had managed to get Margot to sit still at the studio. "Oh, that was easy," I said, "we gave her a picture book to hold." Margot, with a bow in her pretty hair, sits between her brothers in their best sailor suits.

Fräulein Dickgräve's second-grade class in elementary school in Mülheim, 1927.
I am sitting in the third row, second from right. Behind me, slightly to the right,
sits Bernardine Weisshaupt, who gave me this picture at a lecture I gave in
Cologne a few years ago. Joseph (Jojo) Mohl is second from right, front row.

At a restaurant in the countryside at Schlodderdich on a Sunday afternoon in the summer of 1930. I am seated in the centre, holding the soccer ball. In the back row, from left, my brother, Kurt, my mother, my cousin Hannerl Neugarten, and Frau Rosalie Mohl, mother of my friends Heinz, left front, and Walter, right. My sister, Margot, sits to my right (left in the photo); to my left is Martha Simons, a cousin of the Mohls and daughter of Rabbi Dr. Julius Simons. Martha, who now lives in San Francisco, and I are the only survivors of the group.

At the beach of the Mülleneisen Schwimmbad in the Mülheim harbour (1936): (from left) Edith Speier-Holstein, Hannah Mohl, Ilse Moses, Susi Speier-Holstein, and Ruth Speier-Holstein. Edith, Ruth, and their cousin, Hannah, were killed in the Holocaust. Susi and Ilse live in Fair Lawn, New Jersey.

On a country hike, posing on a bridge in Hoffnungsthal, near Cologne, about 1936. (from left) Kurt Rothschild, Heinz and Joseph Mohl (cousins), Miriam Cahn, Marianne Stern, and myself. Kurt Rothschild, now living in Toronto, became a prominent community leader; Heinz, Joseph, and Miriam perished in the Holocaust. I have no knowledge of Marianne's fate.

Two portrait sketches I made (1936). Left: Israel Janowski, cantor of our congregation in Mülheim. Right: Hannah Mohl, at age 12. Her melancholy expression, as I look at the portrait today, seems to prefigure her early death in the Holocaust, which also claimed the life of Cantor Janowski.

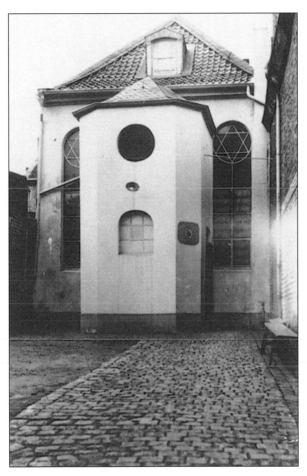

Our synagogue in Köln-Mülheim, situated at the back
of a courtyard, before its destruction—begun in the fires
of *Kristallnacht* 1938 and completed in the frequent
war-time Allied bombings.

Our last formal family portrait, January 1939, days before my hasty departure for Holland. The picture succeeds in portraying us as we wanted to appear, a harmonious family, the epitome of stability and domestic tranquility. Kurt, on my right, debonair and handsome; myself, immersed as usual in a book; Father at the tip of the pyramid holding us together with a smile of satisfaction; Mother and Margot, beautiful, loving, and content. The reality was despair, anguish, and fear of the future. Father and I had returned from Dachau concentration camp only weeks before. The love and warmth of the picture, however, were real.

languages, mathematics, or science. Languages were soundly taught by good linguists who emphasized pronunciation, grammar, vocabulary, and syntax. Mathematics and sciences were also taught on a high level, with an emphasis on abstract concepts and the relationships between the different branches of mathematics. We were trained to read aloud, clearly and with the proper declamatory emphasis. Being able to express concrete and abstract ideas clearly and articulately was of great importance, as was the development of a good writing and speaking style. Students were always encouraged to expand their general knowledge.

Physical training was also very important and several hours a week were allocated to it. It was one subject that I neither enjoyed nor was good at. I loathed the high bar, the parallel bars, the rings, and the entire gymnastic apparatus on which many of my classmates performed with such impressive ease. I had none of their athletic skills. In later years, when the Nazis racial theory dominated the educational system, my inadequacy in sports and athletics simply illustrated the physical inferiority of Jews. I was not too bad in swimming, though. My friends, the Mohl boys, and I had taken swimming lessons at the large indoor pool in the Genoveva Baths. I was proud of my endurance swims, the most advanced requiring a swim of 45 minutes, for which I garnered a few diplomas.

Perhaps my endurance in swimming foreshadowed what became my physical hobby later in my life: long distance running. Jogging—or running distances of three to six miles several times a week—has been my sport for over forty years. Ever since I had stopped playing soccer with my friends in the park, I had not pursued any physical exercise other than the compulsory participation in school gymnastics and physical training. I did continue to enjoy swimming occasionally and indulged a love of hiking that also stems from my youth. At the University of Toronto, I played squash from time to time, usually with my friend and predecessor at Adath Israel, Rabbi Abraham Kelman. Then, after a few years of marriage, came the startling and embarrassing discovery that my physical fitness was at a low level indeed. In 1953, Laura and I moved from the lower duplex apartment at 86 Brunswick Avenue to the upper one that had the additional space our growing

family required. The move entailed carrying some boxes and belongings up a rather steep staircase. I was huffing and puffing. And I was only 33 years old! I was ashamed—and a little worried about the state of my health as I approached middle age. I made a resolution. I was going to exercise.

The YMHA—the Young Men's Hebrew Association—had just completed a beautiful new building at the corner Bloor Street and Spadina Avenue, only a few minutes' walk from our home. I became a member and joined a calisthenics class conducted by a great teacher, Bert Life. My physical condition improved dramatically; I regained strength and endurance. The work-outs that I attended twice a week always included a run. Interval training and other techniques greatly improved my running ability.

The YMHA, having admitted women members, soon became the YM&YWHA, and erected a magnificent building in suburban Toronto. The new building was within easy driving distance of our home, to which we had moved in the winter of 1955, and was close to our synagogue being built in the same area of recent Jewish settlement. The new Y, as it was colloquially called, though officially renamed the Toronto Jewish Community Centre, had a marvellous indoor running track that I regularly enjoyed. I also played badminton with my friend and physician, Dr. Murray Herst.

Gradually, after the untimely death of our instructor, Bert Life, of a brain tumour, I concentrated more and more on running. I increased distance and speed until I could run a mile in less than seven minutes and five miles in thirty-eight. minutes. I tried to run three times a week—difficult on my rabbinic schedule, but possible most of the time. Shortly afterwards, a running partner who would become a good friend, Mona Mausberg, introduced me to off-track outdoor running. In summer and winter I enjoyed various routes through parks and pleasant quiet streets. I had found my hobby, my key to fitness, and my sport. I soon only used indoor tracks if extreme weather conditions made outdoor running impossible.

Running is also great when I am away from home. I associate many memorable runs with places that Laura and I have visited over the years. I have run on the streets of Jerusalem, on the seashore promenade of Tel Aviv, and around the perimeter road of

Kibbutz Lavi on a hilltop in the Galilee; in the Vandelpark of Amsterdam; in James Park in London; along the Rhine in Bonn; by the water in Stanley Park in Vancouver; along the Rideau Canal in Ottawa; on the beaches of Florida; and around Little Lake in Lake Placid.

I am still running. If only my proudly Aryan teachers could see me now!

The German school system began to deteriorate rapidly soon after the Nazis took power in 1933. The party lost no time in assuming control over education and perverting it to serve their political ends. They enforced an emphasis on teaching racial theories and nationalistic propaganda, combined with the revisionist Nazi perspective on history and literature and corrupted the school system. The exclusion of Jewish academics and teachers further impoverished schools and universities.

However, my first three years of high school were pure bliss. I loved to learn. My mind expanded by leaps and bounds. Everything was new and exciting. Although I had more competition than I had had in the elementary school, I was soon recognized by my fellow students and teachers as the Primus, the best student. Yet I was well liked by my comrades. I had the benefit of a good upbringing: I was polite, well-mannered, and always available when my classmates needed help. I did not object if anyone copied from my work and was always willing to explain difficulties to others. My helpfulness led to one funny incident that I remember very clearly. One of our teachers was an older man, with a clever mind, but eccentric, disorganized and not always aware of what was happening in the classroom. I have forgotten his name, but his nickname was Ali Baba. One day, he was giving us a test in class. I was finished quickly, so another student, sitting close to me, asked for my paper. After a while, Ali Baba called each of us to come up to his desk to have the paper marked. My friend had the nerve to march up with my test, but had not expected that Ali Baba would mark the work in red ink. So here was I with the teacher's remarks already on the pages! What was I to do? In mindless desperation, I presented my test, expecting an embarrassing exposure. "Oh, I've already marked yours!" Ali Baba exclaimed. I went back to my seat with a great sense of relief.

It was in the *Quinta*, the second year of high school, that I won a prize in an academic competition. I received an Agfa box camera, which served me well for a number of years. More exciting was the second part of the award: a twenty-minute flight in an airplane over Cologne. Proudly I took my seat in a Junkers aircraft and enjoyed seeing the city from above. I was twelve years old. The flight was my first, of course, and remained my only one for about twenty-five years.

My popularity with my fellow students in Mülheim did not wane over the years. Since I started my periodic visits to Germany in 1983, my classmates have arranged reunions in my honour. They love to refresh the old memories and have showered Laura and me with compliments and gifts. In the last two years, I noted that their ranks, decimated in World War II, have begun to thin out as age and disease take their toll.

Perhaps one of the reasons I was so well-liked by my peers was that my academic excellence was balanced by a speech impediment which had afflicted me since childhood. I stuttered. It worried my parents and, of course, bothered me. The available speech therapy was of no use in my case, because the pattern of my defect was quite unusual. I stuttered in ordinary conversation, but not when the speech therapist wanted to hear it or when I spoke in front of my class. In fact, I was often chosen to recite poetry at school assemblies and never experienced any difficulty. When I was fifteen or sixteen, I was seen a few times by a famous psychiatrist, a Dr. Aschaffenburg, who, among other methods, used hypnosis as therapy. He could not do much for me, though, except assure me that my impediment would probably disappear in adulthood. I often wondered what happened to this gentleman, and then, a few years ago, after one of my lectures in Germany, I was introduced to an elderly psychiatrist in my audience. Explaining his professional background to me, he mentioned that he had been a student of the famous Jewish Dr. Aschaffenburg in Cologne.

I have sometimes speculated whether any of my teachers or fellow students associated my academic proficiency with my being

Jewish. I doubt it, for the only other Jewish boy in our class was Jojo Mohl, who was a very poor student. He was very clumsy, even worse than I in physical training, although he was not bad in soccer. He had neither desire nor ability for scholarship. He remained my friend, though, a loyal member of our intimate group whose members were mostly his cousins. His life ended tragically: shortly before his twentieth birthday, he was arrested by the Nazis and incarcerated in the most infamous Cologne jail. He was given a day's leave to attend his mother's funeral. The next day, the Nazis shot him dead.

Despite the growing political threat and disquieting economic situation, the years from 1930 to 1932 were happy ones for me. Early each morning, I walked up the Wallstrasse, turned into the Buchheimer Strasse at the corner where our second shoe store was located, and then cut diagonally across the square in front of the church to the Adamstrasse where the school entrance was located. The Schubach family, whose daughter Hanna later married my cousin Arthur Kracko and whose younger daughter Else was one of Kurt's girlfriends, lived on the same street near the school. I remember dropping in at their home to enjoy a piece of Mrs. Schubach's cake.

School finished in the early afternoon, but we had a heavy load of home work. Nevertheless, there was also time for friends, play, recreation, or reading. Almost daily for more than a year at least, I took the Mohl's dog, a German shepherd named Chasseau, for a walk on the park-like shore of the Rhine. Chasseau waited for me every afternoon, Friedchen Mohl told me.

Did I have any non-Jewish friends? I had several school friends, but only one of them, as far as I can remember, was a friend in the sense that he came into our home and I into his. Fritz Unterwagner's father had an orthopedic store that sold special shoe inlays, supports, trusses for ruptures, and similar health supplies. Fritz loved everything American and had a good collection of Glenn Miller records. He took to calling himself Fred instead of Fritz. My sister had several non-Jewish friends. On my visit to Germany in 1997, a lady reintroduced herself to me. She had lived in the house across the street and had regularly played with Margot.

Saturday was a school day. That was a problem. I did not write in school, but like all Jewish students, I attended classes. As a result, I could not attend synagogue on Shabbat mornings. However, my male friends and I regularly attended Shabbat afternoon services that our Vorbeter—Herr Janowski—had organized especially for us, I believe. He had succeeded Lehrer Vogel after the political upheaval in our congregation had run its course. He led the prayers, served as the local shochet, and held a class for us on Shabbat afternoon. After we had our bar mitzvah, he trained us to read the Torah at the Shabbat afternoon Mincha service. On Shabbat afternoons, we usually stayed at one of the Mohls' homes, playing table tennis, table soccer and various other games.

It must have been around the time that I entered high school that my father took over his Uncle Max Schild's shoe store in Bonn. Max was the uncle who had taken my father under his wing after Max's brother, my father's father, died and had helped my father open his own business in Mülheim. Now came the time to reciprocate. Uncle Max was in distress; his store was insolvent, and Uncle Max was ill. My father rescued the business, but I know little of the details. Business did not hold my interest. At any rate, it meant that the whole family would make more frequent visits to Bonn on Sundays. Transport was via the fast interurban railway between Cologne and Bonn along the Rhine river. These trips were enjoyable, especially since Olga, Alice, and Else, Uncle Max and Aunt Sophie's three daughters, fussed over Margot and me. Even my big brother, Kurt, enjoyed the trips to Bonn. Uncle Max died a few years later.

Chapter FIFTEEN

Sieg Heil! Hitler Wins

BY 1932, THE POLITICAL SITUATION was frightening. The German economy was in a grave and deepening crisis. Millions were unemployed and the working class became impoverished. The parties of the extreme right and the extreme left were attracting growing masses of followers. Bloody battles between the Communists and the National Socialists raged in the streets. The Nazi party, officially the National Socialist German Workers' Party, led by their *Führer*, Adolf Hitler, was virulently anti-Semitic. While Hitler was in prison after the collapse of an uprising he led in 1923, he wrote the book—the Nazi bible that set out his political beliefs and his proposed program for Germany—*Mein Kampf*. He was quite specific about his solution to the so-called "Jewish Question," but few believed that his threats should be taken seriously. Most Germans thought that it was merely propaganda to enlist the support of the notoriously anti-Semitic German nationalists.

Hitler had a strong appeal among the extreme German patriots and chauvinistic nationalists who were still chafing under the defeat of imperial Germany in World War I. He blamed the world powers and the international Jewish-Bolshevik conspiracy for Germany's miseries, and argued that Jews, in particular, were the root cause of all the misfortunes that Germany had endured; they were the exploitative enemies of Germans and of all superior races. Anti-Semitism was at the core of an elaborate racist theory that the Nazis elevated to the status of the official science. The Aryan races were superior to all others; the Nordic race—which gave the German people its national character—was the human elite. Non-Aryans, especially Jews, were subhuman. As the insidious enemies of the German people, Jews deserved to be excised from the German people without mercy.

The anti-Jewish propaganda of the Nazis was so hysterical in tone and so blatantly and shamelessly false in content, that many reasonable people did not take it seriously and extracted it from

Hitler's social, economic and political program through which he promised to cure Germany's ills. Not all the Germans who voted for the Nazis in growing numbers in successive elections were voting for his anti-Semitic ideas. The leaders of the German industrial and commercial establishment preferred Hitler and his Nazis to the Communist alternative, while the aristocratic military class applauded his appeal to German patriotic pride and imperial chauvinism. German nationalists had never adjusted to the Weimar Republic, the democratic post-war Germany that had risen from the ruins of the German empire; they blamed treason, socialism, and communism for the downfall of the empire, rather than the failure of the German military. Walter Rathenau, the Jewish foreign minister in the Weimar government, had been assassinated by a right-wing extremist in 1923.

I followed the political struggle that went on. Jews were outraged and shocked. Our integrity and honour were violated by the vituperations hurled at us by an increasingly powerful Nazi press that included the *Stürmer*, a newspaper devoted entirely to anti-Semitism. Blatant lies and falsehoods, old and new, were spread by the skilled use of every propaganda tool and fanned the hatred of Jews. "The Big Lie"—the intentional distortion of facts—was perfected by Josef Göbbels, the Nazi propaganda chief, and became the most effective tool of Nazi propaganda. Göbbels was abetted in the project by Alfred Rosenberg, the voluble expert of the new Nazi science of race studies.

The German government was unstable. Chancellors and cabinets seemed to come and go through a revolving door. Elections were held repeatedly, but no political party was able to muster a parliamentary majority. However, each election brought greater victories for the Nazi party. Triumphant Nazi storm troopers paraded provocatively through the streets, arousing ever greater popular admiration for Hitler. The raucous speeches in which Hitler threatened his opponents and promised work and prosperity for Germans, glory for the German Fatherland, and hegemony for the Aryan race were broadcast through radio and film.

German politics was in turmoil. Many leaders tried in vain to stem the Nazi tide, but elections held early in 1933 established Hitler as the leader of the strongest party, which, in coalition with traditional right-wing parties, commanded a majority in the

German parliament. The German president, Paul von Hindenburg, an old-style military hero and avowed nationalist, appointed Hitler as chancellor and gave him the mandate to form a government. Hitler and his Nazi party had legitimately taken over political power.

That date, a turning point of world history, was January 30, 1933.

It was the day that ruptured our lives. Forever.

In less than two months, I was to celebrate my bar mitzvah.

Chapter SIXTEEN

The Revolution

Remagen is a lovely little town on the west bank of the Rhine, a short distance upstream from Bonn. Older people will remember it as the site of a bridge across the Rhine that the retreating German army failed to destroy. It was captured intact by the rapidly advancing American troops who thus managed to establish a bridgehead on the other side of the Rhine, speeding up the final phase of the war.

I visited Remagen during my lecture tour in 1996, when I gave a lecture in the community hall of the Protestant church. Because of its close proximity to Bonn, which still functioned as the capital of the reunited Germany, Remagen is home for many people working for the federal government, as well as for men and women from the famous Bonn University. After the lecture, members of the audience involved me in a thoughtful discussion. There were some penetrating and challenging questions that I tried to answer honestly and thoughtfully. As the discussion had just about run its course, a gentleman stood up. He was a professor at the University of Bonn, and had enlivened our discussion with several comments.

"Rabbi Schild," he said, "You have had a satisfying career as a rabbi in Canada. You have produced a family. Now you are retired. You visit us from time to time and give us insights into Judaism and contemporary Jewish life that are of extreme importance to us. Why don't you come and live with us? Germany needs Jews. Our whole culture, our academic life, our art and literature languish because there are no Jews to provide the leaven, the stimulation. We need you. Come and help us!"

I smiled and explained that although I was willing to teach, lecture, support, and encourage the good people of a new Germany, I could not bring myself to take up permanent residence. Canada was my home and home to my family. I could live in Israel, of course, but I could not leave Canada for Germany. Not after all that had happened...

❖

SOMETIMES I SPECULATE how my life would have unfolded if Hitler had not been an anti-Semite. What would have been the course of Jewish history in the twentieth century? If fascism had not embraced racism—if that can be imagined—what would have become of my family? What if Hitler had never happened? Would I have become a professor of literature or philosophy at a German university? Or a German *Rabbiner*? Or a politician, a writer, a poet? Who knows? Would the State of Israel exist if there had been no Holocaust, no World War II? Would North American Jewry have assimilated and become an endangered community?

Of course, there are no "ifs" in history. Television's History Channel is not interactive. History knows one plot only, unalterable, irreversible, without any rewind or optional endings. In the chain of historical causality, what happened on January 30, 1933, determined the course of world history, the fortunes of the Jewish people, and the parameters of my life.

For the Jews of Germany, the consequences were immediate. Although the Nazis had been provocatively loud and clear in announcing their anti-Jewish agenda, reality caught us by surprise. The vast majority of my parents' generation could not envision Jews losing their rights and status as Germans. Only the most pessimistic imagination could have prepared them for the problems they now had to face. Few people outside the inner circles of the Nazi party realized that Hitler's appointment as chancellor and the transfer of governmental power to his party was only the beginning, not the end, of a revolution. Germany was turned into an absolute dictatorship. Now the whole apparatus of the German state and all aspects of society and its organizational structures became subservient to the will of Adolf Hitler and subject to the arbitrary control of the party he ruled unconditionally. Before long, all other political parties were banned. The Nazi party was the only source of power. The state and all its institutions and branches became the instruments of terror and lawlessness.

This radical revolution doomed any hope that the Nazi government might be short-lived, like so many governments before it. At the beginning, Jews and opponents of the regime gave it, say, a year, at the most. The Nazis would not be able to keep their promises; the disappointed populace would sweep them away in the next election. How naive! It was a miscalculation on the same scale as Hitler's prophecy that the Third Reich he had established would last a thousand years!

The most tragic and fateful error of the German Jews was their failure to understand that hatred of Jews and the plan to eliminate them—first from the German people and eventually from the human race—was central to the racist nature of Nazi ideology and integral to the platform that Hitler had designed in *Mein Kampf*. They also had forgotten—and certainly never told their children—that the history of German nationalism had always been strongly tainted by anti-Semitism, and that even before the Nazi era, many of its spokesmen had hated or despised Jews and wanted to see them ostracized from the German *Volk*.

My parents' generation chose to ignore that history. German Jewry felt secure in the knowledge that Jews had been legally emancipated in their country for more than a century and had become so integrated in almost every sphere of national life that it was hardly possible to imagine Germany without its Jews. My parents never thought of themselves as anything other than German in nationality and culture, differing from the majority of their fellow citizens only in religious observance and traditions. Theirs was a view that was typical for their generation and one that I shared. Even many of the very Orthodox were able to think of Judaism and Germanness as not only compatible, but even mutually enriching. German philosophy and German idealistic thought could blend with a higher understanding of Judaism; conversely, Jewish wisdom, experience, and insight could contribute significantly to the German national ethos.

As a youngster, I fervently shared German patriotism and the mystical love for the Fatherland. Thus, I, and almost all of my contemporaries, were totally unprepared for the impact on our lives of a hail of anti-Jewish decrees and discriminatory disabilities that nullified the gains of emancipation and consigned us once again to the wretchedness of medieval conditions. Nor could we fathom and adjust to the growing intensity of the popular hatred against us, a hatred that was constantly fanned by the media and, as they were rapidly taken over by the Nazi party, institutionalized by all agencies of government and public life.

Almost overnight we became foreigners, outlaws, enemies, lepers—outcasts in our own country.

Even under the Nazi regime, it took time to enact the legislation necessary to cloak the racist practices of the new Germany and the increasing exclusion of the Jews from the community in a mantle of legitimacy. However, the pressure exerted by the Nazi party and the power flaunted by its paramilitary minions—the brown-shirted storm troopers and the dreaded, black-uniformed, elite SS squadrons—had no need to wait for legalities. Their arbitrary excesses against Jews individually and collectively outpaced the passage of the anti-Jewish legislation that was ultimately enshrined in the so-called Nuremberg Laws of 1935.

The persecution of the Jews began as soon as the Nazis came to power. Within a few weeks, the new government proclaimed a one-day boycott of all Jewish businesses. Uniformed storm troopers were posted at the entrance to every Jewish store to intimidate would-be customers. "Germans, do not buy from Jews!" became a permanent official slogan that soon began to exercise a growing influence on the public mind. Still, my parents' shoe stores in Mülheim survived, albeit with a greatly diminished volume of sales and increasing financial difficulties, until liquidation became mandatory after the *Kristallnacht* in November 1938.

Regional variations in the intensity of popular anti-Semitism modified the plight of the local Jewish communities for better or for worse. In some parts of Germany, the Nazi environment gave free rein to intense latent religious or nationalistic anti-Semitism, so that Jews were soon suffering extreme economic distress and experiencing the threat or reality of violent physical persecution. Physical danger affected our family in the village of Ulmbach, and forced my Uncle Felix and Aunt Bertha, as well as their son, Joseph, to flee to the anonymity of a larger city—Frankfurt. In the Rhineland, particularly in Cologne, where people are more *gemütlich*—more laid-back and less fanatical—many people privately sympathized with the Jews and displayed less animosity to their Jewish neighbours. Cologne had lagged behind other major cities in supporting the Nazi rise to power. Konrad Adenauer, a prominent Catholic who became the chancellor of West Germany in the post-war period, was the Lord Mayor of Cologne and exerted a moderating influence, until the Nazis removed him from office as an opponent of the regime. Hitler showed his dissatisfaction with the city by conspicuously delaying his first official visit as chancellor.

Thus, my family was somewhat less exposed to the harshness of anti-Jewish policies. Of course, fear of the ruthless terror, that the Nazi regime used to punish all opponents from the very beginning, effectively paralyzed any thought of opposing the anti-Jewish legislation and official acts. Nevertheless, many people in Cologne did not stop buying in Jewish stores and continued to use the services of Jewish professionals as long as they were allowed to practice. That was not for very long, however. Over the course of a few years, Jews were systematically eliminated from the justice system, the legal profession, teaching, medicine, the media, the arts and entertainment. Jews had been successful in all these areas, as well as in commerce, especially under the democratic Weimar Republic after World War I. The Nazi propaganda machine incessantly branded Jewish achievement and success as proof that Jews had come to dominate, exploit, manipulate and abuse the German nation.

The Jews of Germany, helpless, shocked, and bewildered, watched as a majority of the German people, abandoning rationality, civility, tradition, democracy, decency, and compassion, enthusiastically embraced the new order. They hailed Hitler as their Führer, their supreme leader, a providential champion of German destiny. They worshipped him as a god, a divine redeemer, who commanded absolute, unquestioning obedience. No sacrifice for the Führer could be too great.

Opposition to the regime was brutally quashed. Leaders and activists of the now-outlawed opposition parties were incarcerated in concentration camps, an innovation of Nazi atrocity and ruthlessness. New words, spoken furtively in whispers, entered the language: *Kah-Tzett*, as Germans pronounce the letters KZ, short for *Konzentrationslager*; *Schutzhaft*, protective custody, the mocking Nazi euphemism for arbitrary arrest of innocent individuals who were thus "protected" behind the electrified wires and death strips from the just wrath of the people; Dachau, Sachsenhausen, the names of the first horror camps. We talked in hushed tones about the dreaded paradigm of terror: the knock on the door in the middle of night; Gestapo officers, the secret state police, come to arrest Jews and suspected political opponents, who then disappeared into the camps; the sealed coffins in which their bodies were returned to their families with the explanation that they had been shot while attempting to flee.

All opposition melted away or went underground. People were afraid to even whisper criticism of the government, frightened of possible informers in their own family and circle of friends. Terror had become a most effective instrument of political and social control.

Aside from this current of fear, most Germans had little to complain about. Hitler created jobs, raised German triumphal pride to new heights, mesmerized the masses with a revival of the Teutonic ethos that included resplendent militias, uniforms, flags, parades, benefits for the workers, re-armament and restoration of the military, defiance of the world, and a relaxation of moral restraints. Jews were pilloried as the scapegoats who were responsible for all the misery and wretchedness of the shameful past and the remaining problems of the present, such as the world reaction to the excesses of the German regime. Men and women joined the Nazi party and its branches by the millions to enjoy the benefits that were granted to the faithful and to glory proudly in being German, members of the master race. A new dawn had risen for the German people; their Führer would lead them to a glorious destiny. "Perish Judah!" "Deutschland über Alles!"

Of course, my own young life was terribly disrupted by the Nazi revolution. How long could I cling to my self-definition as a German youth? How long did I want to resist the erosion of my love and loyalty for Germany? Yet the wealth of German culture, its music, literature, its spirit, its philosophy—it was all mine! It belonged to me! Why should I not defy those who wanted to deprive me of my German heritage and alienate me from my cultural roots?

The resolution of this hurtful spiritual dilemma was a curious paradox: on the one hand, my peers and I turned to our Jewish heritage and became more deeply involved in it. On the other hand, over the next few years, young Jewish people coalesced to form a ghettoized German-Jewish youth movement, immune to the contamination of their ideals by Nazi thought and fascist ideology, a community whose members became spiritual hold-outs, the last of the Mohicans, the last faithful exponents of what had been a better, truer German culture.

It was a paradox that could not last. The community had to dissolve. For many young Jews, emigration broke their link with their past. Those who were young enough to adjust created a new value system in their new home or attached themselves to a different society with its own cultural and spiritual values. For most of the others, death in the Holocaust, the ultimate refutation of the German-Jewish symbiosis, was their own final solution.

These issues were still far from our minds as I, together with my family and friends, approached the celebration of my bar mitzvah in March 1933, six weeks into the Nazi regime. We were certainly not in a mood to celebrate; we were very worried and uneasy. But we were not yet ready to despair, for we had not yet felt the full force of anti-Jewish policies. German governments had come and gone in the first two years of the 1930s, none lasting more than a few months. Why should Hitler fare any better? Come next winter and the usual seasonal increase in unemployment, the Hitler regime will be gone, said Abraham Mohl, echoing the optimistic hope of the majority of Jews. It took him and others several years to face up to the fact that Hitler was different, that our existence was threatened by an all-powerful dictatorship that the German people could no longer overthrow even had they wanted to—and they did not. My father, though more realistic than others, put his trust in the rule of law and his personal integrity. "I pay my taxes; I abide by the rules; I obey the laws and carry on my business honestly—so what can they do to me?" Little did he and all the others understand that, under the new regime, laws were no longer designed to protect the innocent and just. No longer did the members of the "sub-human" Jewish race or other "enemies of the people" have any legal recourse or appeal to fairness and human rights.

Prudence and apprehension required a subdued celebration of Jewish family events. My bar mitzvah did not reach the joyful peak of Kurt's, seven years earlier. One of the first Nazi decrees had been the prohibition of *shechita*, the Jewish method of slaughtering food animals. This happened only a few weeks before my bar mitzvah and forced us to revise the menu for the celebration. Kosher meat was not available, but for the family bar mitzvah dinner, we were able to order kosher cold cuts from Holland.

I acquitted myself adequately of my ritual duties as a bar mitzvah. I had been carefully prepared by Lehrer Vogel, who taught me the tropes for the Torah and the Haftarah reading so I was able to read any Torah portion or Haftarah. In fact, I read my first Haftarah in the synagogue a few weeks before my bar mitzvah: it was the difficult Haftarah of *Shemot*. On my bar mitzvah Shabbat I read the Torah portion of *Kee Tissa* from the third section on, the first two being too long. I remember that I gave a speech—that was something I always liked. We had a festive dinner at home; on the next day, Sunday afternoon, I had a party for all my friends.

I had become a man, for the purposes of Jewish obligations. My bar mitzvah observance was a significant focus in the context of my Jewish education and my growing commitment to religious observance. Every morning, before starting out for school, I put my tefillin on and said the morning prayers.

After Leopold Vogel retired, Mr. Oskar Simons, the Mohl children's uncle, took over our religious instruction. He took a much more intensive and ideological approach, emphasizing observance and knowledge of Jewish religious law. Along with carefully selected Bible texts, we studied many parts of the *Kitzur*, the abbreviated *Shulchan Aruch*, a practical compendium of religious practice. We read it in Hebrew, of course, thus extending our vocabulary. Mr. Simons also introduced us to the study of Talmud. We learned excerpts from the tractate *Berachot*. I became familiar with some of the basic Talmudic vocabulary and terminology.

Later, Rabbi Dr. Julius Simons became my teacher and mentor. Although he was Oskar's brother, he was quite different in outlook and personality. I consider him to have been my first true rabbi. He was Orthodox, yet modern; learned, yet widely educated; devout, but not fanatic. He had a patient sympathetic understanding for individuals at all religious levels. Since his children became my close friends, my contact with Dr. Simons continued in his own home, which was upstairs from the synagogue of Cologne-Deutz, his home congregation.

Dr. Simons had a very beneficial influence on me. For the first time, I learned Jewish history in a systematic manner and was introduced to Jewish theology. Being cast out, vilified, and humiliated by our environment provided a powerful incentive to seek solace in Judaism. However, I had not yet learned that Torah could form the basis for one's *Weltanschauung*, for a comprehensive philosophy of life and world view. I still depended on my high school teachers and on the books I read to interpret my world. My reading became more adult and gradually I was drawn to serious literature.

Soon after my bar mitzvah, awakening emotions led to new experiences. I discovered romantic love. I have never been a cool rationalist. The search for truth was always more exciting to me than its possession. Dry scholarship was never my ideal. Much as I saw myself as a creature of rational thought, I have also always been a romantic and mystic individual. I am a bipolar person. Reason and emotion have always competed within me just as the biblical twins Jacob and Esau wrestled in the womb of their mother, Rebecca.

Part Two

Exile

Chapter *ONE*

Under the Swastika

*I*F I DID NOT KNOW what to expect at school on the day after the Nazi ascension to power on January 30, 1933, it was a dilemma shared by most students and teachers. Teachers were probably in the more precarious position because they had to explain, to comment, to lead, to offer guidance—and perhaps only a few knew how risky it was to express their opinion. Which way was the new wind blowing? Surely, at past faculty meetings, lively discussions on the political issues must have taken place. Some teachers must have been ridiculed or ostracized by their colleagues for swallowing the fascist garbage and accepting that charlatan Hitler as their saviour; now, it was their turn to gloat, while the others silently cursed the turn events had taken and, perhaps, regretted their criticism of the Nazis. Some decent and sensitive teachers may have looked ahead with loathing, dreading having to work under the arrogant eyes of Nazi colleagues who would be in a new position of power on the faculty.

The handful of Jewish students at the Mülheim *Gymnasium* were ill at ease. We felt, I guess, as if we had lost a war. Our enemies had won and we had no idea how they would treat us. So we just pretended that nothing much had happened, carrying on, cautiously, keeping a low profile and staying out of trouble as much as possible. The other students did not have much to worry about unless their parents or other family members were known to be political opponents of the Nazis; they could afford to just wait and see.

Our teachers' reactions varied widely. One greeted the class with a caustic or sarcastic remark; another tried to joke about the changes we ought to expect: swastikas, stricter supervision, jackboots, military discipline. Some were more serious, asking for support for new challenging initiatives—or sharing their misgivings about the future. The latter would have reason to rue their words. The party loved informers. As time went on, pupils informed on their teachers and children on their parents.

The tone had been set right away by a sudden and ominous

event that shocked the students. One of our teachers, who had made no secret of his leftist political leanings, simply disappeared from our school on the very first day of the new regime. No explanation was ever offered. Was he told to stay at home? Had he been fired? Had he been arrested? We never found out. No one ever asked out loud. My guess, which I kept to myself, was that some of his colleagues had seen to his disappearance. In all probability, party members on the faculty had been preparing for the takeover of the school in anticipation of the power they would soon have to dictate to the school administration.

As I have said before, the Nazis lost no time in taking control of the entire education system. Opponents of the regime and Jews were purged from teaching positions. The vast majority of teachers—afraid of jeopardizing their careers—joined the Nazi party, regardless of their privately held beliefs. One of the first innovations introduced in the classroom was the mandatory use of the Nazi salute at the beginning of each session. The salute—the words "Heil Hitler!" spoken while standing with the right arm stretched out just above shoulder height—was decreed to be the German greeting everywhere for all occasions, everywhere—on the street, at work, and at home. The Hitler salute put Jews in a dilemma. To participate in the salute, or to respond to it, would be taken as blasphemy or mockery. To refuse or to ignore it would be construed as disrespect or subversion. In school, we decided to stand during the salute, but to not say the words or raise our arms. That pretty well became the practice for Jews wherever they were under Nazi rule.

In the course of the following years, the educational system became another victim of the Nazi ideology that saw schools only as a means to inculcate the next generation with unconditional loyalty to the party and to the Nazi state. The goal was not to teach young people to seek truth and knowledge and to examine ideas critically, but to provide the rationale for blind obedience to the fuhrer and to engender unbridled devotion to Nazi ideology. A new religion deified people, land, blood, and state. A new ethic was to be taught in which ruthless strength was virtue, and compassion revealed moral weakness. Racial studies were given supremacy on the science curriculum. This pseudo-science that was designed to support the Nazi racial theories included the identification of racial types and their characteristics. Naturally, the Jews were at the bottom of the racial hierarchy, while the superiority of the Nordic master race destined Germans to become the rulers of the world. "Today, Germany is ours," the marching columns of Hitler Youth sang, "and tomorrow the whole world!" The teaching of history and literature was adjusted to the Nazi objectives. History was revised to support the political claims of Nazi Germany and Jewish contributions were expunged from the historical record. As Jews were demonized, Jewish writers and artists were excised from the curriculum or banned as degenerate.

At the beginning, there were teachers who could scarcely hide their discomfort with the new practices and the intrusion into the class room of Nazi race theories and chauvinistic propaganda. A few teachers tried to be especially nice to me and to other Jewish students. I remember one teacher apologizing to me—discreetly, in private—for what he was compelled to teach. On the other hand, many teachers who had belonged to the Nazi party all along, now proudly wore their membership button on their lapel and taught school dressed in their brown, storm-trooper uniform. Even those teachers, however, tried to be fair to me personally. Perhaps to some teachers' chagrin, I remained the student who best understood what they taught us in German language and literature, as well as excelling in French, English, and other subjects.

My classmates did not seem to be infected by the Nazi virus in their relationship to me, either, even those who openly identified themselves as Nazis. I was teased a little about being Jewish and about my similarity—or lack of it—to the cruel caricature that was now the official portrait of a Jew ("Well, Schild, how many Aryan girls did you violate last night?"), but, generally, my comrades were good-natured and my friends remained my friends. Some of my classmates realized what was happening and tried to be sympathetic and encouraging. Naturally, they were all still willing to copy from my work and pick my Jewish brain.

The number of Hitler Youth uniforms in the classroom, if few at first, grew quickly. All other youth and student organizations were dissolved, causing a flurry of resentment—especially among students who belonged to religious youth organizations. Instead, (Aryan) students were pressured to join the Hitler Jugend. One of the first students to appear in the uniform of the Hitler Youth was my friend Fred Unterwagner, the American jazz fan. As I mentioned previously, Saturday was a school day in Germany and, like the rest of the Jewish students, I attended school. However, I did not write on the Sabbath, when writing is forbidden by Jewish law. Around age ten or eleven, I grew more conscientious in my Shabbat observance, and started to also respect the Sabbath prohibition against carrying anything through the public domain. Fred Unterwagner used to carry my books to school for me on Saturdays. But one day, I cannot remember whether it was before or after the Nazi takeover, an article appeared in the main Nazi newspaper, the *Völkischer Beobachter*, scathingly condemning this blatant violation of German honour. What kind of a school would permit an Aryan boy to demean himself by carrying books for a Jew? I do not recall that the article mentioned our names, so I would guess that this incident happened before January 30, 1933. I do not suspect that the piece in the newspaper motivated Fred to join the Hitler Youth, but, naturally, our personal relationship cooled. Overt friendships between Jews and non-Jews became very problematic and any show of friendship with Aryans of the opposite sex was extremely dangerous. Interracial relations were criminalized, branded as *Rassenschande*, a shameful contamination of racial integrity, and were severely punished.

An attractive girl about my age, named Mali Mager, lived across the street from me. Her parents had a wholesale tobacco business diagonally across from our store. She often stood in their doorway and we exchanged shy glances and discreet, long-distance greetings whenever I happened to pass by. We never actually said a word to each other. One day, Fred Unterwagner—I remember he was in uniform—told me that he was dating Mali Mager and that she had confided to him that she liked me. "You'd better watch out for *Rassenschande*!" he teased me with a loud laugh. For me, it was a scary jest.

That does not end the story of Fred Unterwagner. In 1972, when Laura and I made a short stop in Mülheim while driving from Switzerland to the Netherlands—my first visit to Germany after the war—I dropped in on Fred Unterwagner. He had taken over his father's business and seemed glad to see me. I was appalled, however, when he compared the suffering of the population during

the Allied air attacks on Cologne to the experiences of the Jews during the Holocaust. He did attend the first class reunion held in my honour in 1982, but none of the subsequent ones. My class-mates did not regret his absence, explaining to me that Fred had been a "real" Nazi during their years at school and that his sym-pathies were probably still with the movement. On a later visit and reunion in 1996, I heard that he had died.

❖

One of the cherished privileges of high school was the scholar's identity card. It entitled students to a 50 percent reduction in the admission charge to the opera house, the municipal theatre, and the concert hall. Students were expected and encouraged to broaden their interests by attending artistic and cultural events, especially the performance of the classical plays that were often discussed in class. I enjoyed this privilege as long as I could. My parents also liked the opera, and Kurt, the musician, was, of course, the family expert.

Perhaps the loss of the opportunity to attend the opera seems trivial, seen in retrospect against the background of genocide, but small details like that can best describe the conditions under which I grew up and to which my parents had to adapt. To say we lived under an increasingly constrictive atmosphere of oppression that slowly suffocated us is an abstract metaphor. The reality was that hateful brown and black uniforms were everywhere. My parents must have struggled with constant chicanery in business, a hostile bureaucracy, dwindling customers, and social ostracism. We watched helplessly as the Nazi government intensified their hold on all aspect of public and private life. Every edition of every news-paper, every broadcast on the German radio—we did not dare tune in to foreign stations—every public event, every school assembly and celebration proclaimed the glory of the Führer, the reviving economy, the rising prestige of Germany. Inevitably, along with the assertions came the refrain, repeated over and over, excoriating the Jews of Germany, as well as the international Bolshevik-Jewish con-spiracy.

Jews had to be circumspect in public. We had to learn not to attract attention. Not to be conspicuous. To be on your best behav-iour. The list of our restrictions, enacted by law or initiated by private zeal and party pressure, grew and grew. Signs that read *"Juden unerwünscht"*—Jews not wanted—increasingly appeared over the entrances to restaurants, recreational facilities, and places of commerce and entertainment. Our horizons contracted. It did not take long before I had heard my last opera and watched my last drama performance. German culture—or what was left of it—was out of bounds for Jews.

And yet. As I look back on the years that followed my bar mitzvah, I am swept by memories of an exciting time. There was pain, frustration, anger, fury; but there was also search and discovery, adventures within and without. There was friendship and love and loneliness, sweet loneliness. There was learning and growing, taking and giving. There was Sturm und Drang, storm and thrust—watchwords of the German romantic movement—and yearning and trembling; there was sun and rain, there were hills and valleys, rivers and roads and wooded paths; there was poetry and music, and shreds of happiness, like blue patches between storm-tossed clouds, and there was stillness for dreams and fantasy. There were books to help me escape beyond the ugliness, to take me beyond the bondage, to a level of clarity and freedom where my mind could stretch and my soul could roam and my heart could feel, feel.

Chapter *TWO*

Transitions

A STRANGE FASCINATION TOOK HOLD OF ME in the six-week interval between my bar mitzvah and my sister's eleventh birthday. At my bar mitzvah party for my friends, everything had been normal: the boys teased the girls, while the girls whispered secrets in each other's ears to make the boys mad. By the time the same group got together to celebrate my sister's birthday, I had mysteriously changed. I had eyes and ears for only one girl, Ruth Speier-Holstein, the oldest of our family doctor's three daughters. How she had blossomed into young womanhood! I had started to notice it during the preceding weeks and I felt deluged by emotions about which I had heard and read, but had never experienced before.

A beautiful friendship ensued, utterly innocent and romantic. We sought each other's company whenever we could. We were rarely alone, but whenever all the kids got together at parties, or in the synagogue, or at someone's home, or on excursions, or at the swimming pool, we were always together. We talked a lot about love in the abstract, and about other ideals, such as truth and loyalty, about adventures in foreign lands, explorers, and pioneers, but we never had the temerity to say that we were in love with each other. We compared our school work and we read the same books; on the occasional walk by ourselves, we pretended to be heroes from the adventure novels we both liked to read.

Was my affection for Ruth merely a sideshow staged by the biological forces that scripted the rapid changes taking place in my mind? Was the quickening of my senses and my enhanced receptivity to romantic notions and esthetic pleasure the effect of the hormonal activity that nature programs in this phase of growing up? I know how science would answer this question, but the poet in me reverses cause and effect: it was my feeling for Ruth that set off the emotional fireworks and triggered the powerful chemistry that metamorphosed my inner life. My emotions became more intense; my feeling heart responded to so many new stimuli. I was happy when I was with Ruth; I missed her when too many days passed without a chance to see her. New hurts, new tortures infiltrated my emotional repertoire; new definitions of bliss crystallized in my mind. I claim that this transforming flood of emotional phenomena was released by my friendship with Ruth, and who dares to say otherwise?

At the same time, my taste in literature was changing. I was becoming more idealistic, more noble, more compassionate. After Ruth, there would be other friendships, both romantic and platonic, and I learned how complicated interpersonal relationships can be. I tasted joy and jealousy, delight and disappointment. I discovered how the dialogue of friends, male or female, can help and heal, and how, with a friend at your side, you can stride on the heights of the earth.

Strangely, I have portraits of Ruth's two sisters in my photo album, but the only photo I have of Ruth is a small group snapshot. It was taken on the grassy spit of land that shelters the harbour of Mülheim from the river current. There was a commercial swimming area there, owned by a crusty old Mülheim type, Herr Mülleneisen, who refused to bar Jewish kids from his beach. Though it was rather primitive and not too clean, we went there now and then to swim with our friends. Ruth's father had some reservations about allowing his daughters to swim in mixed company as some religious authorities frown on this practice, but he relented. Ruth was a strong swimmer and we enjoyed swimming side by side. The snapshot shows a group of girls in simple black bathing suits: Ruth, her sister Edith, Hanna Mohl, and Ilse Moses. Alas, Ruth's face is hardly visible.

Recently in Cologne, a lady accosted me after a lecture. She had bought the German edition of my book, World Through My Window, *and had read about Ruth in the first chapter. She told me that Ruth Speier-Holstein had been in her class at the* Lyzeum *and showed me a photo. I was shocked. Yes, that was Ruth, exactly. But it was so different from the image that was stored in my memory. I remember her face, freckles spreading in summer time from her nose over her cheeks, but in my memory she is not as plain-looking as the face in the photo. In my memory, perhaps, she has the aura of the martyr that she became.*

❖

I really would like to believe that it was Ruth who set in motion a process that gradually weaned me from my more childish friendship with the boys in the Mohl family. Ruth has no burial place, no tombstone. Let it be her memorial that this gentle, pure, romantic and thoughtful girl, idealized in the mind of a thirteen-year old, helped him break out of the confines of childhood in Mülheim—so familiar, so defined, so concrete, so commonplace—and allowed him to emerge in a more universal space that encouraged abstraction, experiment, search, growth, and mystery. I still live in that space.

The physical safety of their children had always been one of my parents' major concerns. It was one of the reasons that Margot and I had a nanny when we were small. We were not allowed to play on the street; Anna took us to a park. We did not associate with the boys and girls the adults called *Gassenkinder*, or street children. My parents also considered bicycles to be much too dangerous to ride in city traffic. How I envied my school comrades who were not so restricted by protective parents! When the Mohl boys all got bicycles, I felt left out. Fortunately, Jojo's older siblings found an old, but very serviceable bicycle for me in the storage area of their business. After a few weeks of watching me ride the old bike, my parents bought me a beautiful new one. I suppose they realized that the dangers of riding a bicycle was insignificant when measured against the risks of living under the Nazis!

My bicycle became a very important part of me, indispensable for mobility and independence Now I could roam the countryside surrounding Cologne with my friends. I could get to Cologne more easily and participate in new activities offered by the Cologne Jewish community, a lucky escape from the tightening net of anti-Semitic restrictions around us. My bicycle was among the few effects that would eventually accompany me to Holland and England—I rode it through London in the wartime black-out.

Gradually, although I still attended high school in Mülheim, the focus of my social life shifted to Cologne. Dr. Speier-Holstein was not only our physician and Ruth's father, but he was also a deeply religious and widely learned Jew, and the spiritual mentor of our young circle. He had urged us to join the No'ar Agudas Yisrael, the youth branch of the world-wide Agudah organization, a bulwark of strict Orthodoxy. The Agudah was opposed to Zionism, because they could not accept the Zionist objective of the self-redemption of the Jewish people. Nor did the Agudah condone membership in a non-Orthodox umbrella organization like the Zionist movement. Nevertheless, the Agudah, independently of the Zionist World Organization, had launched its own project to build settlements in the Land of Israel, since living in the promised land is in itself a meritorious condition, a mitzvah. Today, the Agudah, its ideology little changed, is a powerful party in Israel.

There was an Orthodox alternative to the Agudah, the Bachad. The name was an acronym for Covenant of Orthodox Pioneers. Bachad, and its parent organization, the Mizrachi, although Orthodox, were part of the Zionist family, and the relative merits of Agudah and Mizrachi were hotly debated in our circle. The Zionist side was represented by Dr. Kurt Bamberger, a brilliant chemist working for the famous chemical firm I.G. Farben, who had settled in Mülheim in order to live close to his workplace.

With some of my friends, including Ruth, I became active in the Jewish youth community of Cologne. We had the benefit of well-educated, articulate Jewish youth leaders, teachers, and rabbis, and from them, I gradually acquired a more profound understanding of Judaism. It began to dawn on me that Torah—the Jewish tradition in its totality—contained all the elements from which to construct one's *Weltanschauung*, one's view of the world and of human life. This was no sudden discovery, no flash of illumination, but an intellectual development that extended over several more years.

During the ensuing years, we also found a replacement for the cultural institutions, such as stage and concert hall, from which we had been evicted as Jews. Hundreds of Jewish artists and entertainers, singers, musicians, directors, lecturers, professors, and scientists, had been deprived of their audiences, and the Jüdischer Kulturbund—the Jewish Cultural Federation—was founded to bring together Jewish audiences and Jewish performers, academics, and artists. In my middle teens, I enjoyed great lectures by Jewish historians and philosophers, wonderful performances by fine artists, and lively discussions by religious and secular thinkers. They often had to make do with make-shift stages or unsuitable halls, but their offerings were of a superior intellectual and artistic quality.

There were few occasions for carefree fun; life was serious and full of problems; I took no dancing lessons. Our attitude to conventional behaviour and bourgeois norms was decisively influenced by the idealistic youth movement that had been so strong among German youth before the rise of the Nazis. Despite a tendency toward self-segregation among the Agudah Youth, and the social quarantine of Jews in general, my peers and I were not immune to many of the positive values of the youth movement. Its romanticism and its disdain for bourgeois values had a profound impact on the members of the Jewish youth movement. Again, this was a paradoxical situation, in that Jews became the custodians of German tradition. The spirit of the youth movement was inimical to the Nazis, although they preserved some of its forms. The Nazis had wanted to eradicate its romantic pathos, its *Weltschmerz*—the universal pain of being—from the character of German youth and replace it with the tough, hard-edged, self-assertive Nietzschean ethos of fascism. It was among the Jewish youth that the spirit of the movement, the Bund—the covenant of youth—lived on. We disdained anything as philistine and bourgeois as ballroom dancing and the formalities of middle-class lifestyle. I would never be caught with an umbrella, for instance! I don't use one to this day.

We grew up under harassing conditions; we were victims of the meanest persecution. Our life was a tragedy, yet tragedy, as I knew from my reading, was the stuff of good literature. I developed my own variation of Descartes: I feel, therefore I live. Emotional experience was not to be judged in terms of its quality—on a scale from sweet to bitter, happy to sad—but in terms of its intensity: how deeply could I feel, how profoundly did feelings grasp me. One feels sadness and pain more incisively and deeply than joy and happiness. So I made a virtue out of drinking from the cup of bitterness. Were not most of the true heroes of history and literature tragic figures?

If this sounds hysterical, confused, or contradictory, so it was. I was chafing under the emotional pain that the society around me inflicted on my community and I was struggling with turbulent inner conflicts: competing spiritual and intellectual forces, conflicting philosophies of life, friends and relationships pulling me in different directions. Years later, when my ship was sailing in calmer waters, I wrote a poem in which I worried about the sudden stillness within, about the extinction of the tumult. I comforted myself with the prediction that such fermentation as I had undergone must produce a good wine. At the time, however, I was about to begin a new ordeal: the effects of being forced to emigrate.

Had German Jews been able or willing to read the writing on the wall, a mass exodus from Germany would have followed the Nazi assumption of power. A few did leave immediately. The first to flee—if they were able to escape before the Nazis had them arrested—were individuals whose past prominence in German politics or other sensitive areas targeted them as likely victims of Nazi reprisals. Next to leave were Jewish families who had little to lose, who had no property or business to leave behind, or who were recent immigrants from eastern Europe, and therefore not as rooted in German soil. The early emigrants were fortunate, for the neighbouring countries like Holland, Belgium, France, and Britain had not yet closed their doors to refugees. That would happen a few years later, when the distress of German and Austrian Jews had become so desperate that it threatened to trigger a stampede.

When European countries were no longer willing to accept refugees, Jews went farther afield, to Africa, and South America. Naturally, the most desired destination was the United States, but a fixed quota system continued to restrict severely the number of German-born Jews who were eligible to enter. Nonetheless, a large contingent of German Jews settled in the United States over the next few years. Canada, in contrast, stone-walled. "As for Jews, none is too many!"—the infamous quotation from the files of the Canadian government said it all.

Meanwhile, my parents and many of my friends' families were still clinging to the hope of political change in Germany. After reality had shattered that hope, they leaned on another broken reed: the suggestion that Jews might be able to survive in Germany under Nazi rule as they had during the Middle Ages: in ghettoes, with fewer material goods, with less freedom, perhaps, but, at least, able to survive in a familiar environment, speaking a familiar language, and allowed to keep a portion of the fruits of their labour and enterprise. So they took the chance of waiting a little longer.

Alas, as the stream of emigration began to swell, the gates to even the distant and less desirable havens of refuge closed one after the other. And then it was too late.

Like nearly all the young people in my circle, I anxiously watched for political developments in Europe. Of course, my sources of information were limited to the Nazi-controlled media and government spokespersons, along with the occasional rumour, passed furtively around, originating from someone who had dared to listen to Radio Luxembourg or another foreign broadcast. For a time, my juvenile naïveté persuaded me to hope that the Nazi regime might still be overthrown. Not by a German opposition—the vast majority of Germans had now embraced Hitler and his party enthusiastically—but I was convinced that the European powers could not possibly allow German militarism to rear its head again so soon after World War I. The sad truth, however, was that the resolve of British and French leaders melted before the fiery will of the German dictator. The Western powers preferred to turn a blind eye to Hitler's goal of achieving hegemony over all Europe and beyond.

The test of Europe's resolve was not long in coming. As part of the peace treaty after World War I, the western part of German Rhineland, which borders on France and the Low Countries, was to remain demilitarized. In 1935, Hitler took the bold gamble of revoking this provision of the treaty. Confident that the Western powers were intimidated by the military machine he had already built up in two short years, he ordered the German army into the Rhineland.

I stood on the bridge in Mülheim among hundreds of other spectators as heavily armed German troops, on motorcycles, trucks, and armoured vehicles, rolled over the bridge into the demilitarized zone on the west bank of the Rhine. I felt sure that, this time, Hitler had gone too far. In a few days, I remember telling my parents, French and British forces would arrive to teach Hitler a lesson. But the European powers did no more than meekly protest. Hitler knew he had won the gamble and continued to prepare for a military expansion of the Reich.

In response, the French put their trust in an illusion. They built the Maginot line, an impregnable system of fortifications along the border that, they asserted, would stop any attempted military onslaught against France. This would also save the French the trouble and expense of rebuilding their own war machine to match Germany's. Did the French generals and politicians really believe it?

It became more and more evident that the only hope for German Jews lay in emigration. The Germans put no obstacles in the way of Jewish emigrants, except to impose increasing restrictions on the amount of goods and money the fugitives could take with them. Soon, most Jews were either preparing to leave or were desperately searching for a place of refuge. The increasing volume of emigration added still more bitterness to the sadness of our lives. When we are young, our friends often mean more to us than family. It was depressing to lose so many friends.

There was no sweetness in the sorrow of parting. Although we were happy for those who were able to leave, saying good-bye to relatives and friends, perhaps forever, was gut-wrenching. Especially friends. If one went to Argentina, and another to South Africa, what chance would there ever be again to share thoughts, feelings, and experiences? It was not only a wrenching experience for those who were left behind, but also for those who were leaving. Many left parents, grandparents, siblings, and other relatives behind. Nor was it easy to tear oneself away from surroundings that had become part of us: the city, the river, the landscape. But at least there was hope for a new life. I resisted the chance to create new personal relationships. Why make an emotional commitment to new friends when we had to anticipate the heartbreak of separation. How well I remember!

Although I had no trouble academically in my high school, my situation as the only Jewish student in my class—Jojo had quit long ago—became increasingly difficult and absurd. How could I feel comfortable in the Nazi system that had taken over education as a means to prepare members of the master race for its glorious destiny. Cologne had a Jewish high school, the Jawneh.[1] So, my parents and I consulted with some of my high school teachers whose sincere concern for my future welfare we could trust. They advised me to leave the *Gymnasium* in Mülheim and continue my education at the Jewish *Gymnasium* in Cologne.

[1]The name, pronounced "yavneh," perpetuates the tradition of a site of ancient Jewish learning.

Chapter *THREE*

The Jawneh

On a cool but sunny afternoon in June of 1993, I stood beside an ornamental fountain that adorned a little square in the city of Cologne. The square was formed by the contours of a handsome low-slung commercial building, which houses elegant boutiques, an art gallery, and a tony restaurant. The modern, luxury S.A.S. Hotel loomed over the little square from across a narrow curving roadway. The hotel's imposing bulk could not intimidate an ancient chestnut tree whose giant angular limbs spread a leafy canopy over the decorative cobblestone pavement on which I stood.

For me and for a group of other men and women who had gathered in the square, the old chestnut tree was all that remained of a distant past. Half a century ago, the tree had stood in the centre of the schoolyard of Cologne's Jewish high school, the Jawneh.

The Jawneh was founded by the Adass Jeschurun Congregation, whose synagogue had stood on the site usurped by the hotel, the restaurant, and the newly created square. No trace remains of the school or of the large synagogue, except for the chestnut tree—and, yes, for the name sign of the square. The square has been named after Dr. Erich Klibanski, and his biography, condensed into one sentence, has been squeezed onto the street sign at the corner. Dr. Klibanski was the heroic director of the Jawneh whose tenacious efforts were instrumental in saving more than a hundred of the school's students from certain death. His desperate efforts succeeded in arranging the students' transfer to England. Instead of saving his own life and that of his family during the rescue operation, he returned to Cologne to stay at the helm of the school. The end came when he and the last remaining students of the school were deported from Cologne. The schoolyard of the Jawneh was used as the place where the Jews were assembled for transport to their doom. While they were on the death train, the Klibanskis managed to write a post card addressed to non-Jewish friends in Cologne. They threw the *card out of a window while the train was stopped at a station. An unknown person mailed it. It became the last sign of life of the family. Dr. Klibanski, his wife, and his children were murdered by the Nazis on their arrival in Minsk.*

We were in Erich Klibanski Square to dedicate the fountain to the memory of the Jews of Cologne who were killed during the Holocaust. In particular, a sculpture of the Lion of Judah and soon-to-be-added plaques would identify the fountain as a memorial to more than a thousand young children—including the students of the Jawneh—who had been on the last transports. The dedication ceremony was the climax of a week-long reunion that had brought together members of the former Jewish community of Cologne from many parts of the globe. Quite a few of them had been students of the Jawneh. We—the members of the group and their spouses— were joined by pupils of a local school and a school choir, by public dignitaries, ordinary citizens, and members of the present Jewish community. I had been invited to give the dedication address.

The most senior person in the reunion group was Cantor Philip Modell from California, who had been the last music teacher at the Jawneh and had emigrated just in time to escape the final catastrophe. In his last year at the school, in an effort to raise the students' spirits, he had written a beautiful musical play performed by the students. Now, at our dedication ceremony, the school choir, made up entirely of Christian children, sang one of his songs that had been first heard fifty-three years before at one of the school's last assemblies.

❖

I TRANSFERRED TO THE JAWNEH during the 1935–36 school year, relieved more than sad to get away from the *Gymnasium* in Mülheim. I looked forward to an exciting change, a great challenge, and a new experience. The Jawneh high school was part of the institutional structure of the distinct Orthodox community, the *Austrittsgemeinde*, rather than the main Jewish community of Cologne, the *Grossgemeinde*, also referred to as an *Einheitsgemeinde*, or unity congregation.

Religious communities of all denominations in Germany were not private organizations and the main religious denominations in Germany—including the Jewish one—were officially recognized by the state, which collected a religion tax from all citizens who belonged to a recognized religion, and allocated the proceeds to the various religious communities. Naturally, this also meant that the religious organizations had to accept some measure of state control. This system, which seems repugnant to those raised to believe in a separation of church and state, had some distinct advantages for organized religion. It gave rabbis and cantors the status of public officials with pension provisions similar to state officials, and made the elected representatives and lay leaders of the Jewish community subject to supervision by the appropriate state ministry.

Jews who wanted the Orthodox community to remain separate, of course, refused to pay taxes that supported a Jewish community they neither recognized as legitimate nor wanted to be part of. After a long struggle against the Jewish establishment and against the state authorities, the determined separatists had won the right to establish their own religious institutions apart from the main community. Yet the political wrangling within the Jewish community went on for ever and, I believe, complicated the amalgamation of the Jewish community of Mülheim with the Cologne community. Naturally, the rise of Hitler and the Nazis had put a damper on the political infighting. All Jews, religious or not, and even the numerous converts to Christianity, were targeted as enemies of the German people. Inevitably, the plight of Jewish students in the general school system became increasingly uncomfortable and precarious, especially in some smaller cities. While the idea of a separate Jewish high school had not been very popular, except among the Orthodox, it was now the only solution for Jewish students like me.

The only Jewish *Gymnasium* in Cologne was the Orthodox Jawneh and non-Orthodox Jewish parents were in a dilemma. At this critical juncture, however, the Jawneh offered to admit Jewish boys and girls, regardless of their religious background. Anxious non-Orthodox parents received assurances that the school and its faculty would be tolerant and understanding, and that no pressure would be applied to enforce religious conformity. Thanks to the amazing ability and dedication of Dr. Klibanski, that promise was kept. In general, German Orthodoxy was not extreme or exclusive. The Jawneh flourished with the influx of new students. The study of Torah, which included the study of Hebrew, was an important part of the curriculum, but the philosophy of the school viewed Torah as compatible with the pursuit of secular and scientific studies at the highest levels. The school's objective was an integrated education, positively Jewish but encompassing the best of human civilization.

It may seem strange today, but the wearing of kipas, or skull-caps, although mandatory for boys during Jewish studies, was not allowed during secular classes. When I and other new pupils from the religious right appeared with head coverings, Dr. Klibanski himself ordered us to take them off. Incidentally, the word *kipa* was still unknown; German Jews called it a *käppchen*, the diminutive of the German word for cap.

The teaching faculty of the school was of the highest calibre. Since Jews had been purged from teaching positions in the general school system, Dr. Klibanski had been able to recruit the best teachers for languages, mathematics, the sciences, art, and literature, and most of our teachers were skilled pedagogues with impeccable academic credentials. Jewish subjects, such as Bible, commentaries, and Mishna, were also taught by fine scholars, some of them rabbis. However, I was surprised by the lack of modern lab facilities and equipment, to which I had been accustomed at the Mülheim *Gymnasium*. In this respect, the financially challenged Jawneh lagged behind the schools in the general system.

It did not bother me that my new school was far from home; I did not mind at all riding my bicycle. It took me about forty minutes to pedal across the Rhine on the Mülheim bridge, head south along the river, and then follow the Ring, the semi-circular road around the city core, to the school. Sometimes I took the streetcar. Another adjustment was also pleasant: getting used to the small, co-educational classes of the Jawneh. I found it much more enjoyable to have girls as well as boys as classmates and I am sure it was beneficial for both sexes.

Academically, the Jawneh was an island oasis in the educational system of the city. Its curriculum had not been recast by the Nazi dictatorship whose political, social, and military objectives determined what could and should be taught in schools. At the Jawneh, history and literature were still taught as in pre-Hitler Germany. Unlike teachers and students in all the other high schools—and universities—we did not have to pretend that the works of German-Jewish authors and thinkers had never existed, or merely demonstrated the degeneracy of the Jewish mind. Among the authors and poets we could still read and discuss was Heinrich Heine whose work had been banned from the regular school curriculum because he was Jewish. Heine, caught in the conflict between his Jewish origins and his destiny as a German writer, between cynicism and romanticism, between a love for things German and contempt for some German attributes, served us in some ways as a paradigm of our own predicament.

We could still listen to the many important voices which the Nazis had stilled, and absorb liberal ideas which the Nazis had banished. Moreover, we could still include in our reading and our discourse the contemporary Jewish writers, poets and thinkers who shared our existential despair and felt crushed by the same forces and conflicts that we did. They helped us find solace and inspiration that flowed from our own Jewish sources and from our links to the history and the destiny of the Jewish people.

After living with the poisonous propaganda, distortions, and deceits of the Nazi system and with the pinpricks of daily humiliations, the Jawneh was a refuge, a verdant oasis of healing, a paradise that offered the intoxicating fruit of the tree of new knowledge. It was relief to be in an all-Jewish environment after the complicated relationship I experienced with my Aryan comrades in Mülheim. Most of my classmates had meant well and were probably sincere in their protestations of friendship and comradeship, but the tensions of the last year had just been too great. My new school comrades ranged from Orthodox, like my chaverim from the Agudah, to members of the Marxist-Zionist Hashomer Hatzair Youth Organization. It made for an exciting mix and passionate debates in class and out.

Amidst all the pressures and humiliations of living under the heel of the Nazis, the Jawneh offered us a grand opportunity to learn and to grow. Looking back, I am amazed how we were able, together with our teachers and mentors, under inhuman pressure from a hostile environment, to form an exciting, vibrant community of Jewish individuals. With mutual encouragement, a sharing of our bitter fortune, and supported by mutual solidarity, we embarked on a search for truth and a quest for values that could, at least for the moment, neutralize the falsehood, the evil, and the ugliness that ruled triumphant in the world beyond our school yard.

Soon the chestnut tree would be the only visible memento of this community.

Chapter *FOUR*

Cologne Years

*I*CANNOT CONTRADICT THE SCIENTIFIC CONSENSUS that young humans, just like animals and plants, grow and unfold according to genetically encoded instructions. Physical and biological changes that I experienced before and after I entered puberty were biologically conditioned. Nevertheless, I am convinced that the explosive developmental rush that followed my transfer from the *Gymnasium* in Mülheim to the Jawneh was due to stimuli that came from outside myself. So fast that I could almost see the changes taking place, my transition to a new scholastic environment profoundly altered my spiritual profile.

I had never before found myself in an all-Jewish environment and released from the pressure of being the only Jewish student in a Nazi-dominated school atmosphere, I responded to a new sense of emotional and intellectual freedom. It was a heady experience. New teachers, new books, new friends, new classmates and new ideas made for excitement and growth. I did not remain at the Jawneh for long—less than two years—but the Jawneh remained part of me forever. The juxtaposition of Jewish subjects and secular ideas, literature, and science stimulated thought. We boldly pursued ideas that were presented by gifted and passionate teachers or suggested in our reading: political theories, Zionism, philosophy, art, ethics, and piety.

The transfer to the Jawneh was not without problems, at first. I was an newcomer to a established hierarchy of young scholars. Most of the Jawneh students had been at the school long before me, while I had to adjust to a new and different school environment and tradition. I was challenged more than ever before. Teachers did not know me. I was no longer the star pupil. I had to match serious, gifted students reared in a tradition of learning, who, unlike my former Aryan comrades in Mülheim, had few external diversions to distract them.

I had to struggle, especially at the beginning, with my vanity. While I was very good in most subjects, there was always someone better than I in each specialty. One member of my class was a mathematical genius, a quiet person who was a sharp, logical thinker, but not very imaginative. Another fellow student could trump me in political and religious debates, but he had trouble in languages and mathematics. He was a fervent, articulate Marxist who eventually made aliyah and still lives on a kibbutz.

I saw him again, after sixty years, on a visit to Israel in 1996. By chance, a member of my congregation had met him on a visit to his kibbutz and, while talking with him, discovered that the old kibbutznik had been to school with his Toronto rabbi! He brought me back a note and we arranged to meet on my next trip to Israel. How he had changed! The youthful firebrand, the revolutionary radical, was a calm, polite, rather conventional, phlegmatic Israeli!

One member of the class, David Alster, made me especially jealous: a brilliant, sharp-tongued, linguistically gifted, accomplished musician, who was very learned in Jewish matters, and had an outgoing, domineering character. However, he was weak in mathematics and other subjects that required precise, logical thinking. He struck me as arrogant and superficial and his verbosity bothered me, but he was a powerhouse in class and a leading personality in the school. My judgment of him, as I realized later, was not only uncharitable, but also distorted by my jealousy.

David Alster lived in New York for a number of years, where he continued making music, although teaching was his main career. His home is now in Haifa and we had a reunion there some years ago. I invited him to give a lecture on Israeli music to my tour group.

Thus, when I joined the Jawneh community, I faced an academic challenge as well as an ethical test. Was I able to play a humbler role with good grace and cheerfulness? Would I be mature enough to realize that humility is not a sort of pretension but an acceptance of reality? However, I was able to find my place as a student: I was very good across the academic spectrum. While others surpassed me in specific subjects, I probably had the best average. I showed a special aptitude for the English language and had a mastery of written German. I also tried quite seriously to be a nice person, kind and thoughtful to others, sensitive, gentle, and—well, I had an artistic, romantic flair, though much less flamboyant than David Alster. After a while I came to be known and gained the appreciation and confidence of classmates and students in the lower grades, who came to me with their problems and relied on me for moral support and friendly encouragement. I was never lonely, except when, in the romantic fashion, I sought loneliness for thinking and quiet inspiration.

On the walls of my home and my synagogue study hang a number of sketches, many of them portraits, in pencil, chalk, and ink. The stylized signature at the bottom right corner identifies me as the artist; the date establishes that my artistic career began while I was a student of the Jawneh. To my regret, this career only spanned a few years. I blame inimical circumstances later in my life for damping this creative spark. Some of my friends keep encouraging me to take pencil and paper in hand again. I have tried a few times, but the time has not yet been right. I hope it will be some day.

The art teacher at the Jawneh discovered my talent and helped me to develop it. His name was Ludwig Meidner, a well-known German painter of the Expressionist school. The Nazis had condemned and banned his work as "degenerate"—as they did the work of all Jewish and many other modern artists. A tortured soul, whose paintings expressed his agony and despair, Meidner could no longer sell his paintings and had lost his livelihood. He was glad, therefore, to be offered a position as art teacher at the Jawneh. He taught me that art is not just skill and technique, but an intuitive expression of the self; that drawing a scene, a still-life, or a portrait means filtering what you see through your own feelings; and that a successful portrait, if the artist lets intuition take control of eye and hand, will reflect the inner personality of the subject rather than being merely an outward likeness.

I loved to sketch and soon practiced my new-found art outside of the formal art periods at school. I did portrait sketches of some of my fellow students, and even of Mr. Israel Janowski, our cantor in Mülheim. I sketched landscapes during excursions in the country-side, often in the company of a girl who shared my interest. She was a student at the Jawneh, one year behind me: a very fine, idealistic person, athletic and statuesque, a secular Zionist. She would soon leave school to attend a *hachsharah*—a training program to prepare for Palestine—and make aliyah while I was still in Cologne. Her name was Ruth Levi. After a few post cards and a letter or two, our correspondence dried up.

Three decades later, when I started to visit Israel regularly, I used to stare at the name Ruth Levi on a war memorial commemorating individuals who fell in the War of Independence. It was on the wall of the synagogue I usually attend when I am in Tel Aviv on Shabbat; it memorializes sons and daughters of synagogue members, who mostly came from Germany. It would have been just like her to volunteer for a dangerous mission in the war. I never tried to trace her; with a name as common as Ruth Levi that would have been difficult. Only recently I asked another Israeli Jawneh alumnus about her. He had indeed known her; she had survived the wars, married, and lived on a kibbutz, but had, unfortunately, died a few years before.

My time at the Jawneh—more than one year, but less than two—was crowded with wonderful experiences. Looking back, I find it difficult to understand how so much was crammed into so short a period. We had fabulous classes in literature, French, and English; we studied art and architecture in their historical contexts. I wrote prose and poetry— I loved hexameters—and translated English and Hebrew poetry into German. I remember writing a long essay on the problems of translating. My one complaint about instruction at the Jawneh was that I did not like our Latin teacher's method. In Mülheim, we focussed on a passive knowledge of the language and we made rapid progress in reading Latin literature, but at the Jawneh, we spent a great deal of time translating into Latin, which I considered a waste of time. I still think I was right.

I took extra classes—*shiurim*—with rabbis and other educators. The Adass Jeschurun Congregation that sponsored the Jawneh also maintained a small institute for training religious teachers. I benefitted greatly from contact with some of the students, as well as with some of the faculty. Rabbi David Carlebach was the head of this seminar and I was fortunate to study with him and with other teachers. Amazingly, I also found time to participate in the youth movement. I became a certified youth leader in the Agudah Youth—I still have the passport-like identity card issued to Jewish organizations by the Nazi youth administration; I had time for my art, for family gatherings, for giving private lessons in French and English, and for a host of other activities.

Above all, I made time for my friends. I led a double or triple life. I retained my old friends in Mülheim. My first romantic friend, Ruth Speier-Holstein, was now my classmate at the Jawneh, but the nature of our relationship had changed. We remained close friends and continued to enjoy each other's company.

Then there were the friends I made in the youth groups. Not surprisingly, many of these were girls. We had long and serious discussions about life's problems, philosophy and religion, and personal relationships. We debated the relative priority of the individual and the community. We talked about authors, their books and their ideas, about art and artists, poetry and music, truth and beauty, reality and appearance, mysticism and rationalism. Often we talked about our prospects for the future, our plans for emigration. We shared our inner anguish and the sorrow of having our families torn apart by the stressful circumstances of our lives. We compared fears, frustrations, loneliness, and despair, and sought comfort and strength and wisdom together. We bared our souls and poured out our hearts. Among my friends were also young people who had taken refuge in Cologne—or in Mülheim—from the more virulent persecution of Jews in small towns and villages.

For years I have had the reputation among my Toronto friends that I am very fond of travel, of exploring, hiking. The reputation is well deserved. The inclination to enjoy nature and scenery, and the yen to walk or drive through the countryside, as well as the skill of using maps, were bred into me. Wanderlust, a prevalent German attribute, was very much a part of life in my youth. Exploring the forests, the hills, and the valleys of the region surrounding Cologne was a regular activity for most youth organizations. When we were in a large group, we usually wandered on foot. On private excursions with closer friends, we rode our bikes. We had to be careful not to arouse too much attention and to be on our best behaviour, always avoiding places where the presence of Jews might be provocative. However, we had nerve and were lucky, I suppose. We lived in a region where violent anti-Semitism was not rampant. Nevertheless, fear and anxiety were always present because we were surrounded by anti-Jewish publicity, billboards, slogans, and newspaper displays, and were subjected, day after day, to restrictions and humiliations.

One bicycle trip particularly stands out in my memory, not only because it was my first overnight bicycle tour, but also because it almost did not take place on account of a very sad family event. It must have been in the summer of 1936 when my old friends the Mohls and I decided to take a bicycle trip to Frankfurt. We were going to stop near Koblenz on the first night and spend the second night at the home of a girl in Mainz—Ruth Scheuer—whom we knew from the time she had lived with relatives in Mülheim. She had become friendly with our group, especially with Heinz Mohl.

Several days before our planned departure, a terrible thing happened. My uncle Emil Kracko disappeared. He suffered from what would presumably be diagnosed today as Alzheimer's disease; he was disoriented and would wander off occasionally. Usually he came back, either on his own or accompanied by a friendly policeman or neighbour who had found him wandering. After all, Mülheim was not so big. This time, however, he did not return and remained lost for several days. When he was finally found, he was quite ill and died a few days later. His funeral was on the day we had planned to leave for our bicycle trip. Of course, I had to attend the funeral, but I felt terrible that our trip would be aborted. We could not start out a day later, since we had to be back in school. My parents, however, came to the rescue with a compromise plan: on the day after the funeral, we would take our bicycles by train to Koblenz, a day's journey by bike, and continue from there.

It turned out to be a beautiful trip. Our worry that we might not find overnight accommodation was unfounded. For the two or three nights that we required it, we found guest rooms in private homes, as many travellers did. Had we not been Jewish, we could have stayed in any of the numerous youth hostels that provided popular, inexpensive, and convenient lodging for thousands of young people. But they did not admit Jews, of course. On the return trip we stopped off at a landmark that I had never seen before: the Laacher See in the Eifel Mountains. I had my art materials with me and brought home a beautiful sketch of the lake; the drawing still hangs in our house.

When I arrived home from our bicycle tour, a friend of Margot's and mine, Hannah Mayer, was waiting for my return. My sister had left school a short time before and had gone to work in a business office located in the *Hochhaus*, the first modern skyscraper in Cologne. The firm where she worked was owned by the Mayer brothers. The family came from Gelsenkirchen, a city not far from Cologne, where another brother was a practising pediatrician. His two daughters, Hannah and Gisela, attended the Jawneh, and Hannah was in my class. Through her uncles, who were Margot's bosses, she became very friendly with my sister and me, and often visited in our home.

Although she was in the working world, Margot created her own ties with the Jawneh circle. She came under the special influence of a very exceptional scholar and passionate teacher, Rabbi Dr. Sigmund Stein, who eventually died a martyr's death. His teaching and personal example became vitally important for Margot during her last years in Cologne, before she was deported to Riga with our parents. Margot's genuine personal piety, inner strength, and saintliness owed much to Dr. Stein, and she, in turn, felt eternally grateful to him.

I have so many memory fragments that I am unable to place chronologically. They are held together by geography—belonging to Cologne and the period that began with my entrance into the Jawneh in 1935 and did not quite end when I left Cologne, because I still came home for vacations. Most of these memories have to do with my relationships to various people.

Eli Munk was a close friend in my Jawneh circle, a scion of a renowned rabbinic family. We were re-united in England where we saw each other quite often; after that, we lost track. One of my mentors in the Agudah was Erich Wallach, who, I believe, died of natural causes at a young age. There were also the three sons of the Königshöfer family. I met one of them at the Jawneh reunion in Cologne a few year ago. He had travelled there from Israel and we enjoyed refreshing our shared memories. Tragically, he was killed in a traffic accident just a few weeks after he returned from Cologne.

One of my good friends in our youth organization was Margot Klein. She later switched from the Agudah to Mizrachi, went to a *hachsharah* in Britain, married Moshe Sigler, and made aliyah with him from England about 1942. They live in Jerusalem and are dear friends whose company we enjoy on each visit. They moved from a religious kibbutz, Tirat Tzvi, to Jerusalem before the State of Israel was born. Moshe was among the brave defenders of Jerusalem during the War of Independence. He is passionately devoted to Israel, learned, and an excellent amateur guide to Jerusalem. We cherish our friendship with them, their children, and their grandchildren. My sister has also been close to Margot Sigler over the years, so the Siglers have practically become part of our extended family.

Ernst Simons, the son of Rabbi Dr. Julius Simons, was my best friend for a long time and one of my regular companions in 1936 and 1937. He also liked my sister, Margot, while I was very fond of his sister Martha. Martha introduced me to her friend, Helmi Loeb, with whom I developed a close and mature friendship. Helmi was proud that she was not an "intellectual" like me and most of my friends, but was very practical, worldly-wise and down-to-earth, a perfect friend for a dreamer like me. While I appreciated her efficient directness, she admired my knowledge and poetic flair. For a while, we tried to study Spanish together. Martha's younger sister, Ruth, was a cute, lively, and very funny girl, a friend of Helmi's younger sister, Rita. Sigmund Loeb, the girls' father, had been a successful businessman who was now faced with ruin. When the Loeb family was preparing for emigration to the United States, they retained me to give them English lessons.

Martha, Helmi, and I spent many Sunday afternoons together, until emigration parted us. Martha's family, the Simons, went to Holland. Helmi was able to find refuge for a time in France and later joined her family in the United States. On one of our first visits to the United States, Laura and I visited the Loeb family in Asbury Park, New Jersey. When Kurt lived in New York, after his emigration from Germany, he got in touch with Helmi, although he had only known her slightly, through me. They remained good friends until my brother left New York. Helmi eventually married another Kurt, Kurt Berndt, and lived in North Carolina. We used to visit them often on motor trips to the south, but our friendship unfortunately ended, quite unnecessarily, over some sharp personal disagreement.

Quite coincidentally, when Laura and I were visiting Martha in San Francisco three years ago, Rita Loeb happened to be in California and phoned Martha. It was an exciting surprise to speak to her, for the first time since 1937.

As I have mentioned before, unfortunately, the Germans caught up with the Simons family when Nazis occupied the Netherlands. Dr. Julius Simons, his wife, Veronika, and their oldest son, Hermann, perished in Auschwitz. Martha was liberated by Canadian troops from the Dutch concentration camp in Westerbork, just in time to be saved from the fate of her parents. Ruth Simons managed to survive by going into hiding and posing as a non-Jew. My friend Ernst was near death when he was liberated in Bergen-Belsen. Kurt Simons, Helmi's friend, also survived until he was killed in the fatal car accident while driving with British officers to find a Torah scroll for Jewish camp survivors to use in services.

Ernst, who had married during the Holocaust, lived in the United States for a short period after the war. He then returned to Cologne and had a distinguished professional career in education, culminating in the position of chief administrator of the state school system. When he retired about ten years ago, a school in Cologne was named after him. He has been, and continues to be, a prominent leader in the Jewish community. He conducts tours of the synagogue for non-Jewish groups, particularly for school children, and he interprets Judaism and the Jewish way of life to countless listeners in churches, schools, and social organizations. His children live in Israel. Ernst and his wife, Ans, divide their time between homes in Jerusalem and Cologne.

Martha, whose husband, Erich Jonas, died some years ago, lives in San Francisco. We have remained friends all through the years. Ruth and her late husband, Naftali Amsel, lived in New York for about seventeen years. She now makes her home in

Amsterdam. We had several reunions with Martha and Ruth, sep-
arately, over the years. Finally, the three of us were all together
when the two sisters were guests at our golden wedding anniversary
celebration on January 1, 1995.

Other interesting friends must also be mentioned. I have an interesting snapshot taken of me on one of our hikes in the country when
I was about sixteen years old. I am sitting on the wooden railing of
a little bridge over a creek, wearing knickerbockers, standard clothing for hikes, and a French beret, a "Basque cap". One of my friends
in the picture is Kurt Rothschild, the son of a highly regarded
Orthodox family in Cologne. Our friendship began in the Agudah.
Kurt had an outstanding professional and business career in Canada
and has been a prominent influential communal leader. He lives in
Toronto, when he is not in Jerusalem. Interestingly enough, he is
one of the most prominent world leaders of Mizrachi, serving as
president of Canadian Mizrachi, and also as president of the
Canadian Zionist Federation. Strange, that our friendship began
when both of us were active in the non-Zionist Agudah Youth
organization!

Also in the picture is Heinz Mohl and a girl whose name was
Marianne Stern. The other person in the photo is Miriam Cahn.
Miriam was a very conflicted young person. She was the sister, two
years younger, of Jettchen Cahn, my classmate at the Jawneh and
the daughter of one of our teachers. In the eyes of a casual and
superficial beholder, Miriam was not beautiful. Her face was long,
her eyes very deep-set, and her very straight nose appeared to push
her mouth too far from her eyes. She usually wore a sad expression
that reflected her disposition: not angry, but sad and lonely. She felt
inferior to her sister, who though not pretty either, was very lively,
outspoken, and popular. Miriam was quiet, aware of her ungainly
looks, and rather melancholy. Yet her face was unusual, interesting
and moving, perhaps even beautiful, if you knew her.

Miriam was very fond of me and liked my company. One afternoon—I believe it was Shabbat and we had just finished a study session—I found myself walking with her. We were strolling in the
Botanical Gardens when Miriam opened up her heart to me. In tears,
she told me how she felt about me and how sorry she was that her

feelings were not mutual. Her sadness deeply moved me. A tragic beauty transmuted her face. That afternoon I learned anew how friendship is linked to obligation. I learned that one may become responsible for a person by not loving them as much as by loving them. I felt more than compassion.

Perhaps that afternoon changed our relationship, but we had run out of time. In a few weeks, I was to leave Cologne for Würzburg and Miriam was also about to leave Cologne. Perhaps the impending leave-taking had given her the courage or the desperation to speak. I received some letters from her, which I kept, but I don't remember if I ever saw her again after I left Cologne. She died in the Holocaust, with her sister and her mother.

One new friend was a bright, happy young lady, about my age or a year younger. Betty Stern was a relative of Mrs. Bertha Mohl who had fled from Nazi terror in her village to live with the Mohls. We became very close friends. She had a beautiful, serene face, a tall, husky physique, and was very intelligent, resourceful, sensitive, and artistic. We decided—or perhaps she did—that we should not spoil our relationship or complicate our lives with romance; ours was to be an unselfish, mutually supportive, platonic relationship. Our friendship began at a time when emigration was on everybody's mind—romantic ties might just lead to more pain. Betty was trying to get to England as a domestic—the only way that she could hope to receive a visa. I helped her with her English lessons. Our relationship continued. All that remains of it, for reasons that I will explain later, is a photograph and a beautiful poem that Betty wrote on the back.

Chapter *FIVE*

The Rush to Exit

A PASSAGE FROM DISBELIEF TO DESPAIR—that describes, in very general terms, the process that German Jews underwent between 1933 and 1938. First, there was disbelief: the Hitler regime could not last, or, if it did, it would not implement the extreme anti-Jewish program of the Nazi party or enshrine it in legislation. In the course of the first three years, this delusion gradually faded. Inexorably, on all levels of public life, Jews were deprived of position, civil rights, legal protection, and economic opportunity. Before long, it became clear that the Third Reich, which Hitler had prophesied would endure a thousand years, was there to stay; Jews could no longer make plans for the future based on the false hope that it would crumble. It also became increasingly obvious that anti-Jewish measures were being broadened and intensified. The hope that Jews might be tolerated as a segregated second-class minority became also untenable. No doubt remained that the regime was serious about making Germany *judenrein*—free of Jews—although very few would have anticipated that this objective was going to be extended to all of Europe and, possibly, to the world, or that it would be pursued as a systematic process of brutal genocide.

Gradually, we came to accept that emigration was the only solution. Individuals—Jews and also many non-Jews—who had been politically active, tried to flee the country immediately. They were accepted as refugees by other European countries. Jewish families or individuals who had no career, business, property, or other non-transferable assets to leave behind also found new opportunities in Holland, Belgium, France, Britain, or other similarly desirable destinations. Other Jews saw the light—or rather the darkness—early and pulled up stakes to go to Palestine, the United States, South Africa, South America, and Australia, even if it meant turning their backs on position, property, or profession and severing personal ties and roots.

As the stream of refugees began to swell, most European countries tightened their immigrations restrictions and closed their borders. The boat was full. Even Palestine, under the British mandate, introduced quotas to keep Jews out. The United States accepted only a small number of German-born immigrants, limited by an annual quota that had been fixed long ago, when the United States had set quotas for the natives of all other countries. Jews scrambled to register with the American consulate in Stuttgart, speculating hopefully that, with time, they would find relatives or friends in the United States who would be prepared to sponsor them and to sign the required affidavit. The American consulate in Stuttgart issued numbers to all applicants. Soon, the waiting list exceeded the quota for several years to come. Applicants knew that unless America changed the rules—as it never did—it would be years before their number came up. A cruel fate indeed. A low number was a chance to live. The higher your number, the smaller your chances of survival in this lottery of death. Many Jews in eastern Europe and the Balkans—traditional countries of origin for Jewish migrants—as well as many Austrian Jews, became frightened of Nazi expansionism or anticipated the spillover effect of Nazism on their countries, where anti-Semitism was indigenous. They joined the throngs of Jews clamouring for a refuge or crowding the remaining lanes of migration, shuttling from country to country.

The potential flood of refugees alarmed the Western democracies. Conferences were called to discuss and solve the refugee problem, raising the hopes of the trapped Jews. It was to no avail. Nothing was solved; no country volunteered to accept Jewish refugees. The much touted international conference at Evian in Switzerland, convened with so much fanfare, only confirmed the global abandonment of the Jews in continental Europe and deepened the despair of those trapped inside it. A cruel jest was circulating. Who has faith in Evian? Just read the word backwards: N-A-I-V-E!

Germany did nothing to inhibit the exodus of its Jews. On the contrary, in the early years of the Hitler regime, Jews were allowed to ship or take with them most of their personal belongings, such as furniture, appliances, bicycles, and carpets. I remember how early emigrants had their bulky belongings packed in huge crates for shipment by sea to Buenos Aires, Cape Town, or other overseas destinations. Later, motivated by their desire to make Jews as miserable and wretched as they could, the Germans placed increasingly tight limits on money and other assets that could be taken out of the country. Finally, emigrants, such as myself, were allowed only to take a bare minimum of personal effects, such as clothing and books, and ten mark in cash. I had one small suitcase, a small wooden box, and, fortunately, my used bicycle. By that time, however, many people would have been glad to escape with their shirts on their backs.

Most people in situations similar to my parents' failed to understand what was happening. Their properties, their businesses, their roots in the country, their fear that they would be destitute if they left Germany deterred them from taking the steps to liquidate what they could and to move on, as persecuted Jews had done for nearly two thousand years. Especially after the "civilized" European countries closed their gates to immigrants, my parents and thousands of others weighed their prospects as immigrants in strange countries such as the Dominican Republic, Uruguay, and Madagascar against their chances of survival in the Third Reich. By the time the reality of despair had sunk in, finding a prospective place of refuge had become impossibly difficult, time-consuming, and frustrating. People became despondent. The number of suicides rose spectacularly.

I cannot recall that my parents had taken any definite steps toward emigration before 1937. Kurt had secured a number from the American consulate, but by the time my parents did the same, their wait-list number was hopelessly high.

Some of our relatives had been smarter or luckier. The first to leave were my Uncle Willi and Aunt Else Neugarten, my mother's brother and sister-in-law. Uncle Willi had tried a number of businesses with little lasting success. Their latest effort, in a town called Dinslaken, had just failed, despite my father's attempt to help out. Dinslaken was close to the Dutch border, and so Willi and Else, with their beautiful daughter, Hannerl, and infant son, Hank, managed to get across. The year was 1934, I believe. Willi and Else had nothing, except their enterprise and skill. I have already described how they built a successful ladies' skirts manufacturing company in Amsterdam.

About 1936, my cousins Kurt and Edith Moses, brother and sister, left for Asuncion, Paraguay. My cousin Walter Neugarten emigrated to South Africa, brought his widowed father, Uncle Gustaf Neugarten, to Cape Town and established a successful ladies' wear factory. Unfortunately, Walter died young, before his dad, but not before he had married and had children. Another cousin, Ilse Neugarten, was able to find refuge in Belgium.

My mother's sister, Aunt Nettchen Kracko, whose husband had died, was perhaps the most fortunate. Her son Arthur was an engineer, working as a marine engine installer for a large international diesel engine company in Cologne. When the company, a major German firm, could no longer employ a Jewish engineer, they had posted him to England to supervise the installation of their engines in British ships. Arthur managed to remain in England, he founded his own marine engine company and prospered. He had married a girl from Mülheim, Hanna Schubach, whose sister, Else, was one of my brother's closest friends. Not long ago, Laura and I attended, Arthur's granddaughter's wedding in London, England. Unfortunately, neither Arthur nor Hanna lived to be there. Another son, Erich, was able to emigrate to the United States with his wife, Selma. By dint of shared hard work, they were very successful in business and became the parents of a fine, large Jewish family. Of all our maternal cousins, Erich and family have remained the closest to us.

Hertha Kracko, the only daughter of the family, married a German Jew, Juan Kariel, who had emigrated to Argentina in the early 1930s. When the Olympic Games were held in Berlin in 1936, Juan took a chance and returned to Germany, hoping to find a wife. He did; my beautiful cousin Hertha. Soon, Hertha was able to bring her mother, Aunt Nettchen, to Buenos Aires, where she lived to a ripe old age. We were reunited with her several times at celebrations with Erich's family, who lived in New Rochelle, New York. Hertha visited us several times in Toronto. Spry and adventurous, she travelled extensively until the onset of her final illness. She died in 1992.

Unfortunately, the youngest of the Krackos, Walter, did not escape his doom. He was imprisoned by the Nazis for an alleged racial violation. Instead of being released after serving a prison sentence, he was taken to a concentration camp and killed.

Another cousin who managed to emigrate in time was Hilde Baum, the daughter of my Uncle Gustaf and Aunt Frieda, my mother's sister. Frieda died young in 1934, mourned deeply by the whole family, when Hilde was still in her early twenties. Hilde, beautiful and chic, made it to England, and from there, eventually, to the United States. She lived in Montclair, New Jersey, and married. Like her mother, she contracted cancer and died at an early age. I do not know what happened to her father.

Uncle Felix, my father's only surviving brother, and his wife, Tante Bertha, and their son, my cousin Joseph Schild, had to leave Ulmbach because of rabid anti-Semitism among the local population. Joseph left Ulmbach first, in 1934, and entered a *hachsharah* in Frankfurt. His parents followed him to Frankfurt about a year later. Joseph then decided to try to get to the United States. A branch of our grandmother's family, by the name of Katz, had emigrated to New York near the beginning of the century and the Schilds in Ulmbach had remained in touch with them over the years. The Katz family agreed to assume the responsibility for their distant cousin Joseph Schild and signed an affidavit for him. Joseph was registered with the American consulate and was able to leave Germany for New York in 1937. He was known as Seppel in Ulmbach, but he became Joe in America. As soon as he could, cousin Joe persuaded the same relatives to sponsor my brother, Kurt. They agreed—with the proviso that Kurt marry their daughter. Cousin Joseph, knowing both my brother and the girl, was certain that Kurt would end up disavowing the arrangement, but saving Kurt's life was so important to him that he set his moral scruples aside. He convinced Kurt to agree to the condition, the deal was made, and Kurt's immigration visa was approved. However, by the time his immigration number came up, in April 1940, World War II had already started. Fortunately for Kurt, neither the United States nor Italy had yet entered the war, so Kurt was able to book passage to New York on an Italian ocean liner. He took a train to Genoa and embarked for the New World on the Italian liner *Leonardo Da Vinci*. Cousin Joe was there to welcome him and to share his rented room with him until Kurt could get out on his own.

Meanwhile Joe's parents—Uncle Felix and Aunt Bertha—had been able to persuade a wealthy American cousin of Aunt Bertha's to sponsor them. Alas, their immigration number at the United States Consulate in Stuttgart came up even later in 1940 than Kurt's. By the time they received their visas, Italian passenger boats were no longer crossing the Atlantic and Joe was unable to arrange passage for his parents. Uncle Felix and Aunt Bertha took a desperate gamble. They packed whatever they could carry, took a train to Berlin, and, after bribing a railway official, got on a train to Moscow while Germany and the Soviet Union were still at peace. They continue the arduous train trek through Siberia, with repeated interruptions occasioned by dangerous conditions surrounding them and by lack of money to pay the fare to the next station. Joe borrowed whatever money he could to send to his parents en route. After a journey of several months, they finally reached Japan, which had not yet entered the war. Joe borrowed more money and booked their passage to San Francisco. From there, they took a bus to New York and were eventually reunited with their son and their nephew. Joseph served in the United States army in the Pacific theatre during the war. He returned safely, married, and with his wife, Norma, produced a fine family. We have been very close over the years and continue to be so.

My parents, unfortunately, had waited too long. Even if they had found a relative willing to sign the all-important affidavit, their registration number with the American consulate was too high. It would not have come up until sometime in 1941. By that time, the jaws of the Holocaust had closed on them.

At the end of 1936, it had become obvious that my sister and I were in jeopardy because my parents were not willing to send us, their two younger children, into the world alone, as some others had done. We wrote letters to American yeshivot and universities, but without the intercession of an influential person, they were lost in the flood of similarly desperate requests from thousands of Jewish students in Germany.

The frantic search for an escape from Germany pervaded our daily lives. At the Jawneh high school, the dream of its director, Dr. Klibanski, was to relocate the entire school to Britain. He established some useful links with educational institutions in England and began to work out a plan that would eventually take a substantial number of Jawneh students to England. Meanwhile, since German universities were closed to Jews—as were all professional careers that required high school matriculation—the Jawneh decided to drop the German high school curriculum and to prepare its senior students for the British matriculation exams.

Chapter *SIX*

Abitur

FOR ME, THE MAJOR CHANGE in the educational policy of the Jawneh, the switchover from the German *Abitur* to the British matriculation, presented a great dilemma. I was only one year away from the *Abitur*, the comprehensive examination that completes the high school program and is recognized by most universities in the world. The *Abitur* would not get me admitted to a German university under the Nazi regime, but neither did I have any chance of emigrating to England at that point. I was so close to the completion of my high school program and had been so successful at it that it seemed a pity not to be able to finish.

I tried the new British curriculum at the Jawneh, but it did not appeal to me. It seemed to lack flair, vision, and inspiration. English literature was taught in such a pedantic fashion that it was as if we had to count the trees without being allowed to enjoy the forest. Instead of essays to challenge our thinking and imagination, we had to do précis again and again. Mathematics also consisted of repeating boring exercises.

So, my classmate David Alster, who felt similarly disappointed, and I applied to the school administration of the city of Cologne for re-admission to a *Gymnasium*. We asked for the chance to enter the *Prima*, the final year of high school. We were prepared to go to any school that would have us. It seemed hopeless and irrational. But a minor miracle happened. David and I were accepted. We would complete our final high school year, 1937–8, as students at the Realgymnasium Spiesergasse, a highly regarded school in Cologne.

With fear and trepidation, we again entered a classroom in a regular German school. If anything, the curriculum was even more focused on the needs of the Third Reich than it had been before I had left my school in Mülheim. Most of my classmates expected to enlist in the German army upon graduation and to be trained as officers. Some looked forward to careers in the navy or air force; yet others came from backgrounds that had instilled in them guarded reservations toward the regime.

All in all, David and I had little trouble and were somehow respected by our peers. Some teachers went out of their way to show us sympathy and make things easier for us. I even continued to sketch. At least one of my classmates, whose facial features deviated alarmingly from the Nordic ideal and who for this reason may have harboured special empathy for Jews, sat for a portrait which still hangs in our home today.

The year passed quickly. I was busy with my studies and my Jewish and social activities in the Jawneh circle of which I remained part. Saturday was a school day again. Since it was too far to walk from Mülheim to the school, I spent Friday nights with the Simons family in Deutz, enjoying my growing friendship with Martha, and—in a different way, of course—with her brother Ernst. Then, on Saturday morning, I crossed the bridge over the Rhine and walked through the city to the school. I often spent afternoons with my friend Kurt Rothschild, whose home was not far from the school.

Soon the final exams were at hand. The class assembled to receive the examination schedule. No! it can't be—but it was: to my utter distress, one exam was scheduled for Saturday. I would not write on Shabbat. I was devastated. Had it all been in vain, then? So close to my goal, I would not reach it, for writing on Shabbat was out of the question.

With a courage born of desperation, I raised my hand. "Herr Studienrat, Alster and I cannot write exams on Saturday." Silence. "That's right. I hadn't thought of it," the teacher answered. "We'll change the schedule and hold the exam on another day." And so, in Nazi Germany in 1938, a high school changed its examination schedule to suit two observant Jewish students. Nobody demurred, complained, or ran to party headquarters. A miracle, indeed.

I passed the examinations with high marks and got my diploma and my report. The only subject in which my professor had reduced my mark to "satisfactory" was German, where I am sure I rated top marks. He apologized privately; it was just not politically correct to give a Jewish student "very good" in German.

❖

In the course of time, the wisdom of my decision to try for the Abitur *was borne out. In 1943 I submitted my* Abitur *diploma to the University of Toronto—Canada was still at war with Germany—and I was accepted without having to write any entrance exams.*

It was the spring of 1938. A crucial period in my life had ended. I had finished high school. I had come a long way in my religious growth as a Jew and in my development, I hoped, as a thinking and sensitive human being, in defiance of the pressures of the Nazi environment. "*Cogito, ergo sum*—I think; therefore, I am." Descartes' dictum confirmed the reality of my existence. I not only thought, but I felt, strove, and searched. I was an educated person—*gebildet*, as they say in German. On my own and with my teachers and friends, I had read and discussed important parts of German and world literature. We had explored many themes of philosophy from Heraclitus and Plato to Nietzsche and Kierkegaard and had re-invented great thoughts.

Our debates and discussions had ranged from the sublime and abstract to the practicalities of our lives and our particular plight as persecuted Jews. Our minds had wrestled with the here and now, with infinity and eternity, with being, existence, reality, truth, and beauty. We had tried to bridge the cosmic dichotomies: reason and emotion, form and substance, friendship and love, life and art, duty and freedom, individual and community, language and thought, God and the world, revelation and discovery. Our minds had soared, expanding into many directions at once. And then, suddenly, the storm and thrust seemed to subside, and I was frightened by the sudden stillness and calm inside. I wrote a little poem to reassure myself: the stormy process of fermentation through which I had lived must ultimately produce an excellent wine.

Which books and authors had most affected my outlook and philosophy of life? There were many. Goethe's *Faust*, of course, had made a lasting impact on my thinking. I was enthralled by Heinrich Heine, the conflicted Jew, and saw life through the eyes of Dostoevski. I read Stefan Zweig and Thomas Mann and many others of the moderns; *Peer Gynt* by Ibsen had a powerful effect on my own search for the Self and it made me think about the clash of self-realization and commitments to others, the conflict of self-love and altruistic love. I was deeply affected by Hugo von Hoffmansthal's rhymed play, *Death and the Fool*, about the man who only realizes at the moment of death he has not lived, and by the author's enigmatic postscript about the glory of Man: that he can read what was not even written, find meaning in what is meaningless, and find a way in eternal darkness. I felt in accord with the contemporary Jewish poets who, in the raging sea of hatred, found a shelter island of solace in the collective soul of the Jewish people and its heroic history. And then there were the mystics, like Angelus Silesius, Meister Eckhardt...

My subsequent spiritual development estranged me from many of these influences. I consciously tried to discard everything German. I raged against my tormentors, who had broken up my world and were murdering my people. The effect of my reaction was a partial amnesia that erased a great deal from my memory. It eroded my love of German and my proficiency in the language. I learned Yiddish and ultimately substituted English as the language in which I could best express myself. I am convinced that the decay of the German compartment in my mind was not merely due to disuse, but to my conscious revolt against its power over me. Only much later in my life was I able to build a new bridge to my youth in Germany and reconcile the two parts of my life.

No matter. In the spring of 1938, that was not the problem. I had done well. I was mature. I had the *Abitur*. But what good would it do for me? The outlook was grim; there seemed to be no future. My success in finishing high school was an atypical accident against the general background of Jewish despair. Nazi Germany was triumphant, glorying in its new-found economic strength and military power. It was a strong nation, solidly behind the Führer, united, proud, and prosperous. "Today, Germany is ours," sang the marching columns of uniformed Nazi youth, "and tomorrow the whole world."

For Jews, the future looked bleak. For my parents, the worries of a declining business mingled with nagging despair of the future. What was going to become of us?

Part THREE

Transition

Chapter *ONE*

Würzburg

In Denison Square, once upon a time a fleck of green in the heart of Toronto's old Jewish district, there remains a small synagogue, popularly known as the Kiever Shule, that is now protected as a historical monument and is maintained by the community as a museum. It was still an active place of worship when Laura Saxe and I were married there on the last day of 1944. The wedding party included two people whose participation symbolized the decisive impact on my life of an eight-month period in 1938. One had come from Ottawa, where he was a cantor, to sing the wedding service. The other was my best man. The years from 1938 to 1944 had been tumultuous. They seemed like an eternity when I lived through them. Yet they did not dim the lustre of those eight months in Würzburg.

❖

ONTHS BEFORE MY GRADUATION from high school, my parents and I agonized over a difficult decision that we had to make. What was I going to do next? The outlook was grim. My parents were struggling hard to wrest a living from our shoe stores, at a time when it was treasonous for the majority of the public to buy anything from a Jew.

What kind of a future should I prepare for? And how could I do it? My wish was to continue my studies at an institute of higher learning—but where? Jews were barred from German universities. My efforts to be admitted to a school outside of Germany had been fruitless, so far. I had no chance to leave Germany for the time being. And what should I study? My studies at the Jawneh and my extra-curricular activities had stimulated my interest in Jewish learning.

Two institutions of higher Jewish learning were still functioning in Germany: the Rabbinical Seminary in Berlin and the Jewish Teachers' Seminary in Würzburg. Why we opted for the latter is not clear to me now. Quite possibly my parents' shrinking financial resources played a role, or, perhaps, the teaching profession seemed more practical for me. At any rate, the Israelitische Lehrerbildungs-anstalt in Würzburg, about 350 kilometres south of Cologne, accepted me as a student for the academic year starting in March 1938.

For the first time, I would leave the shelter of my parents' home to live on my own in a distant city. I had to take leave of my friends and my childhood chums in Mülheim. In the interval between my *Abitur* exams and the start of the new year at the Teachers' Seminary, I had become friends with Edith Speier-Holstein, Ruth's younger sister. She was part of our youth group, we went on group excursions together, and, since she was one of my sister's girl friends, I often saw her in our home. Ever since she was about fourteen years old, she had had a crush on me, but she was too young for me to take her seriously. I used to tease her when she would prattle to her friends about her romantic fantasies and she would chide me for hurting her by my indifference. At sixteen, however, she was no longer a child, but a very beautiful young woman. I was smitten.

A deep melancholy had descended on Edith. Life seemed hope-less and pointless to her. She saw no purpose in further schooling and had decided to enroll in a Jewish Institute for Household Science in Frankfurt—really a training program for domestics. Humiliating and demeaning as it might be for well-educated Jewish girls, a position as a domestic servant in England or Belgium, if one could only find one, was one of the few remaining means of obtain-ing at least a temporary entrance visa.

Edith's household science course started about the same time as my semester in Würzburg. Her parents were glad that we would take the same train to Frankfurt, where I would change trains. It was an unforgettable journey. Instead of sitting in a compartment with other people, Edith and I stood face to face by a window in the cor-ridor of the railway coach for most of the five-hour ride. We spoke to each other out of the depth of our young souls. At last we had met each other, but it was not a happy ending. It was the end of what had not been and the beginning of what would not be. We opened our hearts. We talked about our fears, the hopelessness of our condi-tion. We confided to each other the darkness of our spirits. We stood on the edge of nothingness together. We knew, and we said, that there would be no tomorrow for us, only regrets for finding each other too late. And yet at the edge of nothingness, the world dissolving before our eyes, before we said goodbye to one another, we celebrated in that train a sacred moment of recognition and mystery. I am sure the thought never occurred to us; the word was never mentioned, but looking back at that moment from this distance, the phrase suicide pact comes to my mind. Did we really celebrate death on the train? Before we die, let us drink together from the cup of cosmic sadness...

I do not remember whether I saw Edith again after we said good-bye in Frankfurt. The memory of this journey remained with me. If it was a death pact, I did not keep my part of the bargain, although I came close before the year was over. Edith did. I have heard that two or three years later, she died, together with her father, under the wheels of an SS officer's command car while they were being transported to an extermination camp. It was, supposedly, a suicide to escape a fate worse than death. Was our train ride to Frankfurt in her last thoughts? Poor Edith. What an end for her father, the healer, the humanist, the pious, learned Jew.

I stopped in Frankfurt long enough to visit an older friend, Abraham Nelken. He had lived in Cologne for some time to attend the Teachers' Seminary associated with the Jawneh and I had studied privately with him. He invited me to his home in Frankfurt to introduce me to a young man, living in the same apartment house as he, who would be a fellow student at the Würzburg Seminary. This young man had attended the seminary for several years already and could help me get adjusted. His name was Albert Pappenheim. Little did we imagine at that brief meeting that our future lives were going to be closely intertwined; that we were destined to be close comrades, friends and colleagues for a lifetime and that it would ultimately be my lot, obedient to his dying wish, to offer the eulogy at his funeral in January 1984.[1]

I did not find it easy to adjust to my new life in Würzburg. The seminary was not geared to students like me, who had completed their high school education elsewhere and had come for a post-secondary program. To all intents and purposes, the Teachers' Seminary was a Jewish high school, combining a secular and Jewish study program, augmented by the addition of courses in pedagogic

[1]See Erwin Schild, *World through My Window*, p.64 ff.

and educational psychology. Most of the students had started at the high school entrance level, as Albert Pappenheim had. At my age, I was a newly arrived outsider among a group that had grown together over several years.

At first, I found the atmosphere that pervaded secular learning very provincial and pedestrian, quite unexciting. Of course, I was biased and conceited. Many of the students came from small towns and villages in the area around Würzburg and from other regions in southern Germany, and it was their style and mannerisms that alienated me in the beginning. The director of the school, Jakob Stoll, struck me as a typical village school master. He may have been that, but he also was a heroic personality of great loyalty and depth, far beyond my perceptions at the time. Although the seminary had been founded many decades earlier, he was the one who managed to preserve it under the most difficult circumstances one can imagine. Many years later, after the defeat of Nazi Germany, the city of Würzburg recognized his greatness and paid him posthumous tribute.

My adjustment difficulties were aggravated by the rampant anti-Semitism of the population in Würzburg, which was much more overt and violent than had been the case in Cologne. Seminary students had to be cautious and as invisible as possible. When I arrived, students were talking in hushed tones about the terrible beating that the custodian of the seminary had suffered at the hands of the Nazis as retribution for the offensive fact that he, an Aryan, served a Jewish institution.

Nor was it easy for me, having left my parents' home for the first time, to adjust to living in a dormitory. It meant doing without some of the comforts of home. While the female students roomed in private homes, the men were quartered in an ancient building on the Bibrastrasse, in the old part of the city. It had originally been the academic building of the seminary and had been converted to a dormitory when classes were moved to a new modern structure in a new part of the town. Like many other students, I commuted by bicycle, a means of transportation that also allowed us relative freedom of movement for social and recreational purposes. The scenery both in the city of Würzburg and in the surrounding countryside is very beautiful.

There was only one other student, a fine young lady from Hamburg, who, like myself, had entered the seminary after the

Abitur. The two of us were put in our own *Übergangskurs*—transition course—or *Ü-Kurs*, for short. Unlike our peers who had to divide their time between Jewish subjects and the completion of their secular high school curriculum, we were to concentrate primarily on Jewish subjects so that we could catch up to our more advanced colleagues. I enjoyed that very much. It was exactly what I wanted. However, we also had to take a course or two in education, to prepare us to be future teachers. I loathed that part.

My adjustment troubles, while vivid in my memory, must have been of short duration. My stay in Würzburg, interrupted by vacations, only lasted from April to November of 1938, yet it had a decisive impact on my life, on my views of Judaism, and on my spiritual orientation. It forged friendships that lasted a lifetime and is the place of some of the most wonderful memories of my youth. Actually, if I may play my own analyst, my early reactions in Würzburg typified my attitude to every decisive change in my environment. First come the reservations, criticisms, disparagement, and withdrawal, followed by enthusiastic acceptance, integration, and such fervent adoption of the new orientation that I become its staunch champion after the next change in venue. At the Jawneh, I hankered, even if briefly, for the *Gymnasium* in Mülheim; in Würzburg, I was at first unhappy because I missed Cologne; at the yeshiva in London, I started out as the champion of the Würzburg style and approach to study and observance; at the yeshiva in Toronto, I first disparaged the Polish style of Talmud study—inferior, I thought, to the Lithuanian style of London; later on, under the influence of Rabbi Price, I became critical of the Lithuanian approach.

In Würzburg, I soon was part of a wonderful circle of young intelligent Jewish students, enthusiastic, considerate, compassionate, kind, warm, cooperative, and true to the finest values. It was an exceptional community, full of role models to emulate or, at least, to admire. The seminary was an Orthodox institution; Jewish rules and ethics were generally observed, but without coercion. Many, but not nearly all, of the students came from observant backgrounds. Jewish observance had to be respected, yet it was a liberal kind of Orthodoxy. Boys and girls mingled freely and developed friendships and romantic attachments, although I cannot remember any instances of sexual improprieties. Perhaps I was too naïve to notice, but I was not aware of any students rumoured to have sexual relations, nor did I hear any improprieties being discussed. Couples paired off to study together, to go for a walk or a bicycle ride, or simply to spend time together to enjoy conversation, music, literature, and so forth. Informal Torah study circles formed around students who were able to share their advanced knowledge.

Würzburg is a great city for music, famous for its Mozart festivals that are held outdoors in the grounds of the ducal chateau. Of course, Jews were not admitted, but anyone walking on the high ground surrounding the chateau could listen to the music, as some students occasionally dared to do. The conditions of the time were not conducive to frivolity. Students were serious about their work, their growth, and their interpersonal relations.

The dominant personality at the seminary, whose influence pervaded the intellectual and spiritual atmosphere of the school, was its rabbi and spiritual leader, Rabbi Samson Raphael Weiss. It had been a stroke of brilliance on the part of the director, Jakob Stoll, to engage this charismatic and forceful scholar, despite his relative youth. During the selection process, a few years before, Rabbi Weiss' youth had been raised as an argument against his appointment. Wisely, Dr. Stoll argued that if youth was a detriment or shortcoming, it would diminish with every day.

Rabbi Weiss was the very opposite of Director Stoll, who was staid, conventional, and somewhat pedantic. The rabbi was a man of brilliant ideas, masterfully eloquent, dynamic and energetic, powerful, demanding, critical, and capable of biting satire, with a tremendous ability to articulate the flight of his thoughts. He had received his rabbinical training at the world-renowned Mirer yeshiva in Lithuania, where he absorbed not only a tremendous amount of Torah, but also of the Musar philosophy that distinguished several Lithuanian yeshivot. Musar interpreted Torah as a philosophy of life, a self-sufficient system of thought and spiritual life, a *Weltanschauung*, as the Germans call it, a comprehensive view of life and the world. Thus perceived, Torah mandates personal and social ethics and demands an unending quest for self-perfection; it means striving for a knowledge of, and union with, God through intelligent, rational study; it enjoins prayer as an emotional linkage to the Divine, and facilitates a life with God through the observance of the mitzvot. Torah, the world, the people, Israel, and humanity are linked through the mysteries of creation, revelation, and redemption.

My thinking was most strongly affected by the spiritual cosmology associated with the Musar theology of Rabbi Weiss and his disciples. It attempted to solve the difficult problem of a material world—our cosmos—created by a Deity that is entirely spiritual, having no physical substance, out of Nothing. How did matter proceed from God? How could a world take shape and exist if there was no substance; if there was only God ? The theory that became the basis of my world view was the semi-mystical concept of the "Chain of Becoming." In four definable phases the real, material world in which we live emanates from the Infinite: *Atzilut*—(the primeval) Separation (from the infinite spirit); *Bri'a*—Creation (of substance); *Yetzira*—the Forming; *Assiya*—the Making (of finite things and beings). In each successive stage, existence becomes more separate from and independent of its spiritual source, until it finally assumes the physical shape of the material world. The human being has the same antecedent, bearing within himself an ascending channel of spiritually through which his reality flows from its divine source. Rising through this spiritual lineage, Man through the instrumentality of Torah and of the commandments, may take control of the channels of emanation which flow into this world to recreate and maintain it at every moment.

On my first visit back to Cologne, during a vacation from the seminary, I eagerly tried to explain the Chain of Becoming to Ruth Levi, my sketching partner from my time at the Jawneh, while we were on a bike excursion in the countryside. Ruth was a member of Habonim, the socialist branch of Zionism with a materialistic philosophy. I was astounded that the revelation of my new philosophy, which I found so exciting, left Ruth rather cold. I believe my passionate spirituality threw a damper on our relationship.

The radical Judaism of Rabbi Weiss, his discourses, and the discussions led by some of his closest disciples, such as Shammai Zahn, had a deep impact on me. This Judaism was different from the attempts at a symbiosis of Torah and general culture and thought, expounded by the great nineteenth-century rabbi Samson Raphael Hirsch of Frankfurt—after whom Rabbi Weiss was named. This combination of Torah and secular philosophy, particularly of the Germanic idealistic variety, now appeared to have been a lame compromise, refuted and demolished by our experiences under the Nazis. The true Judaism needed nothing outside of itself. Jewish philosophers and theologians throughout all the ages, whose works I now studied for the first time, had made Judaism self-sufficient.

Above all, Rabbi Weiss, who was no stranger to European philosophy and literature, had the gift of being able to expound the Jewish sources to the most sophisticated young Jews like myself who had grown up in the intellectual tradition of Europe. What a revelation for me and for others! I worked hard to improve my Hebrew skills so that I could study the texts that Rabbi Weiss suggested and familiarize myself with the new concepts of Judaism that would enable me to begin the exhilarating exploration of a newly discovered universe. I am using this term quite deliberately: knowledge of Torah and the practice of mitzvot facilitate access to a unified spiritual and physical world and make it possible for us to live in it as Jews and as human beings.

I was turned on, as we would say today. I wanted to study as much Torah as possible and make its pursuit my life work. And yet, my new orientation did not preclude the enjoyment of secular culture. There was room for the enjoyment of good secular literature and for the study of thought systems other than our own. Art and music could still enrich our lives and stretch the firmament above us.

My friends and I had much to discuss. Despite the preponderance of Rabbi Weiss's influence, there was no lack of controversy. Not all the students were as impressed and influenced by him as I was. Looking back now, it seems to me that I belonged to a coterie of the rabbi's followers who tried to absorb as much as possible of his teaching. I certainly did. Others, among them my friend Albert Pappenheim, were a little more critical of his thought, his exuberance, and his relentless poking fun at the conventional German-Jewish Orthodoxy and its philistine, unimaginative followers.

Rabbi Weiss's father was the cantor at my wedding. Until he emigrated from Germany, he had been the senior cantor of Breslau and, eventually, he became a cantor in Ottawa. A fine Torah scholar himself, he used to say that it had been his hope that his sons would follow his footsteps and become cantors as well, thus enjoying—as he did—the leisure time for studying Torah. To his regret, the Creator did not grant them the gift of good voices. So they had to settle for the second best chance to study Torah: the rabbinate!

The faculty of the seminary included several other outstanding personalities. One that I remember most clearly was a highly gifted mathematics teacher who was also a Judaica scholar and taught some Jewish subjects in addition to his official specialty. Our art teacher was a very unusual character, a member of the German aristocracy—Baron Ernst von Manstein. He was a convert to Judaism, a deeply religious person who had married a lady quite a few years older than he because she had also converted to Judaism. Since he was technically an Aryan, he could have escaped persecution, but he chose to share the fate of his co-religionists.

Another remarkable personality on the faculty was the cantor of the Würzburg community, Reuben Eschwege, who was our instructor in the cantorial art. Since teachers in many smaller Jewish communities of Germany had to function as cantors, *Hazanut*—the cantorial skill and repertoire—was an obligatory subject for all male students.

I have a secret way to hold my kipa on my head—a little sewn-on hook that catches in my hair. I learned that secret in Würzburg, from Sybil Berg, a lovely young lady, who crocheted kipas for most of the boys. Sybil, who was called "Silly"—which has none of its English connotation in German—was the good angel of the entire student body, everyone's surrogate mother. I had never met such a person of such unalloyed goodness, angelic, gentle, and unselfish. Her unselfishness was extreme to the point of self-denial, yet she was always happy, beaming, and...nobody's girlfriend. We all loved her. No wonder, before she married and settled in Israel, where she became the mother of a very large Orthodox family, she was a devoted nurse in an English wartime hospital.

The most outstanding disciple of Rabbi Weiss was Shammai Zahn, a person of rare intelligence and sensitivity. Learning from Shammai and studying with him after we met again in London, I absorbed many of the Musar lessons and insights that he had heard from the rabbi. Shammai became later the head of a yeshiva in Sunderland, near Gateshead.

Albert Schild—no relation to me—was the most respected and popular leader among the students, solid, dependable, a sound student and a wonderful person. He was the "postmaster," whose task it was to distribute the students' mail when it arrived at the seminary. I did not take to Albert at first—possibly because of jealousy on my part—but we eventually shared experiences that drew us together and made us the best of friends.

Albert was the best man at my wedding.

Two of Rabbi Weiss's sisters were also students at the seminary and I was very friendly with both of them. The younger was a very sharp intellectual, much like her brother. I corresponded with her for some time after fate separated us. The older one, about my age, was less intellectual, but more impulsive and feminine. We enjoyed a light-hearted friendship that was not without an erotic element, and we remained in touch with one another for many years.

Since only a few relationships among students were "exclusive"—what we call in this country "going steady"—it was quite normal to cultivate friendships with several members of the opposite gender at the same time, even though, perhaps, one relationship might be more special than the others. I acquired a girlfriend pretty quickly. Perhaps it was not an act of choice or selection on my part. It seems to me that I was claimed by one of the young ladies as a newly arrived student who needed help in finding his way in the new environment. She was a vivacious girl, quite outgoing, not to say aggressive, who took possession of me. I enjoyed her attention and her company. I was deeply hurt when after some time—weeks? months?—she ditched me in favour of a bragging show-off, an older student from Leipzig who also came to the seminary after he had completed high school. However, I got over my disappointment and humiliation, surely one of the worst experiences a sensitive young man can suffer.

Generally, I got along well and was friendly with my fellow students, both male and female. Among my closest female friends was Toni Pachtman, still a friend and correspondent today. She was a close friend of another exceptionally fine student, Ze'ev Aron, whom she married in Australia a few years later. My friend Mali Haberman was a very intense person, of strong emotions and a fierce, yet also poetic, mind. We saw each other again in London, but our relationship was gradually eroded by circumstances. She lives in Israel, married to a rabbi. We met once in Jerusalem.

The friends I made in Würzburg eclipsed my childhood friends. My Würzburg friends were now my peers: the young men and women who spoke my language and shared my universe. Summer holidays were probably brief that year and I have only fleeting memories of them. I exchanged letters and post cards with my Würzburg friends. Classes in Würzburg resumed in August so that we could prepare for the High Holidays; the male students at the seminary were a resource for many communities that required cantors.

Singing has never been one of my strong points. I knew some music, because it had been part of the school curriculum. My parents—in the hope that I might emulate Kurt—had made me take piano lessons for about two years, starting when I was about eleven. The seminary curriculum included cantorial singing and familiarized the students with the traditional German-Jewish synagogue modes and melodies. Since this was my first year in such an endeavour, and very likely because of my vocal limitations, I was assigned to a tiny village congregation in Obertulba. It took two short, but slow, train rides and one bus to get there. There was barely a *minyan* for the services. In fact, when one participant had to leave temporarily to attend his calving cow, we had to wait for his return since we had fallen below the requisite number of ten adult males. Nevertheless, my services were gratefully received and correspondingly rewarded. There must have been another week or so of vacation after the High Holidays. A few years ago my Würzburg friend Toni Pachtman-Aaron in Australia sent me a photocopy of a letter that I had written to her after I returned home from my cantorial adventure. I had composed a long ballad in hexameter verse for her, relating in a humorous fashion my experiences as cantor in the little community. I wish a poet could translate it into English.

I returned to Würzburg after the holidays. Little did I know that it was to witness the destruction of the seminary and to become one of the victims in the fiery finish of German Jewry and its institutions.

The Nazis called it *Kristallnacht*.

For me, it was the crushing of a whole world.

Chapter *TWO*

November Pogrom

IN 1938, ADOLF HITLER annexed Austria, thus uniting his jubilant native country with the Third Reich. Triumphant success whetted his appetite for further acquisitions. His next objective was the Sudentenland, a region of Czechoslovakia that had a large German ethnic component and had once been a part of the German Empire. Britain and France had pledged to defend the integrity of Czechoslovakia. War seemed inevitable.

We were certain that war would seal our doom. The Nazis always blamed international Jewry for the hostility of foreign powers to Nazi Germany. An outbreak of armed conflict would unleash new fury against the remaining Jews. War would mean the end of any plan or hope to emigrate.

The academic building of the seminary was close to a main railway line and day by day, we watched trains loaded with tanks, guns, and other war materials roll toward the Czechoslovakian border. The High Holidays were approaching. Rabbi Weiss addressed a final student assembly before they would return home or, as I would, travel to the communities where they would serve on the High Holidays. Rabbi Weiss was at his best; his words were unforgettable. He convinced us that Rosh Hashanah and Yom Kippur were our opportunity to determine our future. The divine judgment on these days of Awe would hinge on our own decisions, on our Teshuvah, the turning and returning to God. He pointed to the window in the direction of the railway line. "Don't think that our fate and the fate of Europe depends on the war machines moving on those tracks. Our fate and the fate of the world is in our hands in this crucial period. Our spirits can rise to the heights where the Almighty judges and determines the destiny of the world. One mitzvah—one act of submission to God's will—can change the course of history." His passionate words cast a spell over his audience. I left convinced that our religious conduct could tip the scales.

And then came the Munich agreement. Neville Chamberlain, the British prime minister, flew to Germany for last-minute negotiations with Hitler and came away waving a signed agreement that, he assured the British, the French, and the rest of the democratic world, would guarantee "Peace in our time." Naïve and misguided as his confidence turned out to be, the Munich deal not only betrayed Czechoslovakia, but encouraged Hitler to believe that the door to world conquest stood open. However, it did postpone the outbreak of war for a year. As it turned out, that delay saved my life and the lives of many others.

It was but a brief respite before disaster.

Before the rise of Nazism, Germany had been the land of promise for the downtrodden Jews of eastern Europe. Many had escaped from the penury and pogroms that threatened their lives in Poland by migrating to Germany. German Jews looked down on the *Ostjuden*, whose Yiddish-accented German and lack of refinements and modern sophistication seemed to compromise the legal and social equality that German Jews had attained. At least, that was what many German Jews thought. Polish Jews, therefore, tended to form their own social and religious circles, distinct from the main stream of the community. Their children, however, who were born or educated in Germany and whose academic aptitude, in typical immigrant fashion, was often superior, found their way into the Jewish and general society. Their presence often added spice to the bland German-Jewish bourgeoisie, and, in many cases, formed a link to a more authentic, less diluted Jewishness.

It was extremely difficult for immigrants to obtain German citizenship. As a result, many immigrants from Poland held onto their Polish citizenship. The Polish authorities had no love for their Jewish expatriates in Germany and made it difficult for them to retain their status as Polish citizens. As a result, the majority of Polish Jews in Germany became stateless, people without citizenship rights in any country.

Germany, meanwhile, began its propaganda war against Poland. Nazi propagandists and historians popularized the notion of the *Drang nach Osten*, the Germans' historic, expansionist thrust to the east. The new Germany required *Lebensraum*, living space, to be found in the fertile regions of the east where the centuries-old presence of German settlers was used to establish German claims. Diplomatic pressure increased and did not bode well for Chamberlain's "peace in our time."

On October 28, a terrible calamity befell the seminary. Without warning, the police rounded up all students of Polish extraction. There were many, including some of the best and brightest students of the seminary—Shammai Zahn and Toni Pachtman were among them. The action was part of a country-wide round-up of Polish and stateless Jews. They were put on trains, taken to the Polish border, and chased across into Poland. The few who had Polish passports were allowed in by the Polish border police. The majority were chased back to the German side of the border, where they were refused re-entry by the German border guards. A stalemate ensued, with thousands of Jews stranded on the narrow strip of no-man's land between the frontiers.

Meanwhile, the atmosphere at the seminary had turned to gloom, despair, and grief at the disappearance of our fellow-students. We did not know what was happening to them and to their families. Of course, nothing was reported in the media. We heard only rumours.

I did not learn the full story of this episode until years later. At the time, all we knew after several days of uncertainty was that our colleagues were coming back. The Poles had been adamant in not allowing Jews without Polish passports into the country and the German authorities had eventually given in and allowed the deportees to return home. Much later I read that the Poles, exasperated by the stalemate at the border, had threatened to expel thousands of ethnic Germans who lived in Poland unless the Germans took the Jews back. And so, much to our relief, most of the students who had gone through this ordeal returned. Perhaps they had jumped from the frying pan into the fire. The end of the seminary—the end of life as we had known it—was rapidly approaching.

Ironically, the expulsion of the Polish Jews had a connection to the last chapter of the seminary. A young German Jewish refugee, Herschel Grynszpan, who had fled to Paris, triggered the final catastrophe. His parents had been among the Polish deportees and, upon learning of his parents' fate, he resolved on a bloody revenge. He went to the German Embassy and shot Ernst von Rath, the third secretary, who remained in critical condition in hospital, hovering between life and death. The German news media reacted with predictable fury to what they called an attack by international Jewry on the German people. It was a crime that called for merciless retribution. We were frightened by the overt incitement to violence. We prayed that von Rath would survive, so that, perhaps, the worst might be averted. But our prayers were not answered. Ernst von Rath died.

We could not study. In hushed tones, we talked about our fears and tried to guess what would happen next. We listened to the radio, scared to death by the Nazi propaganda machine that prodded the populace to vent their outrage at the Jewish criminals. Meanwhile, unknown to us, the Nazi party headquarters, obeying instructions from the chain of command that went right up to Hitler himself, was orchestrating what was later called a justified spontaneous outburst of popular indignation at the dastardly murder of a German diplomat by the Jews. The date was November 9, 1938.

Night fell. With a sense of foreboding and helplessness, we retired to the dormitory building. Why we did not scatter, try to run away or to catch a train home I cannot now understand. Perhaps it seemed too dangerous or futile. Wouldn't anything have been better than waiting passively for the axe to fall? But we had been brought up to believe that our best chance lay in obedience and passivity. The massive wooden gate that protected the entrance to the building and the inner court was closed and barred with extra care.

Around midnight we were alarmed by voices outside. Soon they merged into the clamour of a mob gathering in the narrow street below. The shouts grew louder and more menacing. "Open up, open up!" they shouted. We were trapped. Our bedroom was a ward-like area with about six beds, shelves, and wash basins. Paralyzed with fear, we stayed in our beds. The banging of fists against the door gave way to the thuds of a battering ram. The doors withstood the onslaught for a minute, and then, to the jubilant roar of the mob, the gate broke down. Bedlam ensued. The crash of breaking glass and window panes in the hall ways. The heavy steps of the invaders on the stairs and in the hall. Then the door to our room burst open and a phalanx of shouting devils rushed into the room. "Everybody up! Stand still beside your beds!" The men were carrying axes, hatchets, clubs, shovels, and hammers. I clearly remember my thoughts. Not seeing any guns, I tried to estimate my chances of surviving an attack by the less lethal weapons they carried. Not very good, I thought. My life was over. Suddenly sadness displaced fright. What a pity! I thought. My parents passed fleetingly through my mind; my friends...But only for a moment, for the action began instantly. Hammers, axes, hatchets smashed our furniture to bits, including the wash basins on the wall. I have a vivid recollection of a man smashing a light bulb hanging from the ceiling with a swing of his shovel. Beds were overturned; suitcases opened and their contents scattered. A typewriter was heaved through a closed window landing heavily among the clatter of glass in the courtyard below. Windows and mirrors were reduced to shards. But to our growing astonishment and relief, the orgy of destruction passed without the invaders turning on us. The triumphant mob left the scene.

We spent the rest of the night—this simile always comes to my mind—like the ancient Jews on the ruins of Jerusalem. We did not know what to do. Where could we go in the middle of the night? We were in shock. It did not occur to us to wonder whether this raid might have been a local occurrence. Only much later did we find out that all over Germany and Austria, Jewish dwellings and businesses had been similarly ransacked and that hundreds of synagogues, practically all Jewish institutional buildings, had been destroyed by fire or demolished by other means. However, the orders from higher up had been to confine the destruction to property, although almost a hundred Jews were killed just the same. We did not know it then, but we had lived through *Kristallnacht*, the night of crystal, so named sarcastically by the Nazi perpetrators. We had experienced the fiery portent of the coming annihilation of European Judaism.

We did not venture out into the streets. Finally, the morning dawned. I left the dormitory and made my stealthy way to the seminary building. Perhaps the director and the staff had not yet heard what had happened! Unaware that other Jewish institutional buildings and businesses, as well as many private homes, had been vandalized or destroyed during the night, I was hoping that a semblance of order might be restored again by the seminary teachers. Perhaps the regular morning prayer service might proceed as usual...

My illusions went up literally in flames. Approaching the seminary, I saw a huge bonfire burning in front of the building. From the upper floor windows, uniformed storm troopers were flinging books to the ground: the seminary's library was being burned. As I came closer, I saw that the Torah scrolls from the seminary synagogue were also being consumed on the pyre, a sight that I can never forget.

While the Nazi rampage was going on, I was bold or foolish or desperate enough to enter the building through a side door. I quickly made my way to the prayer room, hoping to find my tallit and tefillin. The room had been ransacked. Prayer books and other articles that had not been consigned to the flames lay scattered about. I was able to retrieve a tallit and a set of tefillin. Then I returned to the dormitory to tell my colleagues what I had seen.

Our helpless predicament—what should we do? where could we go?—did not last very long. A group of uniformed men arrived, lined us up, and marched us out into the street. Between rows of jeering men and women, we were escorted to our destination: the jail.

The details of the next few days are jumbled in my memory, chaotic, dark. Here and there, a flash of recollection illuminates and freezes a scene. Dozens of other local Jews were also being arrested and were arriving at the jail. We managed to glean a few bits of information from them.

For the moment, we were behind bars, safe from the mob. A number of students shared one cell. We talked, prayed, recited psalms. Without prayer books, we had to rely on our memory or those of us who knew psalms by heart. One scene is etched clearly in my memory: reciting Psalm 20 aloud, and the rest of us repeating it verse by verse. *"May the Lord answer you in the day of distress...Some set their trust in chariots, and others in horses, but we rely on the name of the Lord, our God..."*

Of course, we heard no news from the outside. I did not know what had happened to my family or to anyone else. I cannot remember whether we received clothes or other necessities from the outside. We were given food and avoided non-kosher items. During the hardships and horrors of the weeks to come I looked back on the city prison as an oasis of quiet and relative comfort. This interlude ended after a few days. We were taken to a large hall or corridor where a number of Gestapo officers in SS uniforms had set up desks to interview the prisoners. Some of the students were luckier than others. Those who were age sixteen or younger were sent home, released. Albert Pappenheim was among them.

My interview, like that of my fellows, was very brief. After names, home addresses, and similar particulars were taken down, we were asked the key question: Is there any reason why you should not be taken into "protective custody" in a concentration camp? A vise of fear clamped around my stomach. Concentration camp! Protective custody! These were the dreaded tools of state terror. I tried to protest. I had done nothing wrong! I was a harmless student. I would go back home to Cologne since the seminary was closed down...

The face in the black uniform did not even look up from the paper work. With studied, disdainful indifference, he went on. "You have no objection then. Sign here." It was all orderly and legal. I had no choice.

Outside the buses were waiting. Destination: Dachau.

Chapter *THREE*

Dachau

TRAUMA OFTEN BLOTS OUT unbearable memories. My recollections of Dachau are sketchy, with many blanks. Yet certain feelings and scenes have remained in my consciousness and emerge—often unbidden. The black fear, the physical pain, the constant hunger, the exhaustion, the mental torment, the dark despair, the grinding humiliation, the loss of every shred of human dignity.

The ride from Würzburg to Dachau took many hours. Several buses travelled in convoy with armed guards on each one. Escape was impossible. I kept hoping for a road accident. If the bus crashed, there might be a chance to flee. But, of course, nothing happened. Daylight had faded as the buses rolled through the gates of the infamous Dachau camp site. Its very name, spoken only in whispers, was synonymous with terror. It was the place where the Nazis took care of their enemies—the destination of the doomed.

I remember that we stood lined up in a column for hours. Huge, dark shapes of buildings loomed in the blackness of the night, menacing, mysterious. I had a desperate need to urinate.

We were eventually processed. It seemed like a fever dream. Under the supervision of prowling SS men, the so-called camp elders—mostly long-term political prisoners—did the required work. All our belongings were taken away, but in a typically German orderly fashion. Our heads were shaved. The seminarians looked in disbelief as handsome friends suddenly turned into inmates of a penal colony. We went through cold showers, being hosed down at the end by the inmate orderlies. Our own clothes were confiscated. I put on the rough, striped, prison camp uniform that was too thin to ward off the cold November wind coming down from the Bavarian mountains. Somehow I managed to hold on to a sleeveless sweater that my mother had crocheted for me. I wore it on my skin under my threadbare shirt.

When they had finished processing us, we were marched off in a platoon to the barracks, or block, to which our group had been assigned and where new horrors awaited us. In the middle of the barracks, there were trough-like sinks with water faucets and some latrines. I expected to find a kind of bunk to sleep on. Nothing of the sort. Prisoners slept on wooden platforms covered with a thin layer of straw.

Some of my friends and I climbed up to a narrow platform high in a corner of the barracks, where there was room for about three people. Instead, six or seven of us had to squeeze into the impossibly narrow space. Next to me was Albert Schild. We tried to encourage each other amid that scene of horror. We slept in our clothes, folding our thin jackets to serve as pillows. On a ledge along the wall there was a tiny space to store our tin bowl and spoon, and to keep the little piece of bread we received in the morning—if we wanted to save it for later in the day.

Thousands of prisoners were being processed from many different parts of Germany and Austria. The operation lasted into the next day, I seem to recall. The newcomers were under the immediate charge of a group elder, a veteran prisoner whose red triangle on the front of his camp uniform marked him as a political prisoner. We wore the yellow Star of David that was the symbol of the Jewish inmates. The group elders reported to the block elder. Many of these men showed the degrading effects of survival in Dachau: they were abusive and brutal, emulating the model of the SS officers to whom they answered. Others still retained their humanity and even showed sympathy for their Jewish charges. I remember a young man, one of the group elders, who had been imprisoned as a Communist youth leader. He was only twenty-three years old, and had already been an inmate for five years.

During the reception process—it must have been on the day after our arrival—one of the older men in our group, a resident of Würzburg, could not control his anger at the abusive conduct of one of the SS officers who was supervising the proceedings. The man, white-haired and dignified, had been a decorated veteran of the German army in World War I. Emboldened by this background, he protested to the officer, saying, "I risked my life fighting for this country while you were still peeing in your pants!" The SS officer raised his gloved fist and flattened the gentleman with one punch. One of the camp elders remarked a little later that the SS officer must have been in a good mood that morning; otherwise he would have shot the man on the spot! I think it was the same gentleman—or perhaps it was another fellow prisoner—who told me that one day in Dachau was worse than four years in the trenches of the Great War.

Other scenes come to my mind. We were lined up outside of our block when an SS officer strode by with a pair of tefillin that a prisoner had tried to smuggle into camp. The officer had opened the capsule and was looking at one of the little parchment scrolls that he had taken out. "Is there a rabbi here?" he asked gruffly. Somebody raised his arm. It was a Rabbi Bamberger, if my memory serves me right. "Come here! Read this!" The rabbi, in a steady, sonorous voice began to read in Hebrew: "*Shma Yisrael...*" "No," yelled the Nazi. "In German!" The rabbi continued with dignified calm. "You must love the Lord your God with all your heart, with your entire life and with all your strength..." "Stop!" shouted the Nazi, "you are lying!" But he did not touch the rabbi.

The daily routine in the camp was pure and deliberate torture. We were roused from fitful sleep very early in the morning for roll call outside the barracks, standing in the freezing air. Then the bread ration was handed out and a dark liquid reminiscent of coffee. Should I eat the entire piece of bread or save some for later? Will it be stolen? We were never given enough food to still our hunger. The main meal, again handed out in the open, was a piece of *Blutwurst*, the most inferior kind of sausage, and potatoes, which were dumped in a heap on the ground. After the distribution of the food, we scrounged on the earth for left-over potato peels. In the evening, there might be some kind of watery soup to eat with a piece of bread—if you had saved any.

At first, the seminary students and other observant Jews were reluctant to eat the sausage. A rabbi in our block—he was also from the Würzburg area—insisted that we do. "Do everything necessary to survive," he counselled us. We knew, of course, that he was right and so, we ate. I must admit shamefully that I could not help but savour that horrible pork product containing mainly blood and other waste products. Incidentally, the rabbi did not follow his own instructions; he did not eat. He could only be certain that his dispensation was objective if he did not profit from it himself—he had to be sure that his advice to us was not driven by his own hunger. How, and whether, he survived, I do not know.

The most dreaded part of the day was the general roll call. Early every morning, we would march to the *Appellplatz*, the large, square parade ground where the entire camp, drawn up in groups and blocks, waited to be counted. The administration building and the barracks housing the SS troops adjoined the square. We had to stand at attention for hours under the watchful inspection of the guards who made their way through the ranks eager to mete out physical punishment for the slightest infraction. Or an officer might torture us by making us perform agonizingly slow knee bends and other physically painful exercises, mercilessly putting his riding boots to any man who could not do what was commanded, regardless of age or physical condition. Roll call could take hours. Each group was counted again and again, it seems, until all were accounted for. We had to stand motionlessly at attention. Often the cold was bitter. To speak was strictly forbidden and cruelly punished. If anyone fainted, no one was allowed to try to help. The poor victim would lie there until he rallied on his own or until roll call was over. We had no gloves; I soon had frostbite on my fingers.

Except for a short break around noon and, possibly, an hour or so before lights out, we spent the rest of the day marching in columns through the streets of the camp under the watchful eyes of the elders, up and down, around the block, or along the perimeter. There we could see the fence beyond a grassy border area, a very elaborate barbed-wire barricade, and, on the inside, the fearsome electric fence. A number of watchtowers were placed along the perimeter, the machine guns clearly visible. The grass area was off limits; if anyone set foot on it, the machine guns started. Some desperate people committed suicide by running for the fence. Most were cut down by bullets before they could reach the high voltage fence.

A transport of Jews from Vienna arrived and were added to our group. Some of them were in terrible physical condition, having suffered savage beatings and horrible tortures at the hand of their captors. Many did not survive the sadistic atrocities inflicted on them after their arrest. I remember a man whose bruises and broken bones made it nearly impossible for him to walk. A few of the younger prisoners tried to cover up for him. Once I carried him to the roll call on my back.

One evening, as I was standing in front of our barracks during the time allowed for our personal chores, a man called out to me through the window of the next barracks. "Erwin, Erwin Schild!" I was startled. It was "Uncle" Juppeman, the elder Joseph Mohl from Mülheim. He was the first person from my hometown that I had seen. Like me, he had been arrested during *Kristallnacht*. Unfortunately, the news from home was devastating. My father had also been arrested and was here in Dachau. I was shattered. Naturally, through contact with prisoners from other parts of the country, we had heard that the events in Würzburg had been parallelled in communities all over Germany. Somehow, I had hoped that my father had been spared. Mr. Mohl was able to give me the number of the barracks to which he had been assigned.

There was no opportunity to try to visit him that evening. We could only walk about on our own at certain times. The next day, I waited with desperate impatience for a chance to make the visit without endangering myself or my father or incurring the displeasure of the group elders. Finally, I was able to look for him. I saw my dad before he saw me. His group elder was just giving him a rough push. He looked pitiful in his miserable uniform. I tried to hide the sinking feeling in the pit of my stomach, my fury, my despair, my mental anguish. And my poor dad—the look on his face when he saw me! Of course, he had not known what had happened to me, but neither of us were prepared for a reunion—and a very fleeting one at that—in Dachau. It was very hard. My father broke down and cried.

I was unable to visit my dad again, nor could he visit me. Our meeting had taken place quite some time after our arrival in Dachau. A few days later, to my wholehearted relief, I was informed by a neighbour that he had been released.

I only found out much later what had happened. One of the decrees passed by the government to avenge the assassination of the German ambassadorial secretary had called for the immediate transfer of all remaining Jewish firms to Aryans. My mother had to liquidate our shoe stores and "sell" the business to a buyer designated by the authorities. Although my mother was a businesswoman, she insisted that she was unable to look after the transaction and the legal requirements without my father. The Gestapo agreed and issued the order for his release and return to Cologne. He was saved—for the moment—by the German passion for order and legal correctness.

For me, the drudgery, the pain, the despair, the exhaustion, the hunger, the freezing cold went on. Days seemed like years, weeks like centuries. It was December. Winter was rapidly approaching. The cold wind from the Alps grew colder. The grey of the camp, the monotony of the camp routine, the aches in our bodies and minds, grew more threatening. I feared for my health, for my life. The thought recurred: if I ever get out of here, I will never again complain about any hardship. Whatever the future, if there will be one, it can never again be as bad.

There was also a glimmer of hope for me. My father had not, of course, been the only person released. Every morning now, as we assembled in front of our barrack, the elder read out a short list of names. Some lucky people were about to be set free. We did not know why, just as we did not know why we were in Dachau, except for the fact that we were simply among the thousands of Jewish men whose imprisonment was an act of revenge against the Jewish people. Would all of us be eventually released? Before we died? There were no answers.

One night I had a strange dream. I was swimming in a wide river ahead of a huge ocean liner. I knew it was the mouth of the Hudson River and the ship was entering New York harbour. When I woke up, I had a terribly painful sore throat, a throbbing headache, and, I was sure, a high fever. Could I make it to the roll call? To report sick and to be taken to the infirmary was like a death sentence. No one had ever come back from there. I stumbled out of the door for the morning line-up. The group elder read the few names on the list. My comrades rushed me, congratulated me. My name had been read out. I had hardly heard it.

But it was true. New energy streamed into my body. Quick, quick; the lucky few were about to be marched off to the administration building. Quick. Let me take off my shirt—I still had my mother's sweater; let me give it to one of my friends...

The events that followed are hazy. I was worried about being inspected by the medical officer. Sick people, or people showing physical traces of maltreatment, were not allowed back into the world. The officer can't see my burning throat, I said to myself. Please, don't let him find out that I have a fever. And I must hide the fingers with the open frost bites. Panic. What if he sees them and sends me back? No use despairing. Pull yourself together. Look good. I did! I passed! A Nazi officer informed me I was being released on condition that I leave Germany as soon as possible. He did not set a time limit, but he warned me that I would be back in Dachau for ever if I did not leave Germany soon enough. Next I got back my own clothes and whatever I had with me when I arrived in the camp. What a relief to wear normal clothes!

I don't remember much else. I was sent back to Würzburg. Did I travel by bus? By train? How long had I been away? Five weeks? Five centuries? I dimly remember getting to the house of one of my women friends from the seminary, who lived in Würzburg and stayed after the seminary had closed down. Was it Mali Habermann? I only remember vaguely. I must have called my parents from there, picked up what personal belongings had survived the destruction of the seminary, and then I must have taken the train to Cologne. But I have no memory of it. Nothing. I must have been in a fever or a trauma-induced trance. I have a fragmentary memory of coming home, of being embraced, physically and emotionally. Kurt and Margot were there.

Kurt had been fortunate, and very brave. He did not look Jewish, but was blond, handsome, and socially adept. Before *Kristallnacht*, he had been working in a retail store in Giessen, a city in central Germany. He had evaded arrest, mingled in the crowds, and called home. He was told of father's arrest and that my mother had been unable to contact me in Würzburg. Kurt decided to see for himself whether he could find me and bring me home. Daringly, he took the train, mingled with Nazi officers in the railway car without arousing any suspicion. In Würzburg, he found out what had happened to me and that his mission was impossible. He took the train home to Cologne to be with our mother in her terrible desperate anxiety.

Now I found out why I had been released from custody. In Cologne, the consul for the Dominican Republic either had compassion for the Jews or saw an opportunity to gain financially from their plight. Possibly, it was a combination of the two. The Dominican Republic had been one of the few countries all along that was willing to take some male German Jewish refugees. At any rate, for a payment of three or five marks, the consulate would issue an affidavit to the effect that, upon attendance at the consular office, the person named in the document was eligible for an immigration visa to the Dominican Republic. A number of Jews arrested in Cologne after *Kristallnacht* were released on the strength of this affidavit—until the Gestapo realized that the document had no official validity. My mother had obtained an affidavit in my name and sent it to the Gestapo in Würzburg, who, miraculously, accepted it at face value and authorized my release.

For a moment, I did not worry about the future. My hair had begun to grow since the last shave; I was wearing regular clothes! Ah! the pleasure of sleeping in a real bed, of eating a meal at a table from plates with fork and knife!

Tomorrow, I thought, I'll start worrying again.

Chapter *FOUR*

Escape

A MONG MY MOST TREASURED MEMORABILIA is a picture postcard
that my cousin Joe Schild gave me a few years ago. The picture
is a view of the approach to the Rhine bridge at Mülheim, a location
not far from my parent's house. But the picture is quite unimportant;
the significance of the card lies in the fact that every member of my
family—my father, my mother, my brother, my sister and I—wrote
a few words on the card and sent it to my cousin in New York. The
words are innocuous; Margot and I merely wrote regards and signed
our first names. But when my cousin received the card, in January
1939, he got the message: the few words each of us wrote meant that
we were all together at home again after the harrowing events of
Kristallnacht, and that my father and I had returned from Dachau.

It also meant that we were appealing to him to follow up as
urgently as possible the efforts he was making to facilitate my
brother's emigration to the United States. Kurt had written to him
right after *Kristallnacht* and obliquely alluded to our imprisonment.
Now Kurt wrote that he was spending the weekend at home—a hint
that his job in Giessen no longer existed—and that he was sending
regards to my cousin's relatives, the family whom Joe had asked to
provide an affidavit for my brother. My father wrote a cryptic
remark on the card: "Dear Joseph, We are always glad to hear good
news from you; Kurt has kept you informed about us."

I can remember how we sat around the table and wrote the card
while discussing our future prospects. Kurt had a fairly low registration number for the American consulate, and, if cousin Joe were
able to find an eligible sponsor for him, he might be able to emigrate to the United States in about a year. The outlook for the rest
of the family, however, was dim; none of us had any firm prospects
for emigration.

Now, the situation was desperate. *Kristallnacht* had been the
watershed: before November 9, 1938, optimists could hold on to the
delusion that it was possible, even though disagreeable and risky, to

wait in Germany until they could emigrate to a congenial country. Before the night of horror, cautious and conservative people like my parents, who were averse to risking the unknown, might still have weighed the pros and cons of potential destinations in terms of language, economic opportunities, climate, and Jewish life. They might have hesitated to pursue opportunities to emigrate to such places as, say, inner Africa or Outer Mongolia. No such hesitations existed after my incarceration, and my father's, in Dachau. Our business was gone. The Nazis had proved their capacity for unrestrained violence. In Dachau, we had had a foretaste of the future. In Dachau, we had looked into the abyss.

For my parents, business people in their early fifties, the prospects of emigration were bleak, as it was for most of the Jews remaining under the Nazi regime. All countries were increasingly unwilling to accept refugees. The situation was exacerbated by the fact that while in the first few years of the Hitler government Jews could take money and belongings with them, this was no longer allowed; new refugees would inevitably be dependent on the charitable organizations or on the rare benevolence of foreign governments.

In 1938, a conference on the problem of Jewish refugees was convened. From July 6 to 15, 1938, delegates came from thirty-two countries—including the United States, Canada, Britain, France, Holland, Belgium, Australia, New Zealand—and met in Evian, France, on the shores of Lake Geneva. An American news correspondent accurately reflected the tenor of the conference: "Myron C. Taylor...opened proceedings: 'The time has come when governments must act and act promptly.' Most governments represented acted promptly by slamming their doors against Jewish refugees."[1] The world had no room for the several hundred thousand Jews remaining in Germany and Austria who wanted to leave and whom the Nazis were still willing to let go. The United States would not budge from its annual immigration quota for Germany and Austria: 27,370 persons per year. Only the tiny Dominican Republic, whose consul in Cologne had saved me from Dachau, offered to contribute an unspecified area for agricultural settlement. As for the rest of the

[1]See Israel Gutman, ed., *Encyclopedia of the Holocaust*, Vol. 2 (New York: Macmillan Publishing Company; London: Collier Macmillan Publishers, 1995), 455.

world, the Evian Conference conveyed one clear message to the Jews: Sorry, but the lifeboat is full!

My parents had pinned their only hope for getting out of Germany on America, but they were doomed by the quota. Their registration number with the American consulate in Stuttgart was so high that, even if they had found a sponsor, they would not have been eligible for entry until 1942. Even the Dominican Republic only admitted a small number of unmarried men. In the days immediately following the November pogrom, neighbouring countries allowed any fugitives who made it to the border to cross, but then the doors were banged shut once again.

A frightening deadline—literally—hung over me. My release from the concentration camp had been conditional on my emigration. Fear, abject fear, possessed me. I felt like an animal trying to escape from the hunters who were closing in. I was willing to go anywhere to get out of Germany. But where? Students were sometimes exempted from immigration restrictions. With increasing desperation, I wrote letters, sent telegrams, applied to rescue agencies abroad, enlisted in emigration schemes, with no success. The yeshiva in Baltimore agreed to accept me and to apply for a student visa on my behalf, but the process moved at a snail's pace, and how could I wait? A student rescue project organized in Britain under the auspices of the Chief Rabbi looked more promising. Immigration to Britain had been cut off long ago, but there was still a chance for students. Be patient! Wait! Maybe next month. But I can't wait a month! Maybe next week. Patience! Hope!

The Agudah operated a *hachsharah* in Enschede, Holland, just a few kilometres from the Dutch-German border. I had been a leader in the Agudat Israel Youth Movement. I thought I had a chance to be accepted there. They knew my plight, yet there were so many desperate applicants who had to be out of Germany very soon—or else!

More waiting. More letters, glitches, problems, obstacles. Hurry, please, hurry! Here comes the mailman, for whom we wait every day as Israel waits for the coming of the *Mashiach*.[2] Perhaps today he will bring news of salvation. Again, disappointment, frustration! Send another document, complete one more questionnaire. "We are waiting for the authorities to approve. Hopefully soon."

[2]Hebrew for Messiah

The days go by; the panic in the pit of my stomach grows like a cancer. Get my suitcase ready, just in case! I know I am allowed one suitcase and ten marks. And my bicycle. Who cares? Let me go with the clothes on my back! Just let me in somewhere! My photo album...might as well take it. My own drawings—I am so attached to them. Lots of time to pack; there is nowhere to go yet.

In the midst of all the tension, we reach for some degree of normalcy; we try to do what families do before they break up. We have a photographer take the last family pictures. They remain among my most precious possessions. Here we are, Father, Mother, Kurt, Erwin, and Margot. We are still together, like a happy family. A typical German middle-class family. We are well dressed; Father holds a cigar, Mother smiles in contented contemplation of her dear ones, Kurt looks debonair, Margot is beautiful, and I—the only one of the group still living—am looking at a book or a picture. The photographer did not capture—nor was he expected to—our feeling of sitting on a volcano or on the deck of the Titanic. The floor under our feet looks solid, stable, neither burning nor sinking...

I write letters to my friends. In hopeful anticipation, I take "last" walks or bike rides, taking leave of the Rhine and of the hills, the valleys, the meadows, and heaths of the countryside. I feel a strange ambivalence. I am desperate to get out, yet feel a melancholy pain for what I must leave behind. Secret fears rise up. Will I be whole after I am gone? Will I still be I, if I am divorced from the past, the people, the language, the sky, and the earth?

Stop dreaming! Pull yourself together.

Some hopeful news. The student visa for England will be issued soon—just when, we don't know yet. From Holland, I receive assurances. A special permit is on the way in a matter of days. I find it hard to wait. I can't even care how my parents feel about my leaving. What will happen to them? And to my sister and brother? They have had no luck in their efforts to find a refuge abroad, but they were not in Dachau and are not on probation like me.

Here is the mailman. I can hardly believe it, but here in my trembling hand is the document, the special permit from Holland. I am cleared to cross the border into Holland at Enschede.

Shouldn't I wait for the British visa?

No—no more waiting for me. Holland's permit came first—I'm going!

We buy the railway ticket. I write one last postcard to say good-bye to our former nanny, Anna, that she kept until her death.

Early on January 26, 1939, we are at the station—my parents, my sister, my brother, and a few friends. Everyone is nervous. Into the train. Goodbye, goodbye. Tears choke off words. Farewell. *Auf Wiedersehen*. Soon. Maybe, God willing. The train leaves; I lean out the window, waving back as they wave the last goodbye from the platform. The rails curve. They are gone.

I am impatient for the train to reach the border. We pass through the last German checkpoint. The border police check my documents, my belongings. The photos attract attention and give grounds for some cruel teasing. "Who is this? Your Aryan girl-friend? You are a violator of our race?" They finish with a deadly threat: "Don't you dare ever to come back or you'll be dead!"

Finally, the train moves across the Dutch border. I am safe!

Then the Dutch border guards scrutinize my documents. Sorry, they're not in order. This is a special emergency entrance permit, valid only at a specific border crossing, the other Enschede border crossing a few kilometres away. There are two trains from Cologne to Enschede. You took the wrong one. No problem—we'll just put you on the train back to Germany; and you can transfer to the other train that crosses the border at the right point. I'm terrified. I panic. I can't go back. They'll arrest me; send me back to a concentration camp! I argue, I plead. Look at my papers! I am accepted by the training school in Enschede. Just let me go there!

Consultations. The guards call an inspector. More discussions in Dutch that I cannot understand. A phone call is made to Enschede. I wait, under guard. Finally two gentlemen show up, respected Jewish citizens from Enschede, supporters of the *hachsharah*. A con-versation in Dutch between these two angels and the border police. My documents are endorsed and stamped. My two angels escort me from the border station to their car. I am no longer a persecuted Jew in Germany. I am a refugee. I have been reborn. At last, I am free!

My recollections from Enschede are sparse. The change was overpowering. I needed time to adjust and Enschede was not the right place. It was still winter and there was not much to do at the very rudimentary agricultural training school. Its main purpose, I suspect, was to save young Jews from Germany under the pretext of training them for settlement in Palestine, so the Dutch government would have the assurance that these young refugees would not stay in Holland and become a burden on the country.

I was looking forward to seeing my friend Martha Simons again in Enschede. It had been almost a year since we had enjoyed each other's company in Cologne; it seemed a lot longer. Contrary to my expectations, however, I saw little of Martha there. In fact, when she came to Toronto from San Francisco in 1994 to celebrate our fiftieth wedding anniversary with Laura and me, and we reminisced about the old times, she could not even remember that we had met in Enschede. I do.

My stay at the *hachsharah* turned out to be very short. My clearest recollection is how cold it was in the boys' dormitory. Jewish observance, strictly adhered to in Enschede, requires washing one's hands immediately upon getting up in the morning. It is recommended, therefore, to keep a bowl of water by the bed. I remember that in the morning the water was sometimes frozen.

Altogether I remained in Holland for only about five weeks. I spent part of this time in Amsterdam visiting my Uncle Willi, my mother's brother, my Aunt Else, and their young son, Hank. Their daughter, Hannerl, was already married, I believe. My uncle and aunt were happy that I had escaped from Germany and could visit them in their comfortable home. They had a strong sense of family and took pleasure in showing me their hospitality. In the few short years since they had emigrated to Holland, their business had grown substantially. I was impressed when visiting their large ladies' wear factory. My uncle and aunt were obviously quite well off and thoroughly enjoyed their new-found prosperity. Knowing that I could only have brought ten marks with me from Germany and that I had no source of income, they supplied me with pocket money as long as they could, until the German occupation of the Netherlands separated us.

I enjoyed the sights of Amsterdam and was impressed by the affluent and relaxed Dutch lifestyle, especially by the food. Chocolate flakes on buttered bread was a delicious luxury after almost starving in Dachau two months ago! How could it only have been two months?

Meanwhile, Britain had granted me a student visa, the Jewish Refugee Board having found a place for me in a yeshiva. The documentation followed me to Holland. I did not hesitate—Enschede was much too close to Germany for my comfort. Besides, I really wanted to study in a yeshiva and fulfill the official purpose of the arrangement that the British Chief Rabbi had made with the British authorities. In the light of subsequent events, the decision I made probably saved my life. I had never thought of Holland as more than a way station, grateful as I was for the temporary asylum. I did not know any Dutch and saw no opportunity for continuing my studies.

I took the train and then the channel ferry to England, making the crossing in cool, damp weather. I had finally reached the country where I really wanted to live and whose language and culture I had studied quite intensively. My spirits rose. It seemed as if I was emerging from a fog that had enshrouded me since Dachau. Paradoxically, it was in foggy London that my mind cleared and my memories become sharp and coherent.

Chapter *FIVE*

London

My HEART BEAT A RHYTHM of joyous expectation as the train rolled closer to London. I had arrived! I had come to the end of my journey, to my chosen destination. I had not had much choice in selecting my place of refuge, but Britain, particularly London, would have been my choice if I had had one. Now, to my everlastingly good fortune, I was here. The horror of Dachau, the waiting in Cologne, and the transience of Holland were all behind me. I had reached the country of my preference, the new home that I was only too ready to adopt. I had learned the language. I had studied the literature. I had read Shakespeare, Kipling, Dickens, Shaw, and Wilde. It was the land of fair play, of democracy and aristocracy, of individualism and eccentricity; the land of Parliament and the Magna Carta. I knew about British institutions, its universities—Oxford and Cambridge. Although I had never been there, I felt as if I knew London and its landmarks: Westminster, the Strand, London Bridge, St. Paul's Cathedral, Trafalgar Square, Buckingham Palace, and Hyde Park with its Speakers' Corner. I had read the Chief Rabbi's *Book of Jewish Thoughts*. I had heard of Whitechapel.

And London was the seat of the mightiest world power, the heart of a huge empire. It was the capital of a nation that ruled the oceans of the world, of a realm that included India, vast portions of Africa, and spheres of interests and international mandates in the Middle East and in the farthest Asia. Its language girdled the globe, linking it to my second-choice country, the United States, to far-flung Australia, and to strings of islands in distant seas. Canada? They speak mainly French there, don't they?

My excitement mounted as the train slowed and entered the terminal. And then, I got a little scared. What a relief it was to see a familiar face in the crowds at Victoria Station when I arrived in London! My cousin Arthur Kracko was waiting for me at the gateway to my new country. I had not seen Arthur since he had left Cologne several years before. It was exciting to meet him again in the capital of the British Empire.

As I mentioned earlier, Arthur had been fortunate. He had worked for many years as a diesel engineer at the Deutz Motorenfabrik, a major engine manufacturer in Cologne-Deutz and he had become a specialist in the installation of marine engines. He had married Hanna Schubach, a Mülheim girl. They had a little daughter, Ruth, their only child. Arthur's bosses liked and appreciated his work and kept him on for as long as a prominent industrial firm under the Nazi regime could employ a Jew. When that was no longer possible, the company sent him to England to supervise the installation of the marine engines that they exported to British shipbuilders. When I arrived in London, Arthur had already founded his own marine engine business and had acquired the agency for the German engines. Eventually, when the war broke out, he served in the British armed forces, again utilizing his engineering expertise. After the war, his marine engine company prospered and Arthur reaped the fruit of his diligent work.

All this, however, was still in the future. When Arthur met me at the railway station in the spring of 1939, he was still a struggling immigrant, hard-working, feisty, and energetic. We took the London subway, the Underground—or the tube, as it was more commonly called—to his home. I remember how impressed I was by the nonchalant way in which Arthur handled the huge British coins required for the subway fare. In Germany, coins were carefully guarded in a change purse. Arthur had his coins jangling in his pocket and this is the way I carry change to this day!

Hanna, Arthur's wife, was a fine and gentle lady. Her sister was one of my brother's best friends. Now, for the first time, I met their little daughter, Ruth, who took a great liking to me. Arthur and Hanna assured me that I would always be welcome in their home and offered me whatever help they could give me.

I was anxious to start my new life. My first agenda item was to register at Bloomsbury House, the headquarters of the rescue and refugee organizations—an important place for the many thousands of refugees. Upon presenting myself, I found to my surprise that I had choices other than to resume my studies, notwithstanding the fact that I had been admitted to Britain as a student. But I did not really want to live in a youth hostel while waiting to receive a work permit, as the lady who interviewed me suggested; I genuinely wanted to study, and, specifically, I wanted to study at a yeshiva.

And so it was arranged that I would report the next day to the Yeshiva Torath Emeth, better known as Rabbi Schneider's yeshiva, on Upper Clapton Road in North London. Unfortunately, it was quite far from my cousins' home in the south of London. I would soon find out exactly how far it was, because I covered the distance on my bicycle many times in the ensuing year.

My first discovery was that the yeshiva was not the Würzburg Teachers Seminary! For a *yekke*, a German Jew raised in the distinctive style of German Jewry, the transition to the yeshiva was a real culture shock. Even though Rabbi Schneider's yeshiva had flourished for many years in Frankfurt-am-Main, the unofficial capital of German Jewry, I was suddenly plunged into what was definitely an eastern European environment. Rabbi Moshe Schneider, the *rosh yeshiva*, or head of the yeshiva, was an eastern-European-style rabbi and educator, from his long, unkempt black beard to his manners; from the lack of elegance of his clothing to his simple, elemental piety that informed his passionate and scrupulous observance of the mitzvot. He bore no trace of the cultural refinement and worldly sophistication that characterized the German *rabbiner*. He was blunt, impetuous, loud and impervious to the outside world, not at all interested in, nor familiar with, secular culture. His language was Lithuanian Yiddish, but having lived and taught in Germany, he understood German well, and was quite aware, although critical, of the cultural conditioning of German-Jewish students and of their ingrained proclivities. Yet he was a great, forceful, learned, devout, honest and compassionate person.

Rabbi Schneider came from Memel, where he had been a disciple of Chofetz Chaim, a giant of Jewish scholarship and ethics who was renowned for his lifelong campaign against the prevalent misuse of speech for slander, tale-bearing, idle talk, and similar abuses. Rabbi Schneider, although not an eminent Talmudist, was a committed educator. His first commitment was to Torah—Jewish learning—which he loved with every fibre of his being; his second was to his students. He seemed to devote all his energy to the mission of raising them as scholars and pious Jews. A product of the Musar movement, he held that refinement of character, spiritual nobility, moral purity, self-restraint, and self-control were inseparable from scholarship and piety. He was convinced that, while good character is the result of sincere Torah study, it is, at the same time, the prerequisite for attaining the true understanding of Torah. In Frankfurt, home to many outstanding institutions of Jewish learning, his yeshiva had primarily attracted young men from eastern European Jewish backgrounds. When the decline of those Jewish communities eroded the base of the yeshiva, he had transferred his institution to London, where the community of his original students was augmented by newcomers like myself. With perhaps one or two exceptions, all the students were refugees.

The language of the yeshiva was, of course, Yiddish. At first, I could not understand it, let alone speak it. Fortunately, I have an aptitude for languages and, after about two weeks, I understood most of what I heard. I soon began to speak Yiddish and became quite good at it. The students who had come from Germany still mostly spoke German among themselves, though most of them knew at least some English. The rabbi, on the other hand, did not know a word of English. One of the apocryphal stories circulating among the students turned on the two slips of paper given to the rabbi every Friday before his visit to the public bath house, one with instructions to the bus driver to let him out at the Stoke Newington stop, the other, for the bath attendant, with the words "a little more hot water, please." The rabbi allegedly gave the latter note to the bus driver by mistake.

The yeshiva occupied a large house on Upper Clapton Road, where Rabbi Moshe Schneider lived with his family, his wife, and his three daughters. His son, already a scholar, was studying elsewhere. The rebbetzin and her daughters were kind and understanding. Of course, they had to keep house for the students, so the rebbetzin cooked and baked and kept the building clean with the help of her daughters. For the family and the students, the house provided sleeping quarters, a dining room, and living space. After the influx of new students, Rabbi Schneider was able to rent additional rooms in a largely empty house on near-by Cazenove Road, owned by a Hasidic rabbi who lived there. The older students roomed there, including me.

Rabbi Schneider also obtained the use of a large *bet hamidrash*, or study hall, a block and a half away on Knightsbridge Road. It was a small, local synagogue that saw only limited use and whose owners or officers were happy to support the yeshiva by putting the building at Rabbi Schneider's disposal. The *rebbe*, as we respectfully called him, also had solicited the financial support of a few well-to-do benefactors to supplement the small subsidy that he received from the refugee organization that had placed some of its wards in the yeshiva. Still, although the rabbi tried his best to raise money for the yeshiva in any way he could, there was never enough. Sometimes the shortage of money was so severe that the rabbi had no choice but to send a pair of students into the neighbourhood to canvass from door to door. Since the rabbi considered any distraction from study a sinful waste of time, this was a great and painful sacrifice. Because I knew English, it was my job several times to go collecting. I hated it. One day, when I was sent to collect donations with my friend Shammai Zahn from Würzburg, we just sat in the park with a volume of Talmud and studied; afterwards, we were forced to lie, telling Rabbi Schneider that we had been totally unsuccessful in soliciting any money.

It was a most frugal existence, but the rabbi and his family shared the poverty and our torn or worn-out clothing was mended by the rebbetzin or her daughters. Bread was supplied free by a local Jewish baker, Grodzinsky. At the end of the business day, the yeshiva was allowed to pick up the shop's unsold products and one or two of the students were detailed to carry the large bags. Whenever the bakery did not have any bread left over, there was a shortage at the yeshiva the next morning. And without bread, the rebbetzin could not bake the meat loaf for dinner! When there was enough money, students received sixpence or so for their weekly allowance. If not, there was just enough for the weekly trip to the public bathhouse on Friday afternoon.

However, the frugal way of life did not affect the students too adversely. After all, the way of the Torah, as defined in *Pirqei Avot*, is to "eat bread and salt...sleep on the ground, live in poverty...and you will be happy and it shall be well with you." I remembered the vow I had made in Dachau that if I ever got out, I would never complain about living conditions again. Besides, my uncle in Amsterdam often sent me a few guilders and I even managed to earn a few pence on my own.

Rabbi Schneider liked me, but he also utilized my talents, particularly my knowledge of English. I had little opportunity to perfect my English within the yeshiva, but in rare moments of spare time I sometimes managed to sneak into the local library.

Newspaper English, especially headlines, baffled me for a while, but ordinary literary and spoken English was no problem. Whenever Rabbi Schneider needed a letter written in English, it was my special job—and a great mitzvah, he assured me, because it was for the sake of Torah and its students—to compose and type these letters. Of course, I did not expect to get paid for that, not only because there was no money, but because it would have spoiled the mitzvah. However, being part-time secretary to the Hasidic rabbi in whose house I slept was a different matter. This was the time when it was widely expected that war would break out and there was a need to prepare for the evacuation of children from London—a need that became especially urgent after the war actually started. Many Jewish children were among the evacuees, but amidst the wartime panic, little thought was given to providing a Jewish environment for these children, who were left largely without kosher food and Jewish education. Our landlord, the Hasidic rebbe, claimed to be in the process of establishing a kosher hostel for evacuated Jewish children in Bournemouth, a safe distance from urban London and safe from the expected air attacks. I was retained by the rebbe to compose and write letters to prospective donors, soliciting funds for his evacuation scheme. I doubted whether he really had any plans for his scheme, but I got a few pence for my trouble and that was enough to buy jam, chocolate, and a few other snacks to supplement the meagre yeshiva menu. And, of course, writing these letters of solicitation sharpened my English style and, perhaps, honed a specific skill that turned out to be essential in my later career!

The daily routine of the yeshiva was strict, severe, and—to use a very inappropriate but descriptive word—Spartan. We were expected to be in the *bet hamidrash* at about 5:30 am, at least an hour before the time appointed for morning prayers, so that we might recite *Tehillim* (*Psalms*) as a preparation for concentrated, devout prayer. Being a little late was not too serious, provided it was not more than a quarter of an hour or so, and did not happen too regularly. In that case, the student would be called in for a talk with Reb Moishe Schneider. But if you could honestly claim, as I often could, that you had been up late studying the night before, the reproach would be gentle; you might even be dismissed with a compliment rather than a reprimand.

Morning services took at least an hour and a half. Reb Schneider prayed with deep devotion, punctuating his prayers with loud exclamations, sighs, and shouts, raising his arms and fists in fervent appeals for heavenly mercy. He recited the prayers very slowly, just as we were expected to do, pronouncing each word carefully and correctly. For students like me, who had been brought up in the restrained and formal style of German Orthodoxy, prayer in the yeshiva was an unsettling experience at first. I must admit, however, that after a while I was caught up emotionally in the fervour of prayer. I adopted the eastern European pronunciation of Hebrew and the habit of swaying to and fro and swiveling from side to side as an aid to concentration and intensity. But that did not happen right away. Initially, I felt strange and even repelled in this atmosphere.

After the morning service, we walked back to the yeshiva house and had a sparse breakfast, mainly bread and a beverage. If there was butter on the table, it usually meant that it was Rosh Hodesh, the new moon, and the butter was a treat to mark the semi-festival. I usually ate my jam or marmalade.

After breakfast, we returned to the *bet hamidrash* to study. In the manner of the Lithuanian yeshivot, all the students studied the same tractate, but at their own level of depth and scope. Each day the *rosh yeshiva* would present a *shi'ur*, a learned discussion on a part of the text that the yeshiva was studying, using commentaries, finding new interpretations, and proposing and solving problems arising in the Talmud, the commentaries, and the codes. Most of the time, the students studied in pairs. The term for one's partner was *havrusa*, an Aramaic word meaning companionship.

My *havrusa* was my old friend and colleague from Würzburg, Albert Pappenheim, who had arrived in England about the same time as I. Since he was born and raised in Frankfurt, it was reasonable for him to continue his education at the Schneider yeshiva. While we were different in temperament and in our approach to the learning process, we studied very well together. In a yeshiva environment that seemed relatively alien to both of us, we offered each other the comfort of similar backgrounds and allowed ourselves the luxury of a critical evaluation of our surroundings, putting ourselves a little above it. Sharing our reactions, we were better equipped to cope with the intellectual limitations and the narrow academic horizons of the yeshiva world. Together we were able to smile at some of the strange goings-on. Stubbornly, we held on to our values and opinions and, in our minds, defended the territory that we had staked out in the fields of Jewish studies before coming to the yeshiva. At the same time, we took full advantage of the learning opportunities the yeshiva offered. As our proficiency in Talmud improved, we began to delve more deeply into the commentaries. Volumes piled up on our table as we debated and defended our respective positions.

The approach to Talmud in the Lithuanian yeshivot is analytical, seeking an in-depth understanding of the reasoning, definitions, and rational nuances underlying the Talmudic debates. This contrasts with the method cultivated in many Polish yeshivot, the *pilpul*—literally pepper—method, in which a far-ranging comparative and dialectical approach is preferred. *Pilpul* requires a wide erudition; it delights in sharp, ingenious, and, sometimes contrived, differentiation and encourages mental acrobatics.

The presence of senior students in the *bet hamidrash* was very helpful for our progress in Torah. Their example set a standard of commitment to learning and they freely offered us the benefit of their knowledge. They were able to help the less proficient students when we ran into problems or needed an umpire to resolve our differences. We could listen with a degree of understanding when the senior students discussed—often with the *rosh yeshiva* or other visiting scholars—the problems arising from the texts that we all had been studying. It was quite natural for yeshiva students to continue these debates as we walked between the house and the *bet hamidrash*, at meals or even in our spare time. To discuss possible solutions to a difficult decision in Maimonides' Code or to enter into a debate with the finely honed reasoning of, say, the *K'tzot Hachoshen*[1] while walking in the street was the sign of a true yeshiva student.

In addition to the main tractate, students were encouraged to study a second tractate with less emphasis on depth and analysis and more emphasis on quantity, so as to increase our knowledge of the incredibly varied Talmudic subject matter—often appropriately referred as the *yam ha-Talmud*, the Talmudic ocean—vast and inexhaustible. The study of other Torah subjects, such as Tanach—the books of the Bible, commentaries, and homiletic works, was not

[1] A sharply reasoned commentary on the civil law in the code.

encouraged except on Shabbat or at times when students were too tired to absorb Talmud.

There was one other important subject, however, that all students were required to study in the evening: the literature of the Musar movement. Musar, which translates literally as "admonition", but is closer in meaning to "ethics," was the way to character development, to dedicated Torah study, and to scrupulous piety. The emphasis on Musar was, and remains, typical of the Lithuanian yeshivot and their successor institutions in Israel and America. The objective of Musar study, as advocated by Rabbi Schneider, was not the knowledge or appreciation of this branch of literature, but the inculcation of personal virtues and of zeal and passion in the pursuit of Torah learning and the fulfillment of mitzvot. In essence, we were to study books of personal ethics and elementary theology, guides to pious conduct, and works of admonition exhorting us to pursue personal improvement through diligence in study and observance, self-discipline, altruism, and—the ultimate incentive—the fear and love of God.

Musar had influenced me earlier through the teaching of Rabbi Weiss in Würzburg, but Rabbi Schneider's approach was more simplistic, less intellectual, less philosophical, and much more pragmatic. We were free to choose the works we would study in those evening hours, and while Reb Schneider was sensitive enough to respect my choices that reflected my previous Musar education, he would, nevertheless, express mild disapproval when he looked over my shoulder and saw that I was studying theological works, such as the *Nefesh Hachayim* by Rabbi Chaim of Volozhin and the *Derech Hashem* by Luzatto. "I like plain, simple Musar," he would say. "Why do you need the philosophical Musar?"

Rabbi Schneider had a powerful personality. Piercing black eyes and a long black beard enhanced the forcefulness that derived from a personal, simplistic piety that was impervious to uncertainty or doubt. There was only one way: the way of Torah and unquestioning faith. Each Shabbat afternoon, and occasionally, if there was a special reason, on a weekday, he presented a Musar talk. He usually started with a verse from the Torah portion and a thought suggested by it, and then exhorted us to greater efforts in study and observance, greater fervour in prayer, and greater refinement in personal conduct, modesty, restraint, and civility. As far as he was concerned, nothing gross becomes a scholar of Torah. He often referred to conduct he had observed among the students, praised what was praiseworthy and disparaged objectionable deportment, unworthy of a Torah scholar. If he was aware of problems of belief, of conflicts in a modern world, he did not show it. Nothing but lack of determination, commitment, and persistence stands between us and saintliness. In concrete, graphic terms he called us to the fear of God. If we only remember who we are and what we could be, what God has done for us and what he asks us to do for him, if we only have the will to overcome the temptation of the self, or whatever obstacle the evil impulse puts into our path, we can become perfect and able to love God and serve him in the manner expected of us.

Many students of the yeshiva, mostly those who came from Hungary and Czechoslovakia, did not know any English. Once, a number of students decided to ask Rabbi Schneider to arrange for English lessons. The rabbi was aghast. He asked us to step over to the window: "Look outside!" he said. "Do you see all the people in the street? The taxi driver, the mother wheeling the pram, the garbage man heaving the bins into his truck? They all speak English. Do you think God saved you from Hitler's clutches because He needed more English speakers in London? There is no shortage of English here! There is a shortage of Torah! You are needed here for that. That is the purpose for which God saved you and brought you to this country!"

Fortunately there were several other students who shared a more enlightened view of Torah. Shammai Zahn, disciple of Rabbi Weiss in Würzburg, was a good source of support. And we also had two former students of the Mirer yeshiva. They added an important quality to the notions of piety that I absorbed. One of them, Joseph Epstein, remained one of my mentors in the next chapter of my life. He was a paragon of humility, gentleness, and self-denial. The rebbe rarely criticized Epstein, whose exemplary conduct and maturity elicited his respect and whose choice of Musar works to study—for example, his notes of talks by the Mirer *mashgiach*, the spiritual mentor of the Mir yeshiva—was, therefore, beyond reproach.

On one occasion, Albert Pappenheim and I were singled out by the rabbi in his Musar talk, not only once, but twice. In the first instance, he lavishly praised us by name; in the second, he reproached us—anonymously. It happened when Passover was approaching and the yeshiva needed wine. One of Rabbi Schneider's supporters had in his warehouse a huge flask, holding perhaps twenty gallons of wine. The glass container was protected by a metal cage. The rabbi picked Albert Pappenheim and me to travel to the warehouse in the south of London and bring back the cask, since we knew not only English but were also rumoured—correctly—to be familiar with the geography of London and its transportation system. We gladly accepted this exciting challenge. It was a legitimate excuse from study and an opportunity to spend a day in the city. I was well equipped with maps of London and its bus, Underground, and rail network.

We first stopped off to visit a friend from Würzburg, Henry Bialek, whom we had not seen in a very long time and who was a student at a college in the city. After a pleasant hour with him, we had no trouble reaching our destination. The giant flask was waiting for us. It was so heavy that we had to carry it together; it was also huge in circumference. Our plan was to take it by bus to the Underground station, and then by train to a station near the yeshiva. Alas, however, the container was much too big; the bus driver would not allow us aboard. After consulting the map once more, we carried the contraption to a tram stop, since tram cars had a wide platform at the rear to accommodate our bottle. We were successful in getting to the Underground station, but then, we could not get the monstrous bottle into the train! Our Musar training must have stood us in good stead, or else we would have cursed the thing! Only one alternative remained. Laboriously, we made our weary way to a central railway station and found a train to North London. We finished our assignment by carrying our flask a long distance from the train station to the yeshiva.

The rabbi, in his Musar talk, held us up as an example, extolled our dedication and self-sacrifice for the sake of the yeshiva students and the observance of Pesach. But then came the scolding. At some time during the week, Albert and I—being study partners—had gone to the washroom at the same time and, occupying two adjacent stalls, had talked to each other across the partition. We were not supposed to engage in conversation in a toilet. Unbeknownst to us, Rabbi Schneider had been in the washroom at the same time; we found out when he uttered a loud cough as a sign of his disapproval. Well, at least he did not mention names in this part of his talk. But he impressed on us proper bathroom etiquette, as befits a student of Torah.

The rabbi and I had a few conflicts on some other points, too. After several months, when he was satisfied that I had made good progress in Talmud and in general Halachic knowledge, that I was accustomed to the ways of the yeshiva, and that I was respected by my peers, he hoped that he could influence me to drop some of my "German" habits and adopt more of the pious practice and deportment of the extremely observant students from Hungary, Czechoslovakia, and Poland. One day he zeroed in on my hairstyle. There were quite a few students from Hasidic and similarly "pious" backgrounds among us. Many of them wore *payot*, ear locks of various lengths and styles—curled and spiralling down over the cheek, or tucked behind the ears, or hanging down straight without the curls. Being a Lithuanian, the rosh yeshiva was not too interested in payot, but he strongly advocated short, cropped hair, especially in the front of the head, so that the tefillin would sit right on the scalp, not on a carpet of hair. That, of course, was not the custom among the German students. "I know you are a German *bocher* [Yiddish for young man]; you don't believe in shaving off your hair, and maybe you are right," he suggested; "but imagine how great a *kiddush Hashem* [sanctification of God] it will be if you get your hair cropped short. All your fellow students will follow your example. It would be just magnificent!" Nevertheless, I kept my hair and did not get scalped. Perhaps I knew what my friends outside of the yeshiva would say. And I did have friends.

It was very difficult to get time off from the yeshiva, but I managed. I had relatives and friends to visit. I saw my cousins Arthur and Hanna from time to time, crossing London on my bicycle. Then there were some friends from Cologne, who lived not too far away and I could meet them occasionally on Shabbat, when the yeshiva discipline was not so stringent. And then there were some important friends, young ladies among them, from the seminary in Würzburg. I needed to discuss theological questions that had arisen in my mind as a result of the clash between the philosophies of Würzburg and the yeshiva. These two institutions represented alternative approaches to Judaism, Torah, and observance. Caught up in the fervour of the yeshiva spirit, its exclusionist intensity, and its unequivocal "no" to values outside of the "four ells of Halacha," I was able to restore a balance through my contact with Würzburg friends.

And then there was Betty Stern—my only remaining link to Mülheim, even though she had only lived there for a while. She was the cousin of the Mohl family whom I had taught English, and with whom I had developed a beautiful platonic friendship. Betty had a very hard time in London. An educated, artistically talented, and sensitive person, she had to immigrate as a domestic servant. The lady for whom she worked abused her, but the immigration rules under which Betty had been admitted to Britain reduced her status practically to that of bonded service. Changing her employment was impossible. It was just as difficult for her to get a few hours off as it was for me at the yeshiva, but once in a while, we managed. We took some wonderful walks through Hampstead Heath and other lovely parks. The nature of our relationship may have changed a little, for much later, after both Betty and I had left London, she sent me a beautiful photographic portrait of herself, printed on a large post-card; on the reverse she had written a poem for me. In this poem, Betty extolled the virtues of friendship above those of love. Love may die, she wrote, but friendship, if not spoiled by love, lasts for a lifetime. I used to meet Betty perhaps once in six weeks or so, and I often had to wait for her at our pre-arranged meeting place, because her employer would not let her go on time. Since my free time was also very limited, I could not help being annoyed. One afternoon, I had waited for Betty nearly an hour. Perhaps she had not been able to get out at all, I thought. Disappointed and angry, I had already boarded a bus when I saw Betty rush down the street, but I was too upset to get off the bus at the next stop and walk back. Little did I know that we would never see each other again.

All through this period of time, I was in touch with my parents, siblings, and friends the world over through the mail. Writing letters was an important outlet for my feelings, views, and problems. Many weighty thoughts, doubts, and fears were entrusted to the pages we wrote. I hope that I did not worry my parents by letting them know of my adjustment problems at the yeshiva. Their plight was ever more difficult.

No doubt, I was greatly enriched by the yeshiva, despite my reservations. Yeshiva life, and even the pietistic indoctrination I received, was valuable experience, of lasting benefit to me as a person and, eventually, as a rabbi. It was an experience I would not like to have missed. I also had the privilege of being exposed from time to time to such Torah giants as Rabbi Abramsky, a consummate Halachist, and Rabbi Elija Lopian, a superb exponent of the Lithuanian Musar movement. Both these outstanding personalities occasionally visited the yeshiva for guest lectures. Incidentally, one of Rabbi Lopian's sons married one of Rabbi Schneider's daughters; another daughter married the best senior student of the yeshiva. Above all, I learned a lot of Talmud and acquired a method of studying it. There were other benefits. The deeply spiritual joy of observing Shabbat and festivals, especially the Days of Awe, in the atmosphere of a community of scholars and students made a deep and lasting impression on me. I have not forgotten how we sang and danced on joyous festivals, not loud and raucous and wild, but with gentle and soft voices vibrating with spirituality and a dancing step in which we almost stood still.

I remained in the yeshiva from March 1939 until May 1940. Events over which I had no control ended my attendance there, but not my pursuit of Jewish learning. I continued my studies, more or less following the London yeshiva approach until I arrived in Toronto, where I was exposed to, and influenced by, a different method of Talmud study at the yeshiva of Rabbi Abraham A. Price.

Part FOUR

A World at War

Chapter *ONE*

Blackout

NINETEEN HUNDRED AND THIRTY-NINE—the year Europe plunged into war.

In the yeshiva, life had proceeded normally, each day very much like the one before, a sameness interrupted only by Shabbat and the festivals. Monotony? No. Letters I wrote to my friends show that I was happy to concentrate on my studies. My attitude had changed. During my first weeks at the yeshiva, I had looked for excuses to escape from the routine. No more. Every hour was precious, a unique opportunity to learn. Every day I added to my knowledge of Talmud. I came to enjoy being immersed in Torah study, an experience afforded only to the fortunate few who study at a yeshiva. I was making progress. I caught on to the essence of Talmud study; intuitively and rationally I had made the Lithuanian style of analysis, critique, and dialectic my own. All I needed was more practice, more erudition, more factual knowledge, more experience in Talmud, and then I would be able to hold my own in the creative discussions of the aspiring scholars. My letters indicate that I did not expect to remain at the yeshiva indefinitely and therefore wanted to make the most of my stay. There was talk of founding a yeshiva in Dublin, Ireland, and I was a candidate for this pioneering venture. No longer did I miss reading secular literature or going to the theatre, to museums and galleries that had so strongly attracted me when I was first liberated from the restrictions and discrimination against which I had chafed in Germany, and I was once more a free person in a land of great culture. I was under the spell of Torah study. I did not intend to give up secular learning forever, and I still visited my cousins and met with my friends occasionally, but study was my highest priority.

There was one thing I missed, though, and found it hard to do without: the country hiking excursions I had so enjoyed in Germany. I missed wandering through forests, hills, and valleys. My letters show that I was hoping to visit Scotland somehow in the coming summer, the summer of 1940, where I could stay with some friends at a religious Zionist colony and walk the countryside. I guess you could take me out of Germany, but you could not quite take Germany out of me! I never got to Scotland.

The yeshiva was an island of imperturbable calm in a world of rapidly developing events. Europe was in turmoil. Adolf Hitler, emboldened by the collapse of Anglo-French resistance to his takeover of Czechoslovakia, prepared for further conquest. Now it was Poland that Germany claimed as her undeniable *Lebensraum*. The pressure increased. Britain and France stood firm: an attack on Poland was an attack on them and would be a *casus belli*. They signed a pact of mutual assistance. The line in the sand was drawn. Germany showed no sign of backing down. War seemed inevitable.

The country prepared for war. Important instructions for black-outs were issued. London would be dark, if war came, so as not to guide the German air force to its target. Gas masks were distributed. They were to be carried at all times, if war was declared, since poison gas bombs might be dropped on the civilian population. Plans were made for the evacuation of children from London.

Now even the yeshiva could no longer isolate itself from the world any longer. We tried to carry on normally, but when students talked among themselves, the topic was rarely a problematic decision in Maimonides' Code, but whether there would be war or peace, whether France and Britain would continue to appease Hitler or had finally resolved to resist.

Would Hitler really be bold enough, or mad enough, to provoke a war that would pit the forces of Germany, rebuilt and rearmed during the last five years, against the military power of Britain and France which had defeated Germany just over twenty years before? And how could Hitler take the risk of provoking the vast Soviet Union? The Communist empire, sworn enemy of Nazism and Fascism, could not stand by if its neighbour, Poland, was invaded by Germany. Was Hitler bluffing? Or were the Western allies bluffing, talking bravely and firmly, as they had during the Czechoslovakian crisis, only to retreat ignominiously when words had to be backed up by action?

The students argued and argued. We debated and we prayed. We thought of our loved ones who had remained in Germany and whose hopes to emigrate would be dashed if war broke out. So far, we had been able to keep in touch with family and friends. War would terminate postal connections.

Deep down, I hoped for war. It was the only way to stop Germany and to topple the Hitler regime. The Germans, we knew, were solidly behind the Nazi government that had brought full employment, national pride, power, and glory to the Fatherland. Resistance was sparse; skeptics kept quiet. All Germany marched to the Nazi tune. For Jews, there was no hope or future left. The world had turned its back on the Jews. Only a victorious war waged with firm determination by the combined strength of the most powerful military powers in the world—France, Britain, and the Soviets— could rid the world of the Nazis and, in so doing, save the Jews of Europe. It did not occur to me that the British prime minister, Chamberlain, had appeased Hitler at Munich for any other reason but failure of the will, or naïve political miscalculation. I could not imagine that the motive had been his sense that the Allied military forces were not prepared. I did not dream that the West had allowed its military readiness to erode; that as far as armaments and strategic planning were concerned, Britain and France had relied on the rusty remnants from the World War I, and that their forces were no match for the ultra-modern war machine that Nazi Germany had created.

And then came the bolt of political lightning: the Molotov-Ribbentrop non-aggression pact. Communism, along with the Jews who were accused of creating it, had been Germany's great Satan, the ultimate enemy of Nazism; the Soviet Union was the arch foe, the almost mythological adversary of Germany. And suddenly Hitler and Stalin were accomplices, partners in the projected rape, capture, and division of Poland. The British public and, seemingly also its government, were shocked by this incredible surprise, by the coup the Nazis had pulled off. Nazis and Communists in cahoots! Now, an invasion of Poland would not entangle Germany in a war on two fronts. What would happen now? Would France and Britain honour their word, their commitment to Poland? Or would their will collapse? Weakness or honour; what would win out?

The answer had to come soon. There was not much studying done in the yeshiva that morning of September 1, 1939. The day before, radio and newspaper headlines had flashed the news: Germany had invaded Poland in full force, by air, land, and sea. The mobile Nazi armies, supported by deadly air power the like of which had never before been seen, swept across the borders. We stood around in groups, talking in subdued tones, waiting, waiting for the news that would affect us more deeply, perhaps, than most people in London on that day. We were waiting for the decision that would determine for a long time to come the fate of the people of Britain and, eventually, of millions upon millions of other people on the globe, but most of all, of the Jewish people.

Britain and France had issued an ultimatum to Germany. Stop and withdraw, or we are at war. Did they mean it? Would there be a last minute solution offering an escape? Time was running out.

The door to the *bet hamidrash* opened. A student came in with the news: we were at war.

As if to confirm the news with an ominous warning, the air raid sirens sounded only a few minutes later. But there was no attack. No planes appeared; no bombs were dropped. There would be some time yet to rally forces, to prepare, while Poland was being carved up, violated, destroyed, its forces pulverized, its cities annihilated, its Jews tortured and slaughtered. Only the eastern part, quickly occupied by Russian forces under the Soviet-German agreement, escaped the brutal destruction. There was nothing, it seemed, that Britain and France could do to stop the Germans. But war had been declared and the conquest of Poland would only be its very first phase. For the moment, I felt relieved. Soon the tables will be turned. Germany is no match for Britain and France combined. Of that I was sure. And the British people—I could feel it even through the walls of the yeshiva—were determined to fight to the finish.

Meanwhile we adapted to life under wartime condition. Air attacks on London were expected, especially once the Luftwaffe had finished its job in Poland. Yet there was no talk of evacuating the yeshiva from London, unlike most other schools and colleges. Rabbi Schneider did not believe in it. God—who had saved us from Hitler before—would protect us again. And, of course, we did not have the finances or the connections to relocate the yeshiva without detriment to its operation. The Jewish school children, who were hurriedly evacuated to the countryside, had neither provisions for kosher food nor for Jewish education.

I spoke to Susi Speier-Holstein when, a few weeks after she was evacuated with her school, she came back to London to visit her aunt. She was billeted with a non-Jewish family, had no choice but to eat their food, and she had no connection with anything Jewish.

She was not old enough to look after herself and she was still a ward of the child-refugee organization that had brought her to England. "Erwin, please look after Susi!" her father, Dr. Victor Speier-Holstein, had asked me when I said good-bye to him before I left Mülheim. It hurt me that I was powerless to change Susi's situation, a situation that was typical for thousands of Jewish children.

London at night was dark now. Street lights were out or, where indispensable, dimmed to a minimum. Automobile headlights were hooded so as to emit a mere slit of light, and so was my bicycle lamp. It was a scary business to pedal through London's streets after dark, especially when fog shrouded the contours of buses, cars, and pedestrians. Even walking was not safe. I remember a fellow student returning with a horrible bump on his forehead, the result of a collision with a stationary lamp-post! The windows of every building had to be covered with black drapes or other material that would block all light. Naturally, the rabbi, impatient with all the nuisances and somehow inclined to regard these precautions as irrelevant for a place of Torah, was neglectful and did not black out one of the yeshiva windows properly. But there was no escaping the heavy fine levied for this breach of the rules!

Of course, we knew, or at least hoped, that London was protected by the Royal Air Force and by batteries of anti-aircraft guns. In addition, an airborne balloon barrage formed a protective umbrella over the city: thousands of blimp-shaped balloons tethered by cables to the ground were maintained in a dense pattern all over the city. The balloons and cables were set up to prevent enemy planes from flying over London, or at least to force them to fly so high as to spoil the accuracy of their bombs. Food was rationed, but mainly those food items which the yeshiva could not afford to serve the students in any event. If I am not mistaken, I think that some of the yeshiva students' ration coupons were traded for other necessities—or perhaps for cash.

Wherever we went, we had to take our gas masks with us, ready to put them on whenever the sirens sounded a warning. That presented a problem in regard to the prohibition against carrying articles from one place to another on Shabbat. Of course, since all religious restrictions, except for the most severe—murder, idolatry, and sexual prohibitions—must be waived to save or protect life, carrying a gas mask on Shabbat ought to be permissible. However, as weeks and months passed by without any air attacks, let alone poison gas raids, many of the yeshiva students became inclined to leave their gas masks at home on Shabbat. One day, the famous Dayyan Abramsky, an outstanding authority on Jewish law whose rulings were respected by the most Orthodox circles of British Jewry, visited our yeshiva and gave a lecture. In the discussion period, one of the students put to him the question of the gas masks on Shabbat, since apparently there was no danger to life at this point. Rabbi Abramsky's eyes caught fire. He turned to the window and looked up to the sky. "Do you see the balloons?" he asked rhetorically. "Have you any idea how much money it costs the city every day to keep these balloons in place? And you dare suggest that there is no danger to life! Not only is it allowed to carry the gas masks on Shabbat, but it is obligatory!"

War with Germany meant, of course, that there was no longer any postal service between us and the enemy nation. I could no longer send mail to my parents, family, and friends, or receive mail from them. After a while, we were able to restore communications through intermediaries in neutral countries. My parents wrote to our relatives in Holland, who then relayed the letters to me. I replied by the same route. However, it was complicated and also somewhat dangerous. My correspondents had to be very circumspect in their messages, and I, in return, had to be careful not to rouse the suspicions of the German censorship or to betray the British origin of my letters. Any slip might compromise my correspondents in Germany as spies and place them in extreme jeopardy.

The news from Germany was not good, in any event. My parents had been dispossessed of their home and together with other Jews who remained in Cologne, were assigned to very confined quarters in the city, far from Mülheim and beyond the range of the important support that some non-Jewish friends and neighbours had been able to provide. Not that this support ceased completely. Käthe Roggendorf, the daughter of our former tenants and an important employee in my parents' business, continued to visit and to bring food and clothes to my parents at great risk to herself and her family.

In his carefully worded letters, Father was able to get the message across that he had to work as a labourer. Their new "home" was at 17 Maria-Hilfstrasse. The address still exists, but the building in which my parents spent their last months in Cologne, before their deportation to Riga, Latvia in December 1941 (as I was later to learn), was destroyed in an Allied air attack later in the war. My sister, Margot, lived with them and continued to work as long as she could. I also heard in a long letter from Margot that Edith Speier-Holstein had suffered a serious nervous breakdown, but was recovering. I was very much upset by the news because I felt sure that Edith's distress had to do with my absence.

The only ray of light was the news that, if all went well, Kurt would receive his visa for the United States in March or April of 1940. So far, the United States had not entered the war and emigration to neutral countries was still possible. Transport was difficult, of course, since the customary ports of embarkation for the United States from Germany were closed to international traffic. Italy, though allied with Germany as part of the fascist Axis, was still officially neutral, providing an outlet to the high seas through which a few fortunate souls were able to escape. I heard that some friends' relatives, such as Ilse Moses' mother, had been able to use this route after receiving a visa in the winter of 1939–40.

My parents, Margot, and Kurt were still able to write to our relatives in New York, and I also wrote to them. This channel of communication remained open until the United States entered the war after the attack on Pearl Harbour.

Britain's wartime conditions also affected me in another way. By conventional practice, countries at war confine enemy nationals who have remained in the country, so as to prevent sabotage or espionage. Britain was now host to many thousands of Jewish refugees whose passports were German. There were also large numbers of non-Jewish political refugees from Germany and other exiles in Britain, in addition to businessmen and travellers who, by some chance, found themselves in Britain when war broke out. It seemed foolish, of course, to suspect Jews from Germany of any sympathies with Hitler and to interfere with their freedom. Many refugees were part of the British war effort in one way or another. On the other hand, one could not be so sure of the loyalties of other, non-Jewish Germans. Many, no doubt, were also genuine refugees, yet it might be suspected that under wartime pressures, they could be coerced by undercover German agents to work for Germany. The British authorities, therefore, set up judicial tribunals, before which all

German nationals, including all the refugees, had to appear. They were interviewed by a judge, who then classified his subjects in three categories. Category A was for those who were suspected of German sympathies and therefore liable to internment. In Category C, on the other extreme, were the anti-Nazi refugees whose credentials were so impeccable that no restrictions were to be imposed on them. In between was Category B, to which the majority of refugees were consigned, depending on the judge's whim: they were bona fide refugees, but not entirely cleared of any shadow of unreliability. They were not interned, but could not travel beyond 25 miles of their residence without permission and had to observe some other minor restrictions on their freedom of movement.

When my turn came to appear before the tribunal, the judge did not call my loyalty to Britain into question, nor the gratitude I professed to the country that had offered me refuge. However, when he heard that I was a student at a rabbinical college in London, he remarked that travel restrictions would not constitute any impediment for me. I therefore received a category B grading, as did most of my colleagues at the yeshiva and many of my other friends. From then on, we were to carry with us a passport-like document, called Enemy Alien Registration, with our picture and classification as enemy nationals. At the time, the whole thing seemed quite innocuous, but as it turned out, it would determine the course of my life.

Not much was happening in the war, meanwhile. Journalists and historians would eventually call this phase of the conflict "the phony war." Poland was under the Nazi heel. On the Western front, there was a little sparring across the border and some limited air activity. Otherwise, it seemed quiet, but it was the calm before the storm.

My spirits had sunk when I realized that there was not going to be a quick victory. But life went on and hope remained and we waited anxiously. An ominous sign was the speed and ease of a sudden German attack on Norway and Denmark. German forces quickly succeeded in occupying these countries and turning them into German bases. Fear rose in my throat. There was one piece of good news, though: I heard that Kurt had received his visa for the United States and was on his way to New York on board the Italian liner *Leonardo da Vinci*, out of Genoa.

It was April 1940.

In a few weeks, the phony war would be over. A military hurricane would strike with lightning speed and cover Europe with the roar of titanic battles. It would sweep away all lingering hopes for a speedy victory. My mental picture was of a continental Europe turned into the landscape of a black planet, an earth bleak and desolate under a heaven of sulfurous darkness. Crushed were all the tentative structures that had been taking shape in my mind as I imagined the outlines of a future.

Chapter *TWO*

Behind Barbed Wire— Again

*T*HEY CALLED THE NEW FORM of warfare "blitzkrieg"—lightning war.

While the Germans had built a new war machine from scratch, using all of the latest technology, the generals and strategic planners of the Allied nations seem to have expected the war with Hitler's Germany to be a continuation of World War I. After all, only twenty-one years had passed since the signing of the Treaty of Versailles! The strategy and ordinance that had defeated imperial Germany in World War I, as the 1914 to 1918 conflict was now being called to distinguish it from the new global struggle—implying that it was just the second round of the same conflict—were counted upon to bring down Nazi Germany as well.

The Nazis, however, and the resurrected German military establishment did not play by the old rules. Gone were the fixed front lines of the past. Air power and mobility on the ground, lightning strikes by highly mobile ground forces supported by a modern air force enabled the German armies to advance with unbelievable speed and ruthless efficiency. When the offensive in western Europe began, the Germans rolled over their enemies at an incredible pace, by-passing the totally useless fortifications along the French borders and cutting off large units of Allied forces. Holland and Belgium fell in short order, but not without giving the Nazis the opportunity to demonstrate the lethal efficiency of their air power by levelling Rotterdam.

The much-vaunted British Expeditionary Force, which had been counted on to withstand and eventually defeat any German onslaught, was saved from complete destruction only by a heroic evacuation from Dunkirk. Britain saved most of her manpower, but almost all the equipment had to be left behind, leaving the country vulnerable and exposed. France surrendered after initial resistance and was rewarded by the creation of a truncated French puppet state in the south, usually referred to as Vichy France, after its capital. Northern France, including Paris, became German-occupied territory.

These were dark days in Britain, with even darker days yet to come as the Germans expanded and consolidated their hold over Europe. Only the indomitable courage of Winston Churchill, the British prime minister, was able to rally the spirit of Britain as she stood alone in refusing to surrender or make peace with the triumphant Nazis.

The invincibility of the German forces required an explanation, other than the failure of the Allied military and their strategic thinking. The so-called fifth column, probably more myth than reality, was thought to have been the key to the success of the German blitzkrieg. Clandestine German operatives and sympathizers must have been seeded in the areas to be attacked, blending in with the local population, spying on Allied military installations, guiding German forces by means of radio signals, and facilitating Nazi advances through sabotage. Lurid reports in the British media described the operations of Germany's secret helpers. In one instance, so it was reported, phony nannies in Holland jettisoned their domestic disguise and started shooting with submachine guns hidden in baby carriages. There can be no doubt, the British public reasoned, a whole network of fifth columnists must be spread throughout Britain, secretly communicating with the enemy and waiting for the expected German invasion to begin, when they would create confusion and sabotage British defences.

Members of the Jewish refugee community in Britain were in emotional turmoil. Our worst fears were materializing. Nazi Germany was carrying out its program of global conquest. Our friends and relatives who had taken refuge in Holland, Belgium and France were again in the power of the Nazis and we might be next.

I was close to despair. What was happening to my Uncle Willi and Aunt Else Neugarten in Amsterdam, to their children, my cousins, the beautiful Hannerl and little Hank? What of Uncle Salli and his family in Belgium? What will become of my friend Ruth Speier-Holstein, the Simons family and my other friends who had found refuge in the Netherlands? Hitler's boast of creating the

Thousand-Year German Reich no longer sounded hollow. The only way I could contribute to the fight against the encroaching darkness was to tend the light of Torah, which I studied with increased dedication, and through fervent prayer and loyal obedience to the mitzvot. My religious philosophy, tinged with the mystic elements of some of the theological works I studied, allowed me to see a metaphysical aspect of the struggle against the Nazis. The "other side," as the mystics called the forces of evil, was overwhelming the presence of God. I recalled Rabbi Samson Raphael Weiss's admonition to his students in Würzburg a year and a half ago: we had the capacity to add power to the forces of good. Torah and mitzvot were also part of the war effort.

Our worries over family and friends and our depression over the German victories overshadowed the rage and frustration we felt at the foolish suggestions, made in the British media, that the thousands of refugees to whom Britain had so graciously extended hospitality might be the camouflage for the dreaded secret German operatives. Panic was sweeping the British public. Who knew how many of the so-called refugees were actually German agents, ready to open the gates of Britain to an impending German invasion? The fifth column? They are all over, aren't they? They don't even bother to hide! Don't you hear them speaking German openly, acting just like the Jerries? "Don't speak German in public!" our British friends admonished us. "Be inconspicuous; keep a low profile!"

It was a potent mixture of paranoia, xenophobia, anti-Semitism, and genuine fear that swept through the media. Saner voices spoke out, as well. Was it not bizarre to suspect as potential enemy agents people who had just escaped from Hitler's clutches and would be the first victims if Germany should be victorious? But reason was not going to carry the day. There was precious little the government could do—in addition to the inspirational messages of Winston Churchill—to shore up public confidence in the small measure of security that its depleted armed forces could provide. To remove the threat posed by the existence of a large refugee population was something that could be done. A banner headline over an article in one of the London tabloids dealing with German refugees blared "COLLAR THE LOT!" and the British government decided to do just that.

The students of the yeshiva Torath Emeth were at breakfast, after morning services. The date was May 16, 1940. Kurt had just arrived in New York, one of the last few to escape from Germany via Italy after receiving his long-awaited visa to enter the United States. Just as he gained his longed-for freedom, I was about to lose mine. Two police officers called for me at the yeshiva. After scrutinizing my alien registration documents, they put me under arrest. "Just take a few things," they reassured me, "you'll be back in a couple of days."

I was driven to a large empty building in a London park that was rapidly filling up with other German and Austrian refugees, among them, one after the other, most of the students of my yeshiva. British soldiers bearing rifles with fixed bayonets and machine guns surrounded us. The next day, having slept on the bare floor, we were bussed to the Kempton Park Racetrack, outside London, that had been turned into a makeshift internment camp.

A year and a half after Dachau, I was a prisoner behind barbed wire again.

All German- or Austrian-born males who were not British citizens were being interned. I found myself in the company of such individuals as an Anglican minister whose mother had given birth to him while on a holiday in Germany and had never bothered to claim his British citizenship. His three sons were officers in the British Royal Air Force! He did not know a word of German, nor had it ever occurred to him that born abroad, he was not a British citizen. He was interned.

And so were 30,000 Jews.

The officers who arrested me, as well as the government and military spokesmen, promised the interned refugees and their puzzled and outraged families and friends, that they would be allowed to return home soon. There were also more than a few inquisitive and critical members of the British public, parliament, and press, who were upset that refugees from Nazi Germany and Austria had been unfairly and unnecessarily incarcerated. They, too, were assured by the authorities that our internment was going to be of very brief duration. In a few days, or weeks at the most, the responsible government department would sort everything out. Individuals who might be suspect of harbouring loyalty to Germany and sympathy with the Nazis would remain in custody, so that they could bring no harm to Britain, while the innocent refugees who had escaped from the Nazi persecution would be released to resume their lives and to help their host country achieve victory over the common enemy.

It sounded good, but it wasn't true.

Imagine the panic and confusion in Britain. In the aftermath of the German triumph and the Allied collapse on the continent, the imminent peril of a German invasion, and the menace of the U-boats strangling Britain's maritime supply line; it will come as little surprise that the fate of the unfairly interned Jewish refugees had a very low priority. Britain was under siege. Only what had to be done to defend the brave British Isles from the impending German invasion was urgent. Everything else would wait.

Meanwhile, conditions at our racetrack internment camp were chaotic. The War Office and the British Home Office were at loggerheads as to who was responsible for our upkeep. As a result, we got hardly any food at all during the first few days. Internees who kept kosher had almost nothing to eat. Many internees had been searched by the military and had their valuables taken away. They never saw them again, even though the abuse eventually came to official and public attention.

Physical amenities in the makeshift camp were miserable. We slept on pallets placed on the concrete floors of the racetrack stands, spending the days walking around or sitting in the spectators' seats. There were no horse races to watch, but we were fascinated by the drill exercises of the British regiment and its iron-lunged sergeant-major on the infield. I cannot say that I was scared. Less than two years before I had survived Dachau with its electric fences and watch towers with machine guns. We realized full well, that the British soldiers guarding us were also our only defence against the Germans. Even in this bizarre situation, I blessed Britain and prayed for its troops.

The yeshiva students flocked together at every opportunity for moral and spiritual support. In the Jewish calendar, the time of year was the Sefira, a seven-week period of semi-mourning. As pious yeshiva students, we did not shave during most of these weeks and I remember how itchy my stubbly beard was. In addition to the comradeship of my fellow yeshiva students, I enjoyed meeting some former colleagues from the Würzburg seminary and several other old friends. I met Albert Schild again. We had been somewhat distant as fellow students in Würzburg, but had become very close in Dachau. I had not seen him since my release. He introduced me to his cousin Heini Wolf. Heini, who later adopted Henry as the anglicized form of his name, remained a close friend for many years, until death ended his remarkably successful career as a mathematician in the prime of his life.

We endured internment at the race track for a few weeks. Then we were transferred for a short time to an army camp where conditions were a little better. At least we were housed in barracks and slept on regular bunks. In June we were shipped to the Isle of Man. Here, on the pretty island in the Irish Sea, our surroundings were pleasant and our accommodations comfortable. The army had requisitioned a number of beach front hotels that stood empty because of the war. Compared to the discomforts we had endured before, we lived in luxury, that is, except for the fact that the food was rather skimpy for Kashruth observers.

Nonetheless, I was terrified that any day the Germans might land on the island, which was almost without defences. The troops guarding us had been evacuated from Dunkirk and had lost most of their equipment. They did not even have enough rifles to go around and could not possibly have defended the island against a German sea-borne invasion. We tried to make the best of our situation and to enjoy the comforts our hotels offered, even under military guard. Security was less strict, since escape from the island was impossible. Besides, the military knew full well that the vast majority of us were harmless people, needlessly imprisoned. We were even treated to a bus tour of the island and enjoyed its pleasant scenery. I always wanted to go back some day.

Under the conditions of confusion, tension, and fear that prevailed in Britain, it did not really come as a surprise that one day in July, the commanding officer made an important announcement to the assembled camp population. In order to ease the refugee burden on Britain, and to allow us to be released from our undeserved imprisonment, unmarried internees were going to be sent overseas. He was not at liberty to disclose our destination—that was a military secret—but, he assured us, we were going to a big country where freedom and opportunity were awaiting us.

Did he really believe it? Or, afraid of a mutinous protest against our deportation, was he just trying to pacify us?

We guessed that we were going to Canada—or could it, by some miracle, be the United States, the haven many refugees dreamed of? Although, at that stage, we had little confidence left in British promises, or in their ability to keep them, I was rather happy at the prospect of putting more distance between the Germans and myself. The London blitz had not started yet, but a German invasion of Britain seemed increasingly imminent. The outlook was grim. Our chances of survival were definitely better across the Atlantic.

Chapter *THREE*

Ocean Voyage

By the end of the 1960s, our children were old enough to look after themselves during their parents' occasional absence. Not so my congregation! The membership and ongoing activities had grown so much that a lengthy absence would be a problem. It was, therefore, very difficult to find time for the winter vacations that Laura and I increasingly needed. The solution, before the congregation engaged an assistant rabbi in 1972, was an annual one-week visit to one of the Caribbean islands.

One year, while Laura and I were at our travel agent's office to make arrangements for our yearly escape from winter and the pressures of work, I looked through some brochures on a table in the room. I was stunned to see a prospectus for a cruise on a Polish ship, the S.S. Sobiesky, *showing the lay-out of its decks, cabins and amenities. What an incredible coincidence! I had been on the* Sobiesky *before, more than thirty years ago....*

OUR BRITISH INTERNMENT CAMP commander had been right, it seemed. A few days after he had announced our deportation from Britain, to be followed by release from internment, a ship appeared and ferried us across the Irish Sea to the Liverpool harbour.

Two ocean liners were berthed at the pier. We were lined up at dockside, a long column of a few hundred men, in neat rows of five or six. We were obviously waiting for the order to board one of the ships.

A British officer strode by, counting the rows of our column as he went. How strange it seems in retrospect, but this was the most decisive turning point in my life. The officer stopped just two or three rows behind me and divided our queue: those in front of the break were marched forward to board a Polish ship, the S.S. *Sobiesky*, named for one of Poland's national heroes. The rows behind boarded another ship. Chance, destiny, or providence had decreed that I was on the *Sobiesky*, which, as it turned out, was bound for Canada.

In one twist of fate, the course of my life and my personal geography had been determined for me. Canada was to become my home and the native land of my children, my grandchildren and my great-grandchildren. The other ship, with many of my fellow yeshiva students on board, sailed for Australia.

A chilling note: most of the yeshiva students sent to Australia eventually opted to return to Britain to be released. On the high seas, their boat was torpedoed by the German navy and all were drowned.

My fate had been determined by the close relationship between Britain and its Commonwealth allies, as well as by the fortunes of war. Canada and Australia had offered to ease the economic and military pressure on beleaguered Britain by assuming responsibility for German and Italian prisoners of war and civilian internees. The British military did not have a great number of military prisoners or genuine enemy aliens to send overseas, but seized this welcome opportunity to relieve themselves of the politically and morally difficult problem of thousands of interned Jewish and non-Jewish refugees. Unfortunately, nobody had bothered to inform the unsuspecting "colonies" that the shiploads of prisoners they were now receiving also included innocent refugees from Hitler's Europe. Ottawa and Canberra might balk at hosting refugees who would clamour for immigrant status. They were only expecting military prisoners of war, captured German and Italian merchant seamen, and enemy nationals who would return home after the cessation of hostilities. The inclusion of 2,290—mostly Jewish—refugees from Germany and Austria remained a dirty little secret, at least for the time being.

It was July 1940.

With several hundred other refugees, I now found myself on board of the S.S. *Sobiesky*. The *Sobiesky* had been a passenger liner, a cruise ship. When Poland collapsed under the fury of the German blitzkrieg invasion, the ship had succeeded in evading capture by the Germans and had reached a British port. The British had converted it into a troop transport. Graffiti on our cabin wall bore witness to the ship's mission of evacuating the retreating remnants of British troops from France. A telling comment scribbled in pencil over my bunk by a British soldier during the evacuation from the port of St. Nazaire: "St. Nazaire harbour—May 15, 1940. Goodbye France, and good luck! You'll need it."

Chapter *THREE*

We needed good luck, too; more than we knew. We had heard rumours of a similar transport being sunk by the German navy a few days before. The incident had been kept secret, certainly from us, but would become soon the subject of a vehement debate in the British Parliament, to the embarrassment of the British authorities. The scary fact was that a day before our departure, another ship bound for Canada, carrying interned refugees along with German and Italian prisoners of war had been torpedoed by a German U-boat. Most of the military prisoners, disciplined as they were and trained for such an event, managed to save their lives by getting into the lifeboats; most of the refugees drowned.

Ignorant of these circumstances, I felt pretty safe as the sea voyage began. Our ship was part of a convoy. To reduce the danger of ships being sunk by German U-boats prowling the Atlantic shipping lanes, wartime procedure mandated that ships travel in convoys under the protection of British naval units. One of the ships in our convoy was a huge passenger liner, much larger than the Sobiesky. Rumour had it that this ship was evacuating British women and children to the safety of an overseas dominion; or that a substantial part of the gold reserves of the Bank of England was being taken to safety as a precaution against the expected German invasion. The truth of this rumour was actually confirmed some years after the war.

In any event, our convoy was escorted by several destroyers and one very large battle cruiser. Overhead, the Royal Air Force provided air cover for the first stage of the voyage until our convoy was beyond flying range. The sight of the other ships in the large convoy was reassuring, and we were not too concerned when told that a German radio broadcast had boasted the *Sobiesky* had been sunk. Still, I was occasionally uneasy.

A greater source of discomfort was the fact that we shared the *Sobiesky* not only with the British soldiers guarding us, but also with Italian and German prisoners of war. The sight of Nazi soldiers in such close proximity, even though they were kept on a separate deck, was very unsettling. Being lumped together with them in the minds of the British gave me a horrible, empty feeling. Over the next year, that feeling would become the most painful symptom associated with the mental pathology of internment.

For a few hours, on the first day out, I also had another feeling in the pit of my stomach—fortunately, however, my seasickness was of short duration. I soon enjoyed the hours I spent on deck watching the ocean and the other ships. Food was a problem for the men who did not eat non-kosher food, but we managed. I have a recollection of delicious orange marmalade that was plentiful in the ship's galley. Our accommodations in the cabins were crowded, but there were hints of the luxury that earlier passengers must have enjoyed. I remember taking a bath in sea water that flowed from one of the special taps in the bathroom. Occasionally, the guards were rough. My friend and colleague Albert Pappenheim sported a hole in his raincoat caused by a guard's bayonet when Albert did not obey an order promptly enough.

Our Polish liner developed engine trouble during the voyage, and the whole convoy slowed down for a day or so. Then we were left behind on the hostile ocean, with only one small destroyer remaining as an escort, as we slowly limped on. What a relief it was when we awoke one morning to find ourselves in the beautiful harbour of St. John's, Newfoundland! The ship made the passage from Newfoundland to Quebec City on its own, unescorted. After all, we were in safe waters—the St. Lawrence estuary. Little did we know at the time that German U-boats were already active in the coastal waters. But on July 15, 1940, we docked safely in Quebec City.

Our camp commander on the Isle of Man had told the truth. We had been taken across the Atlantic Ocean to Canada. We had arrived in the New World! Soon we would be free again.

Chapter *FOUR*

Canadian Welcome

THE MOUTH OF THE ST. LAWRENCE RIVER is a majestic portal to the grandeur of Canada. I stood on the deck of the S.S. *Sobiesky*, trying to absorb the spectacular entrance. I watched Anticosti Island glide by. I did not know its name then, but I was awed by the size of a mere island in a river that was larger than some of the countries of Europe. I watched the shores of the narrowing estuary gradually coming close enough to form the shape of a wide river.

My hopes were high and my mood was eager. How would my future unfold in the freedom of this vast country—of which I knew so little? Where would I be able to go, or more realistically, perhaps, where would we be taken to begin our life of freedom in this new world?

Our ship docked in the harbour of Quebec City and our first experience was devastating, a cruel letdown. It became obvious, as our guards escorted us from the ship, that the authorities in charge of our reception were not expecting Jewish refugees from Nazi Germany, but Nazi soldiers and German civilians—in other words, enemies. While the British guards on board our ship had carefully kept the German and Italian prisoners of war separate from the refugees to avoid any untoward incidents, the Canadian military was not aware of any such distinctions, except for the difference between military prisoners and civilians. The former were disciplined, organized men whom the Canadian military could understand and to whom they could relate, soldier to soldier; the civilians were more difficult to handle, a mixture of young and old, unaccustomed to military discipline and procedure. As far as the Canadian military was concerned, all of us were dangerous enemies whom Canada had undertaken to guard.

For that reason, much to our dismay and surprise, security was tight and frightening. We were under the guard of a large contingent of heavily armed Canadian soldiers, with bayonets and machine guns. We felt uncomfortable, to say the least, even though many of the soldiers looked a little comical to us. We were used to the tough-looking, no-nonsense British tommies. The Canadian soldiers awaiting us at the dock were mostly members of the Veterans' Guard, older men who, unfit for duty overseas, were assigned to military operations within Canada, such as guarding POW camps. They were wearing their summer uniforms, sporting unmilitary-looking short pants and short-sleeved shirts.

I have always wondered what these soldiers thought of us, as they watched us disembark. Many of them had never met any Jews and probably had only a very hazy notion of what Jews might be like. What they saw was a mass of European-looking men in civilian dress. They had no reason to question their assumption that the prisoners were all dangerous Nazi sympathizers. Perhaps a few of the more educated ones, especially some officers, might have identified a bunch of young fellows who sported beards, long earlocks, black hats, and long black coats as Jewish—but, then again, their exotic appearance might just be a clever disguise on the part of Nazi fifth columnists. If they recognized us as Jews, and if they knew that Germany was persecuting Jews, it made little difference to them. They were military people; theirs was not to ask questions and to reason why, but to carry out orders that called for treating us humanely and fairly—strictly as captive enemies.

We were hustled through the transfer from the boat to a waiting railway train. All valuables—if we still had any after the searches and confiscations in England—had to be surrendered. At this point, the burly sergeant in charge of a group of younger-looking Canadian soldiers involved in the operation made his appearance. He took one look at the yeshiva students and Hasidim among us, talked to us briefly in Yiddish and seemed to scarcely believe what he saw and heard. Like Joseph in Egypt, who revealed his identity to his brothers, this sergeant revealed himself as a fellow Jew. He promised to inform the Jewish communal leadership of our arrival, as soon as he had a day off to go home to Montreal. In the meantime, he bellowed his orders loudly to us: "Surrender all your valuables, such as money and jewellery." In Yiddish, he added: *"Halt als ding in keshene; vos ir halt in keshene vet keiner nisht gefinnen!*—Hand over all money, please! *Behalt als ding; git kein zach nisht!"* (Keep everything in your pockets! What you keep in your pockets will not be found. Don't give up anything!) That strange incident was a boost for our morale. At least, we had hope that Canadian Jews might soon learn of our existence. Indeed, as we only found out much too late, the sergeant kept his promise. We thought he had forgotten us.

Despite this ray of hope, as our train pulled out of the port of Quebec City and made its way east, we were pretty dejected. Our immediate future looked worse than it had before we left England. The distance from Quebec City to Three Rivers, Quebec, is short by Canadian standards. Yet when I sat in the train that carried me and my fellow prisoners from our port of entry to our first Canadian internment camp, I got another intimation of the vastness of Canadian space. In Europe, we would have seen villages and towns along the line of a comparable rail trip. Here, on my first journey through Canada, I saw lonely farms isolated by long stretches of fields and bush. Some of the images of the journey, recalled in melancholy reveries during the long period of solitude in the camps, lingered in my mind for years. I had seen a girl waving to the train from her farmhouse window. Her image kept coming back and left me with an ache.

I had never heard of a city named Three Rivers—Trois Rivières—which turned out to be our destination. More precisely, it was Camp T, a makeshift internment camp set up in an exhibition building on the town's fairgrounds. We had a sinking feeling as we marched into the camp. In Britain, at least the authorities knew that we were innocent refugees who were interned by some wartime fluke. The Canadian authorities neither knew nor cared. They had undertaken to take custody of German and Austrian enemy aliens. Canada was not going to complicate its responsibility by differentiating between various classes of internees.

The German prisoners of war who were already in the camp when we arrived were more discerning than our Canadian warders. No sooner did they see our bedraggled column marching through the camp gate than they realized who we were and started to taunt us by singing Nazi songs, especially the one that sent shivers of fear down our backs: "When Jewish blood spurts from the knife, it all goes twice as well." Now we were not only depressed over being mistaken for enemies and Nazis, but also terrified at the prospect of being at the mercy of German soldiers as fellow camp inmates. Fortunately, the officer in charge of the camp began to realize that there was a problem and acceded to our plea for segregation from the

German military prisoners. A barrier of barbed wire was hastily thrown up to ensure our physical safety.

Details of life in Camp T are hazy in my mind. I remember how the Kashrut observers in our group tried to advise the camp commander of our dietary peculiarities. We asked for butter instead of the margarine that, in those days, was invariably made of animal fat and had been a staple of camp food in England. The commanding officer haughtily scorned this implied slight of the Canadian dairy industry. "There is no such thing as margarine in this country," he said with pride. In truth, even with the food menu severely restricted for those who would not eat non-kosher items, Canadian food seemed abundant to me after the meagre wartime rations in Britain, especially in our poor yeshiva. I particularly learned to enjoy uncooked wheat flakes with milk, a new taste experience for me.

We also got our first taste of Canadian sport. If we climbed on some tables, we could look out through windows near the ceiling and watch the games being played on an adjacent baseball diamond. We had never seen baseball before.

One day, the Swiss consul visited the camp, as the neutral diplomat representing Germany under the Geneva Convention, to check out the treatment of the German prisoners of war. Our camp commander also offered us the benefit of this protective inspection. Of course, we refused to be seen by the Swiss consul because that would have signified our acceptance of the status of German prisoners of war. Perhaps our refusal helped the Canadian authorities understand who we were—or it may have confused them further. One thing is for certain, it did not impress them enough to reconsider our status. While we refused to be identified as German prisoners, the authorities refused to recognize us as refugees. We were classified as prisoners of war, second class—civilian enemy aliens. We were issued special postal forms on which we could inform our families that we were in British captivity through neutral channels. Of course, everyone in our group refused. We had no contact with the Canadian Jewish community. It was very demoralizing and discouraging. The hope that we might soon be set free in Canada died in our hearts.

We learned much later that the Jewish community had indeed become aware of our presence. The Jewish sergeant had raised the alarm, and the Jewish refugee agencies in Britain lost no time in informing the Canadian Jewish Congress of our plight. However, the Canadian military denied the Jewish community any right to intervene on our behalf. Our internment was not a Jewish matter and of no concern to the Canadian Jewish community, as far as the military and civil authorities were concerned. It was a matter for discussion only between the British and Canadian governments and military authorities. Ignorant of all this, we felt abandoned, disappointed, frustrated, and betrayed.

One ray of light fell into our gloom, at least for the yeshiva students. We miraculously received a shipment of *sefarim*, of books, from our yeshiva in London. The head of our yeshiva, since he had been born in Lithuania and was not a German citizen, had not been interned, and neither had other students born in Hungary, Poland, or Czechoslovakia. Rabbi Moshe Schneider —may his memory be a blessing for us!—had an unerring sense of priorities. What we needed most in internment was not clothing, food, or other amenities. We needed books to study Torah. Of course, our whereabouts were a military secret; so the yeshiva addressed the package to one of our fellow students, care of the internment authorities. By chance, the addressee was not even with us in Canada! He was among those who had been shipped to Australia, but somehow—we were sure it was by providential redirection—the shipment followed us to Camp T. At last we could study again!

We only stayed in Camp T for about a month. On August 12, 1940, we were transferred. Of course, we did not know our destination. It turned out to be a camp in New Brunswick, not very far from Fredericton. Our journey was the longest train ride of my life. Normally, the direct route by train from Three Rivers would cross some part of the United States. Since the United States had not yet entered the war, war prisoners could not be transported through United States territory, so that our train had to take a very circuitous route from Quebec to the Maritimes.

The discomfort of the long train ride in hot summer weather was heightened by the circumstance that Tish'a B'Av, the fast day commemorating the destruction of Jerusalem, began in the evening while we were still rolling through Quebec. Of course, the observant did not eat or drink after nightfall and all through the following relentlessly hot day that found us crossing New Brunswick. It was an ordeal. Finally, in the heat of the summer afternoon, the train stopped at a siding near Ripples, New Brunswick. Everybody out!

Our journey continued on foot, as I and my friends, hungry and dehydrated, dragged ourselves and our luggage along the dusty dirt road through the bush for several endless miles.

At last, nearly in a state of collapse, we arrived at the camp. It was a military camp, designated Camp B, a complex of barracks and other wooden buildings that were obviously not yet finished. One of the things we had already learned in our experience with the military was that usually one hand does not know what the other is doing. The camp was definitely not yet ready for occupancy. Plumbing was just being installed and just one water tap, out in the open, was functioning. To drink or not drink on Tish'a B'Av—that was the question, or rather, it was to line up for a drink or not. I made my decision. Tish'a B'Av did not require that I put my health at risk in the merciless heat, with the sun beating down on our sweating bodies. Besides, water might not be available again after dark, when the fast would be over. So I drank some water, as did many others in our group, and then I resumed fasting for the rest of the day.

Camp B turned out to be our home for almost a year. The camp was primitive and unfinished when we arrived; thanks to labour partly supplied by the inmates, it was gradually transformed into a very comfortable camp, with adequate housing, plumbing, dining hall and kitchens, a recreation hut, and workshops. The irony was that the authorities appeared to have eventually decided that it was too luxurious for non-military interned refugees. So, on June 20, 1941, we were moved out, and German war prisoners were moved in! By that time, there were enough German POWs in Canada to fill the camp.

Chapter *FIVE*

Prison Island

ONE TENTH OF ONE'S LIFE is a long time. While—from the perspective of the present—the time I spent in Canadian internment camps shrinks to the proportion of a brief interlude in my past, it was quite different for the twenty-year-old me. My time in camp stretched and stretched, until it was longer than my stay in London had been. Its long duration, and the uncertainty as to when it would end, brought weariness and depression. Like a growing cancer that gradually crowds out healthy tissue, the lengthening experience of confinement took over the entire frame of the present time. London, Würzburg, Cologne became memories, history, myths. Camp life became the only reality, displacing all else.

How did we live in the internment camp? First of all, I would like to assure the reader that I and the other members of my group did not suffer significant physical hardship in our camps. I know that this statement may be challenged by other former internees. The refugees interned in Canada, depending on the time of their ship's arrival, were dispatched to different camps scattered over eastern Canada and were juggled around according to the needs of the military authorities. In many respects, life in the different camps varied widely. I have heard and read that living conditions were very bad and treatment very harsh in some camps, and that internees suffered physically at least for a time. However, any comparison with Dachau would be specious and irresponsible. We, the internees who came from the S.S. *Sobiesky*, had little cause to complain about the material conditions of our imprisonment.

Generally speaking, our suffering was psychological: firstly, the painful, undeserved deprivation of freedom, and secondly, the mental anguish a Jew must feel to be locked up as a German and as a suspected Nazi sympathizer. Physically, we lived with comforts and discomforts similar to those experienced by recruits in the army. We were housed in austere, but adequate, army barracks, with bunk beds, foot lockers, and—especially in Camp B after it was completed—clean sanitary facilities. We were under military discipline, with daily inspections and military regulations. Some of the rules were annoying or silly for civilians. However, the military command encouraged the inmates to run the camp within the barbed wire through a democratically elected administration. As long as there were no problems, the officers and guards interfered as little as possible. We could make use of facilities for recreation and entertainment. We even created a coffee house, for which our own skilled European bakers, refugees from the Vienna coffee houses, produced great pastries.

The internment authorities also provided the opportunity to work, beyond the work details required for the maintenance and improvement of the camp itself, such as grounds maintenance, sanitation, and work in the dining room, kitchen, and workshops. The manufacture of camouflage nets was a camp industry. While in New Brunswick, we also had forestry work, cutting trees in the woods surrounding the camp. Our pay was twenty cents a day. The work was mandatory.

For the younger camp inmates, a school system was set up with the help of Canadian service organizations. That was, of course, a very important development. The camp population included an abundance of professors, scientists, teachers and scholars—refugees from some of the best European universities. That circumstance not only facilitated an excellent standard of secondary and post-secondary education for the students, but it also enabled the camp community to organize a variety of cultural and educational programs, with the help of numerous artists, musicians, and other talented people. Incidentally, when arrangements were made for students to take their matriculation exams, they achieved excellent results.

The yeshiva students set up our own educational program. This not only enabled us to continue our studies, but we were also able to organize formal and informal study opportunities for other men who were interested in Jewish studies.

Students were exempt from work. Nevertheless, I occasionally went into the woods with the work details and became quite proficient at felling trees with my axe and carrying the trunks on my shoulder to the clearing, where a team of horses picked them up. Especially in the winter, when deep snow covered the bush, it was an exhilarating experience for a bookworm like me.

Work was not always so voluntary. Sometimes, when there were not enough workers to fill the quota, a crusty old sergeant whom we had nicknamed Yankel *der Shtipper* would prowl the camp to nab idle inmates. Although basically good-natured, Yankel the Pusher was liable to ignore the customary exemption from work enjoyed by students. We improvised a signal system to give us advance warning of Yankel's approach, thus enabling us to evade capture. But the system was not foolproof and occasionally I got caught.

While we were treated by the Canadian authorities as regular civilian enemy aliens at the beginning of internment, the Canadian military gradually and grudgingly recognized and conceded that we did not really belong in that category, though what and who we were was not yet defined nor clearly understood. At the urging of the Canadian Jewish community, of refugee advocates, and of the British authorities, who by that time were ready to confess that they had foisted refugees instead of Nazis on the unwary Canadians, some of the most resented restrictions imposed on us were eased. The tightly restricted mailing privileges were relaxed early on, enabling me to start corresponding again with numerous friends and relatives scattered far and wide.

We had a lot of time on our hands, but we also had opportunities to spend it usefully and pleasantly. If we had only known how long our internment was going to last, and how the war was going to end! If not for that terrible uncertainty hanging over our fate and future, internment might have been a kind of adventure, especially for the younger internees like myself. I turned twenty-one while in internment.

The 2,290 interned refugees shipped to Canada from Britain were a mixed group. The great majority of those interned in Camp B, in New Brunswick, were Jewish. Many German and Austrian Jews had long abandoned Shabbat and Kashrut to the same degree as many Canadian and American Jews. On the other hand, there was a sizable minority of Jews who were more or less observant and whose preference or need for kosher food was their common denominator. For the camp administration, this was simply the "kosher group." Some members of this group were very devout and strictly observant men who refused to eat non-kosher food and to break the Shabbat, and tried their utmost to adhere to their accustomed way of life. The core of this group were the yeshiva students whose goal it was, as far as circumstances would permit, to continue their Torah study and to maintain their firm commitment to Jewish law and spirit. I belonged to that group.

As soon as we had been able, we had prevailed on the camp administration to give us extra rations of bread, milk, cereals, and vegetables to make up for the meat and other non-kosher food that we had to refuse. After a few months, when the camp commandant understood our problem and agreed to allow the Jewish community to help solve it, Rabbi Krauss of Fredericton was permitted to visit the camp to establish a kosher kitchen. Fortunately, there were among us men with experience in the meat and restaurant business, who volunteered to work in the kitchen. The supply of kosher meat and other kosher victuals was arranged. After that, our food was good and plentiful.

My friends, the cousins Albert Schild and Heini Wolf, whose parents had owned a meat store in Munich and later in England, were the expert butchers of the kosher department. I do not believe that their skill in this field had any bearing on their later career as mathematicians.

Since the kosher group had to be segregated in the dining room, it became convenient for the camp administration to move its members to one area in the camp. We lived together there and set aside common space for communal and religious needs. We quickly developed into a real, observant Jewish community, almost a miniature of the communities in the Jewish world outside the camp. Our group included a variety of Jewish types, and a wide range of age and occupations. The element that united us was our wish to live according to Jewish tradition, although the group was by no means homogeneous in terms of observance, belief, custom, or Jewish educational background.

Naturally, we had a large number of *yekkes*, German Jews with a reserved formality and an orderly, systematic approach to prayer and observances. In contrast to their stiffness and their love of regularity and order, there was a number of Hasidim, with beards and payot, who preferred spirited spontaneity and emotional impulsiveness. Their particular customs and style differed widely from the German model.

Then there were yeshiva students like myself who, despite our German background, had shed some of our German mannerism and adopted the less sophisticated and more natural eastern-European style that seemed more authentic to us. We tried to adhere to the less ornate style and more ascetic discipline of the Musar movement that emphasized personal restraint, simplicity, and inwardness, rather than to the more sophisticated and esthetic German-Jewish mode which stressed propriety, beauty, and formality. It was an interesting mix with creative differences and stimulating tensions.

We also had a lot of fun. We indulged in a great deal of good-humoured ribbing and teasing, perhaps not quite approved by our more serious "Musarniks". We tried our best to annoy the officially elected honourary *gabbaim*, the dignified and slightly pompous gentlemen who were charged with organizing and supervising religious services. Stout *yekkes* all, they looked askance at the frequent underground Hasidic or yeshiva *minyanim*, or floating prayer groups, whose simple style of prayer—and prayer times—was in contrast to the formal German cantorial artistry, punctuality, and orderliness. There were always lively debates about religious customs and procedures. And there were a few mischievous but good-natured troublemakers who kept us entertained and relieved the monotony.

The yeshiva students and other men with good Jewish academic backgrounds organized Torah and Talmud classes, not only for the yeshiva students themselves, but also for the general membership of the kosher group. We celebrated Shabbat, and the holidays, and enjoyed home-made entertainment on Hanukkah and Purim. I will never forget the beautiful *sukkah* we built of pine trees in Camp B, and the thick blanket of snow that covered it one morning during the week of the festival. On the funny side, there was the wine production before Passover. We got raisins from the kitchen and made wine in milk bottles that we secreted in the space between the ceiling and the roof of our barracks. It was not long before the odour of fermentation became noticeable, much to the consternation of the inspecting officer on his morning rounds. He sniffed the air, looked around for suspicious items, but our hiding place was not discovered. There was a bitter struggle for Shabbat observance, however, that exacted great sacrifice from individuals who were sent to the camp jail for refusing to work on a special detail on Shabbat, in defiance of orders from the commanding officer. Eventually, their struggle was successful.

At this point I must caution the reader against forming an erroneous impression of camp life. True, most of us were recent refugees from Nazi Germany and lucky to be alive. We had plenty of food, fresh air, clean quarters, and within the kosher group, an interesting community with opportunities to continue our education, if we were self-motivated. Yet this picture of camp life ignores our inner turmoil, the angry frustration, and the mental anguish we felt throughout. A comfortable prison is still a prison. To be deprived of freedom, to be kept behind barbed wire and guarded by armed men, even if they are Canadian soldiers, causes a deep psychological ache. To be interned because we were considered to be Germans was even more cruel and absurd, for we were Jews, refugees from Germany, a country that we now hated with furious passion. We were unjustly and unfairly incarcerated. At the same time, we were worried and depressed about the course of the war as we saw Germany triumphant and the Allied cause becoming more desperate.

We were frustrated not only by our imprisonment, but also because official Canada refused to recognize that we were not enemy aliens. We had made two basic demands of the Canadian authorities: we wanted our status changed to that of refugees; and we wanted to be set free without undue further delay. We knew that our demands had the support of several Canadian organizations and prominent individuals, as well as of the British government. Before long, the British government offered us the option of returning to Britain for release and service in an auxiliary army corps. A representative of the British authorities arrived in our camp to make the required arrangements. Some internees exercised this option, but the majority wanted their lives to continue in North America. Europe was no longer home. I chose to stay, hoping to be eventually released in Canada or allowed to immigrate to the United States, where my brother and a few other relatives had preceded me. Naturally, dismissing the option of returning to Britain may have weakened our claim for admission to Canada. However, we remained determined to press the government with the help of our outside supporters. At least, we had the feeling that our voice could no longer be ignored.

At long last, Ottawa relented on one point. As of July 1, 1941—a year after our arrival—we were officially reclassified by the Canadian government as interned refugees. We were no longer enemy aliens! We no longer had to wear the degrading prisoners' uniforms with the large red disk on the back and red stripe along the pant leg, intended to make it easier for our guards to aim properly in case they had to shoot prisoners attempting to escape. The remaining limits on mail privileges, newspapers, radios, and similar security restrictions were also removed. Communications with the outside world became easier, though still subject to censorship. I even was given permission to receive a telephone call from my brother, Kurt, who was then stationed in Georgia.

By and large, I was able to continue my Jewish studies in camp, together with a number of the yeshiva students from London and others who had similar interests. I also read books and cultivated friendships with other internees, whose scholarship in various areas of learning was stimulating and informative. As soon as it was feasible I resumed corresponding with friends from Cologne, Würzburg, or London, who had remained in England, or lived in America and Australia. I did my share of contributing to the intellectual and social life of our group, and helped other students. I do not recall being bored. My Jewish knowledge and my communications skills continued to grow while I was interned.

I was in regular contact through the mails with Kurt, following his progress in his new country and envying his freedom. We shared our anxiety about the fate of our parents and sister. For a time, Kurt had remained in touch by mail with our parents and Margot. In his letters to them, he tried to convey what he was doing and where I was without arousing the suspicions of the German censors. When the United States entered the war after the attack on Pearl Harbour, such contacts ceased, of course.

Among my faithful correspondents was my dear friend Betty Stern, the niece of one of the branches of the Mohl family in Mülheim. As soon as I was allowed to receive mail, her letters cheered me up. Eventually, Betty was able to leave London for the United States. In her letters she always encouraged me to hope that some day soon we would meet again in New York. Instead, one day a letter came from one of her girl friends, telling me that Betty had suddenly taken ill in New York and died. She had often spoken about me, her friend wrote, and I had been in her last thoughts. I was devastated.

When our long-awaited metamorphosis—from interned enemy aliens to interned refugees—took place, we were no longer in Camp

B. On June 20, 1941, ten days before our status changed, we were transferred to Camp I in Quebec. June 20 was a Shabbat. When we were informed of our move, our group strongly protested against being forced to travel on the Sabbath. It was to no avail. We could not budge the army authorities. It was the only time in my life that I travelled on Shabbat. Ironically, our transfer was indirectly related to religious observance. The military authorities had decided that all Kashrut-observing internees were to be consolidated in one location, namely Camp I. Thus the number of our "kosher group" increased through the addition of men from some of the other camps.

Camp I, our new home, was on an island in the Richelieu River. After the long train ride from New Brunswick, a small ferry boat shuttled us from the mainland to Ile-aux-Noix, the Isle of Nuts, a small, pretty island just a little north of where the Richelieu River flows out of Lake Champlain. The island is the site of historic Fort Lennox, a British fortress guarding the approach to Montreal against an invasion from the south. The fort is surrounded by an escarpment and a moat that is crossed by a wooden bridge, leading to the entrance gate. Today, Fort Lennox is a Canadian National Park and I have revisited the island several times. But in 1941, it was our internment camp.

The proximity of Camp I to the city of Montreal was quite irrelevant—it might as well have been on a different continent! The camp was beautifully situated; it was much more pleasant than Camp B, which had been surrounded by dense New Brunswick bush. Our accommodations, however, were much less comfortable than our former camp. While the hut in which I slept was similar to our H-shaped huts in Camp B, the rooms for common activities were largely in the dark and dank stone casements of the fort. Yet we did have a fine *bet hamidrash* for study and prayer in one of the larger, vaulted, stone rooms.

Although we were now officially declared to be refugees, we were still under military guard. The camp gate, however, was kept open during the day and we were allowed to walk unsupervised on the island. We were also allowed to swim in the river under the watchful eyes of a guard. Once I swam across to the mainland, returning quickly when the guard threatened to shoot me for trying to escape. I had no such intention. Where could I have gone without wearing a bathing suit?

Camp life went on; we worked, we studied, we debated, and we enjoyed some diversions, but mainly, we redoubled our efforts to be released. Our reclassification as refugees made continued internment morally untenable. How could they justify keeping refugees behind barbed wire? But there was tremendous resistance to overcome. Right after we arrived in Canada, one of the top-ranking officers walking about in our first camp engaged a group of us in conversation. We asked him about our chances of remaining in Canada. I have never forgotten his reply: "The only way you can remain in Canada is six feet under the ground!"

By all indications, that fine officer had been right. Anti-Semitism had twisted bureaucratic red tape into a solid chain, barring our entry to Canada.

Chapter *SIX*

Free at Last!

Canadians know that citizens of Japanese descent were interned during World War II and unfairly deprived of liberty and property. It was not until decades later that the Canadian government apologized for the blatant racism of these wartime measures and offered restitution. While the Canadian media played an important role in bringing the injustice thus inflicted on Canadians to public attention, the internment of Jewish refugees from Germany and Austria has remained a secret. The story was virtually unknown, even among members of the Jewish communities of Canada. Although a number of excellent books have been published on the subject in the last twenty-five years, and fascinating films have been made and shown in theatres and broadcast on television, many Canadians remain unaware of the drama that took place in our country.[1]

---

[1]Paula Draper, a young Jewish historian at the University of Toronto, wrote two articles in the *Journal of the Canadian Jewish Historical Society* in 1978, while preparing a Ph.D. thesis on this subject. In 1980, a substantial book on the internment, *Deemed Suspect: A Wartime Blunder*, was published by Methuen Publishing Company. The author, Eric Koch, a writer and producer for the Canadian Broadcasting Corporation, was himself one of the internees. Koch's book, an impressive eye-witness account, was the first major work to break the silence. I reviewed his book for the *Journal of Canadian Jewish Historical Society* and expanded my critique into a long essay entitled "A Canadian Footnote to the Holocaust." Some years later, Ted Jones, a school teacher in New Brunswick, came upon the story and wrote a book entitled *Both Sides of the Wire*, in which he juxtaposes the recollections of former internees with those of soldiers and officers who guarded them on the other side. Toronto film maker Harry Rassky was the first to make an interesting film on the subject. He was followed by others. Another Canadian film maker in Nova Scotia turned the book *Both Sides of the Wire* into a documentary film. Another talented film artist, Wendy Oberlander in Vancouver, won recognition with a beautiful, lyrical film inspired by her own late father, who was one of the interned refugees. The name of her film, *Nothing to Be Written Here*, copied from the instruction printed on the prisoner of war

Canadian immigration authorities persisted in their stubborn refusal to release and admit as immigrants a group of people who involuntarily had found themselves on Canadian soil. How absurd this refusal was becomes clear when it is considered against the record of the unparalleled contribution that members of this group made to Canadian society once they were released from internment. Their contribution immeasurably enriched Canadian arts, the academic community, industry and business, and religion. Members of this group included a Nobel Prize winner, a prominent impresario, rabbis and educators, a renowned Jewish philosopher, a Jewish-born Catholic theologian, leaders in the Jewish community, an outstandingly generous benefactor of Queens University in Kingston, and a member of the Quebec Supreme Court. In rising above the anguish and frustration they had to endure as victims of prejudice and official obtuseness, these men bore eloquent witness to the resilient strength of the human spirit.

❖

T HE SUMMER OF 1941 passed slowly. The island was beautiful, surrounded by the calm currents of the Richelieu River. The suffocating shame of being treated as enemies had been lifted. Now we were refugees. Why was my spirit so low?

Fall dyed the foliage on the Isle of Nuts brilliant colours; winter swaddled the ground in white and froze the moat surrounding the fort. We were still interned. Soon, it would be two years, a terribly long time for a twenty-one year old!

Finally, there was some movement. Jewish and non-Jewish humanitarian organizations, and a number of distinguished individuals, spearheaded the struggle for our release. Institutional representatives were allowed to visit the camp and interview individual

letter form which we had to use in the early stages of our internment, eloquently reflects the pathos of the internees' situation.

A film, *The Dunera Boys*, on the similar experiences of Jewish internees in Australia has also been shown on Canadian television.

By far the best and most comprehensive treatment of the story is Paula Draper's Ph.D. thesis. Unfortunately, it has never been published, so that there are only a few copies in existence. Her work is not only sensitive and empathetic, but also painstakingly researched; truly an authoritative presentation of the subject. I hope it will yet be published.

refugees as to their eligibility for release under categories the government had begun to establish. Among our visitors was the late Saul Hayes, who was then a young lawyer and executive director of the Canadian Jewish Congress and masterminded efforts to obtain our release with tremendous personal dedication. Rabbi Abraham Price came from Toronto to visit the yeshiva students in the camp. He was an impressive person, with his neatly trimmed reddish beard and rabbinical Prince Albert coat. The yeshiva students crowded around him as he told us that he was making bold and unconventional attempts to effect the release of the yeshiva students and to bring them to his own yeshiva in Toronto.

The year 1941 was fading and 1942 was soon to begin. Exactly three years ago, I reminded myself, I had been desperately waiting for my exodus from Germany. Now, three years later, I was still not free. I studied; I read; I followed the camp routine lightened by an occasional skate on the frozen moat surrounding the fort, and again waited, waited.

Reports of progress and new promises of freedom trickled in. Indeed, a few internees were released as temporary immigrants. Canadian authorities had, at last, agreed in principle that certain categories of interned refugees, students being one, should become eligible for admission to Canada. However, sponsors would be required to guarantee that students would not become a public charge. The wait continued; but I knew that some people were working on my release.

I had made two decisions already, evidence—I told myself—that I had regained some control of my own life. I had refused to go back to Britain, a choice that I had been offered about a year before. My dread of falling into the hands of the Nazis again precluded my return to Europe. I was not inclined to reenter a country that might still be invaded by Germany. Moreover, Canada was closer to the United States. If given a choice, most European Jews would have preferred to relocate in the New World, and that meant America. At that time, it would certainly have been my choice. Though immigration to the United States was ruled out for the time being, Canada was, at least, as close as I could get. I already had family ties in the United States: my Uncle Felix and Aunt Bertha Schild, a few cousins, and, most importantly, my brother. Kurt had been in the United States for nearly two years and was serving in the United

States army. On January 25, 1942, he was to be married to Beckie Michael of Macon, Georgia. We had no idea where my parents and Margot were, if they were still alive. The war was still going badly for our side, but the entry of the United States had given us new hope.

The second decision had been a little more difficult. As Rabbi Abraham A. Price, the head of the Yeshiva Torath Chaim in Toronto, had told us when he visited our camp, he was negotiating with the Canadian immigration authorities for the release of the interned yeshiva students, and it looked hopeful. At the same time, a committee in Ottawa that had been lobbying bravely for our release had found a sponsor for me and would, if I wanted, apply for my release as a student at an Ottawa university.

I was at a fork in the road.

I chose the yeshiva. I had continued my studies during the internment and my mind was made up. I opted for Torah study in Toronto rather than for the continuation of my secular education in Ottawa. Chance or providence, rather than my own volition, had brought me to Canada. Now, in the snowbound isolation of Fort Lennox on the Ile-aux-Noix, I made the choice that determined the course my life was to follow.

Our time had come. Men were released: farm workers, people with jobs in war-related industries, and students. The camp population began to melt, although deep snow was covering the island when the good news came in January. The release of the yeshiva students to the Toronto yeshiva had been approved. We took a last photo of the yeshiva group on the snow in front of the fort. Our group was too large to be processed all at one time and had to be divided. I was in the second batch.

And so it came to pass, in February 1942, nearly two years after the British police took me from the yeshiva in London for what they had said would be a few days of detention, that I walked through the gates of Camp Lennox, with my little suitcase, to the little boat that would ferry us across the river to St. Paul-sur-Richelieu. A bus drove us from there through the wintry Quebec countryside to Montreal, where a rousing reception awaited us at one of the local yeshivot.

It seemed like a dream. Free at last!

Joyfully we listened to the proffered greetings; we sang and danced with the Montreal yeshiva students and a crowd of well-wishers who had been waiting to celebrate the end of our exile. The radical change from confinement to freedom was overwhelming. Excitement surged through my limbs like an electric shock. Renewed contact with the outside world, from which we had been cut off for so long, set off a current of emotions so powerful that it erased many details. I don't remember where we were and where we spent the night, but whenever I recall that evening I can still feel the ecstasy of triumph and liberation.

In May 1991, the Canadian Jewish Congress convened a reunion, held in Montreal, of the former internees who had remained in Canada. I was invited to give the keynote address. Not all of the surviving "camp boys"—as we used to be called in earlier days—showed up, but for those who came and for spouses and many other guests who attended, I tried to sum up the meaning of our experience as it appeared to me fifty years later.

In my review essay, which had appeared a few years earlier in the Canadian Jewish Historical Society Review, *I called the story of our internment in Canada "A Canadian Footnote to the Holocaust." It was but a footnote because it was dwarfed by the Holocaust, and yet related to it as a footnote to a text. It could only have happened at that time, and only in a world that allowed the Holocaust to happen. It could have happened only because anti-Semitism was widespread, and because the world did not bother to understand Jews.*

British and Canadian officials had been confounded because Jews cannot be classified by the same categories as most other groups of people, by nationality, citizenship, religion, or ethnic origin. Anti-Semitism rubbed salt into our wounded feelings: Canadian officers in charge of the camps made no secret of the fact that they would have vastly preferred to deal with Nazis or patriotic Germans, whom they deemed superior to the whining, complaining, and demanding Jewish rabble.

The ultimate insult, the ultimate failure to comprehend the Jew, was the remark a camp commandant made to the effect that these despicable Jews in his charge did not even possess the decency to love and stand up for their own native country, Germany, but treasonably supported the Allied cause, or at least pretended to!

That still hurts, even fifty years later.

To intern Jews as Germans and as suspected collaborators with the Nazis was an absurdity. No Jew could possibly have any loyalty to the German cause or hope for a German victory. For Jews, a German victory meant death. Jews were existentially anti-German! Our internment was, therefore, a bizarre Jewish shlemiel joke. A Jew imprisoned on the suspicion of being a Nazi is a shlemiel! Kafka could not have dreamt up a more grotesque absurdity.

Our pain was also exquisitely Jewish, unique in the catalogue of emotional torments. It was different from the experience of being a prisoner of war, different even from being in Dachau. In Dachau, you knew you had fallen into the hands of your enemy! Innocent people do sometimes get imprisoned. But to be a Jew locked up as a suspected Nazi has a quality of anguish that is different from being locked up because of a bureaucratic bungle or an asinine law, or mistaken identity, or false suspicion. For all these terrible possibilities, there are precedents in your experience or concepts in your imagination, but not for the infuriating absurdity of being interned by your allies as the enemy, whom you hate even more than they.

I already mentioned that I had made a vow when I was a prisoner in Dachau in November and December 1938: if I should get out alive, which did not appear very likely, I would never allow any future adversity to depress or defeat me. No matter what misfortune I might yet experience, I could never be brought again so low. I have remained true to that vow. It helped me tolerate the insignificant physical discomforts of internment and even the chafing deprivation of freedom. It helped me bear the much more difficult mental anguish, impatience, and frustration.

I hold no grudge against the British. They saved my life. On the whole, internment was not a very tragic experience for me. It removed me from the threat of German bombs that fell on London. It saved me from much more terrible suffering that people experienced during the war. Though painful, my experience of life in internment had some positive value. Above all, it brought me to Canada, all expenses paid!

Canada has more than compensated me for her initial rejection and her hostile indifference to my overtures. The opportunities she

eventually offered me have engendered in me a "true patriot's love"
for her. I sing our national anthem always with deep feeling, and
often with tears welling up in my eyes: to keep Canada glorious
and free and united, I gladly continue to stand on guard!

Part FIVE

Toronto

Chapter *ONE*

Rabbi Price and the Yeshiva

W<small>E TRAVELLED FROM</small> M<small>ONTREAL</small> to Toronto by train. At Union Station, we were met by a number of board members and supporters of Rabbi Price's yeshiva. They escorted us to their cars and drove us to a festive dinner that was waiting for us at the Talmud Torah building on Brunswick Avenue, near College Street. We were impressed by the unaccustomed luxury of private cars. I was driven by a Mr. Sam Kurtz, who was, as I found out later, the administrator of the Talmud Torah. He was one of the finest, wisest, humblest, and most effective servants that the Toronto Jewish community ever had, deserving credit for the subsequent growth of his school into the Associated Hebrew Schools of Toronto. That I was his passenger on my wintry arrival in Toronto was pure chance, of course, but both Mr. Kurtz and I kept the memory of this coincidence alive with mutual satisfaction.

A crowd of Rabbi Price's followers, members of the yeshiva circle, were on hand to greet us. Our arrival in Toronto was hailed as a major event in the traditional community. Rabbi Price welcomed our group of thirty yeshiva students as a significant remnant of European Torah scholars. It was a remnant originally saved by flight to Britain and now liberated from captivity again, thanks to his efforts and the support he had received from his followers.

At the time, his praise may have been a little overblown, since most of us were still too young to have become scholars, but the rabbi had correctly assessed the potential of our group and its stimulating effect on the community. Indeed, among the group were former students of famous yeshivot in Lithuania, Poland, Hungary, and Czechoslovakia. It included a number of pious Hasidic young men recognizable by their garb, beards, and earlocks, along with serious students raised in the traditions of mainstream western- and eastern-

European Orthodoxy. Rabbi Price, Polish-born and educated, had lived for several years in Berlin before fleeing from the Nazis to Paris. He was very familiar with the distinctive strengths and weaknesses of German Torah scholarship and the social conditions of German Jews. He welcomed us and appreciated the influx and influence of well-educated students from German cities and villages.

Before our arrival, Yeshiva Torath Chaim, located in a converted dwelling on the north-west corner of Ulster and Markham Streets, was a small school. That it existed at all was due to the drive, ambition, and genius of Rabbi Price. Its somewhat grandiose description on its letterhead as the Rabbinical College of Toronto was not undeserved. As dean of the yeshiva—one of the rabbi's favourite titles—he had ordained three rabbis: Abraham Kelman, Allan Langner, and Gedalia Felder. The three graduates had already left the yeshiva before we arrived, and had begun their distinguished careers in the rabbinate. Rabbi Kelman occupied a position in Toronto in which I would eventually succeed him; Rabbi Langner had a position in Montreal; Rabbi Felder had become rabbi of the Jewish congregation in Belleville, Ontario, and would grow to be a prolific author of books on Jewish law and a world-renowned scholar.

At the time of our arrival, there were few mature students at the yeshiva. There were three young men from Winnipeg, whose fathers were rabbis in that community and wanted their sons to study with Rabbi Price because his reputation as a brilliant scholar had already spread in the Torah world. There were a number of local youths who studied part-time with the rabbi while attending high school or preparing to go into business. These students, while outnumbered by the newcomers, extended a warm welcome to us and would soon help us adjust to Toronto and to our new life. The yeshiva had also classes for younger elementary or high school students, who received their Jewish education at the yeshiva four days a week after school hours and on Sundays. With our arrival, the yeshiva had now acquired a large number of senior students. This enhancement of the student body raised the profile of the yeshiva and strengthened Rabbi Price's position in the community.

The rabbi's life was dedicated primarily to Torah scholarship. He possessed a sharp and sparkling intellect—penetrating, acute, and analytic—combined with a phenomenal memory and powers of recall. The imaginative, artistic, and romantic sensibilities of the human mind were of lesser interest to him. His mind was mathematical, computer-like, with a genius for spotting or creating connections, finding associations and analogies, and using complex mental maneuvers to build and demolish original hypotheses. Sometimes, I felt, he pushed mental acrobatics to an extreme, ignoring qualitative differences while constructing formal relationships.

The method of Talmudic scholarship that Rabbi Price so brilliantly exemplified was *pilpul*, a casuistic discussion of difficulties and contradictions, real or contrived, whose resolution by means of daring analogies eventually leads to innovative interpretations of texts and the definition of concepts, which, as the *pilpul* discourse demonstrates, may be applied to seemingly unrelated subjects in other texts. What made Rabbi Price's *pilpulim* so fascinating and spectacular was his ability to draw on an incredibly rich store of relevant texts. He knew and remembered all the sources, the Talmuds, the commentaries, the codes, obscure texts— everything seemed to be stored in an inexhaustible memory waiting to be recalled and illuminated by the hypothesis the rabbi would propound. He applied a similar method to his sermons. He had the uncanny ability of discovering the relevance of seemingly unrelated texts to a theme or problem, blazing complicated correlations to philosophy, exegesis, and textual analysis. He dazzled students, listeners, or readers with the complexity of his analysis and surprised them with his proposed ultimate solutions.

Rabbi Price often astounded me with his knowledge of the works of authors that were outside the focus of his interest. He seemed to know everything—whether we were asking him about Yehuda Halevi, Reb Chaim Volozhin, or the *Tanya*. He had read everything and he remembered it. He was a genius. He used to preach on the Sabbath before Passover and on the Sabbath of Repentance for three hours or longer without a break, and he usually managed to conclude his discourse with a message relating to religious observance or to ethics. On occasion, the learned conclusions provided ammunition to settle some scores with his political opponents in the community.

He was a controversial figure in Toronto Jewish community, particularly in the politics of the Orthodox core of the community. I have no desire to delve into the arcane details of the political process that consumed the energies and passion of community activists at that time, nor am I really equipped to deal with them, for my close relationship with Rabbi Price gave me not only a privileged, but also a slanted insight into the controversies. While these disputes are part of the history of our community, they are incidental to my biography, except that a few times I was personally involved in them—to the point of being sued by the editor of a local Yiddish newspaper. In retrospect, these events no longer trigger my passion. The fact that these controversies divided our community at a time when millions of Jews, kith and kin of the local combatants, were being done to death in Europe, relegates the controversial issues to a realm of grotesque irrelevance.

Rabbi Price had been invited to Toronto before the outbreak of World War II, not only to head the yeshiva and to lead the small, but learned, Chevra Shass congregation, but also to spearhead a religious-political faction. The young, prolific, outspoken, dynamic, and audacious scholar, already acknowledged as a rising star on the firmament of Polish Torah scholarship, was imported to counterbalance Rabbi Judah Leib Graubart and, later, Rabbi Jacob Kamenetsky, Lithuanian-style savants. They were the rabbinical authorities of the D'Arcy Talmud Torah and Maharil Graubart yeshiva faction, whose political leader was the fiery Itche Meier Korolnik. The battle arena included the Kehilla, the strife-torn official religious community organization charged with the supervision of Kashruth. Who was the authentic arbiter of Halachah—Jewish religious law—for the community? That was the issue.

Today we would consider the petty, spiteful quarrels of those years embarrassing, to say the least. However, the factional strife created its own momentum and continued for many years. Only after a new generation grew up and had to face critical problems in the wider Jewish world, were the old issues of internecine warfare consigned to the dustbin of history in which the embarrassments of yesterday are forgotten.

Rabbi Price, I must admit, wore partisan blinkers. He could never see any justice on the other side. While his one-sidedness disturbed me, as well as his utter disregard for people who stood in his way or even disagreed with him, I was his loyal disciple. I remain convinced that in most issues he was right. No doubt, he was the stronger and smarter of the antagonists. Yet even after Rabbi Kamenetsky had left Toronto for New York and the sharp edge of the controversy became blunted under his successor, Rabbi David Ochs, Rabbi Price never became nor tried to become the recognized rabbinical authority of Toronto. The reason for his failure was simply that he could not or would not work cooperatively with other lay or rabbinical leaders, or try to ingratiate himself with the communal power brokers. He was not a "committee" person. He affected a disdain for those who considered democratic communal participation a sacred task. I suspect, however, that in his heart of hearts, he was more appreciative of those individuals than he was willing to admit. He was probably painfully aware that his own compulsive need for complete independence and his insistence on unconditional allegiance prevented him from compromising and accepting decisions made by others, and denied him success and recognition in the community.

It may have been sour grapes, but Rabbi Price certainly appeared not to care whether the community as a whole accepted him or not. He had his patrons and followers, among them the wealthy Oelbaum family, headed by Moshe Oelbaum, who had died shortly before our arrival in Toronto. Their support had enabled him to consolidate the yeshiva and, above all, to bring our group to Toronto. A less tenacious and defiant individual would not have been able to do it. As the rabbi told the story, he not only had to overcome the opposition of the notoriously anti-Semitic Canadian immigration officials, but also the skepticism and contrariety of the Canadian Jewish Congress, whose jurisdiction over Jewish public policy the rabbi was unwilling to accept.

It is difficult to ascertain whose version of the events is correct. Rabbi Price claimed that Congress was indifferent, if not hostile, to his efforts to obtain the release of the yeshiva students. According to him, Congress leaders were too timid to confront the government. Perhaps, he conjectured, going all-out in demanding the admission of Orthodox religious students who had nothing tangible to contribute to the all-consuming Canadian war effort that Canadian Jewry wanted to be seen supporting was not a great public relations exercise.

All these allegations were strongly rejected by the Canadian Jewish Congress, although some lively confrontations between Rabbi Price and the powerful Sam Bronfman are matters of record. It is also clear that Congress did not withhold support after the fact. The rabbi's successful determination earned him the admiration, grudging perhaps, of the Canadian Jewish Congress, particularly of Saul Hayes, the organization's notable national director, and the respect of many leading figures in the Jewish community and beyond. The rabbi was revered by some prominent non-Jewish politicians, such as Senator Arthur Roebuck, and by some leading members of the academic community, whose cooperation would later facilitate the entrance of yeshiva students to the University of Toronto. Needless to say, he earned the enduring gratitude and love of the students who were released into the custody of the yeshiva through his dogged efforts.

The Chief—as his students always referred to him with fond irreverence—utilized his acumen not only to build a yeshiva, but also to accumulate, in the course of the years, a large measure of wealth through shrewd real estate investment and efficient management of assets. Unfortunately, Rabbi Price did not solicit my participation in his financial activities, as he did in other areas, nor did he impart his know-how to me.

In most other ways, the Chief was like a father to me and to the other members of our group. He was concerned for our welfare and progress, always sensitive to the needs of young men who had been wrenched away from their families in such difficult circumstances. Although the rabbi was strictly observant and expected his disciples to adhere to Jewish rules and to Jewish spirit, he was not coercive. He understood us. He treated us as responsible adults and was tolerant of our need for general education and for recreation to recover from the emotional ordeal that we had experienced. His piety was tempered—or enhanced—by common sense and by an easy-going sense of humour and geniality that may have been part of his Hasidic heritage. His Halachic opinions were generally liberal and shaped by a sensible, pragmatic perspective, but they were always based on sound and thorough Halachic reasoning, of which he was a master. I am convinced that he deserved the highest rank among his scholarly peers. Again, it was his pugnacious streak, his inability to appreciate opinions contrary to his own, and his brutal frankness that obscured his genius and isolated him. That did not seem to bother him. He corresponded with many renowned members of the Torah world and was satisfied to entrust his reputation as a scholar to the numerous books he wrote. Indeed they are firm evidence of his unique genius.

Chapter *ONE*

Rabbi Price was about 42 years old when I arrived in Toronto. Our close relationship underwent changes in the ensuing decades. Yet when he died during Pesach in 1994, 52 years after I arrived in Toronto, I was the first person—I believe—whom his granddaughter called at dawn.

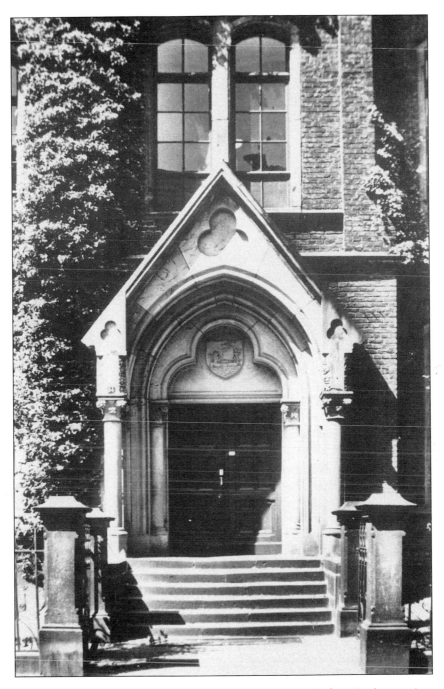

Portal of the high school I attended from 1930 to 1936, the Reform-Realgymnasium Köln-Mülheim.

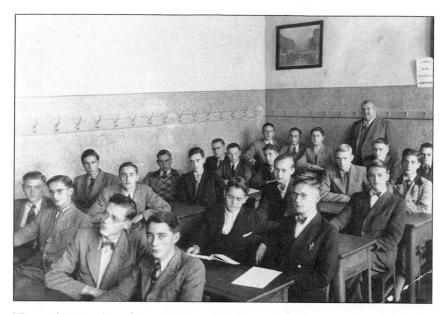

The graduating class of the school in which I was allowed to receive my matriculation, the German *Abitur*. The two Jewish students, David Alster and I, are seated in the corner in the back row.

Former students of the Würzburg Teachers' Seminary, reunited at the London yeshiva in 1939, show their abiding camaraderie in the new environment: (from left) Friedel Perl, Joseph Faust, myself, Albert Pappenheim, and Shammai Zahn.

Betty Stern

Moor-Park April 1940

Portrait of my dear friend Betty Stern, who took refuge with her relatives, the Mohl family, when persecution in her town made life too miserable. Our friendship deepened in London, where the portrait was taken in April 1940. On the back of the photo, shown here, she wrote a poem in praise of friendship. Worried that our platonic relationship might change, Betty extolled friendship as superior to love, entitling her poem "Everlasting!" I was crushed when I received a letter in a Canadian internment camp, informing me of her sudden death from a mysterious illness not long after her arrival in New York.

Everlasting!

Everything in the world is transient
even this picture grows yellow and faint.
Even Love does not last for ever
sometimes it may even turn to hate.
If there is anything permanent
it is Friendship, faithful and strong.
True friendship is an iron bond
that rust can rarely corrode.

...

[If] at some future time by chance
your eyes will fall on this picture again—
You turn it over, and then perhaps
you read these lines after many years.
Then think: though it was dormant
it has remained noble and whole,
Just dust the Friendship off
and it will shine as brilliant as of old.

POST · CARD

Erstrahlt di Freundschaft in altem Glanz!

Unverwüstlich!

Alles ist vergänglich in der Welt,
Selbst dieses Bild vergilbt u. blaßt,
Auch die Liebe nicht ewig hält,
Manchen, den man einst geliebt, man haßt.
Wenn wirklich etwas hat Bestand
Dann ist es Freundschaft, treu u. fest!
Wahrer Freundschaft eisernes Band
Sich selten vom Rost zerfressen läßt.
Eifersucht ist's was an Liebe nagt.
Dagegen ist Freundschaft gefeit,
Die Liebe ist blind! (wie man so sagt)
Freundschaft sieht u. versteht u. verzeiht.
Vertrauen ist ihr Fundament,
Ihre Säulen: Vernunft u. Verstand,
Und wenn die Liebe sie nicht verbrennt
Dann hat sie ewig Bestand.

Vielleicht wird sie, wenn angefraut,
In eine Ecke gestellt,
Mit anderm Gerümpel zugebaut.
Das ist der stete Lauf der Welt!—

Und läßt Du wieder Zufall es heischt,
Dein Blick auf diesem Bilde weilen.
Du wendest es dann um, vielleicht
Und liest nach Jahren diese Zeilen,
Dann denke: wenn auch abgenutzt,
So ist sie doch Edel u. ganz
und wenn nur den Staub erst abgeputzt,

Yeshiva students at their studies in Internment Camp I, Fort Lennox, Ile-aux-Noix, Quebec, 1941. Centre left: Joseph Epstein

At long last, the day of liberation for the yeshiva group bound for Montreal and Toronto. One final group photo in the snow of Ile-aux-Noix, January-February 1942

Susi Speier-Holstein, the youngest and only surviving daughter of Dr. Victor and Lena Speier-Holstein, in England, September 1941. Susi was saved by the "children's transport" that brought a number of very young Jewish children from Germany to Britain. She mailed this charming picture to me in the internment camp to boost my morale.

Courting days in July, 1944. Laura and I shared a delightful excursion by steamboat to Niagara Falls.

Our wedding, December 31, 1944. With bride and groom are (left) my best man, Albert Schild, Laura's maid-of-honour, Rhoda Kay, who later married Albert Pappenheim, my brother, Kurt, corporal in the U.S. army, and his wife, Beckie Schild

Together again—for the first time since we parted in 1939—are the three siblings at Margot's wedding in September 1947 in New York, less than two years after she arrived in the United States. The photo captures a moment of great joy and thankfulness.

Three rabbis celebrating ordination at the Yeshiva Torath Chaim, 1947. Rabbi Abraham A. Price is seated on the left. Standing (from left) are newly ordained Rabbis Erwin Schild, Albert Pappenheim, and Joel Litke.

A new generation is born: smiling mother, Laura Schild, with our first-born, Daniel, in Queen's Park, Toronto, 1946.

Chapter *TWO*

A Long Winter

"WHAT DO YOU LIKE BEST about living in Canada?" asks the young lady who is interviewing me. She is compiling research data for a thesis relating to the adjustment of immigrants. My answer is spontaneous, unpremeditated. I don't have to think. The word shoots right out of my mouth. "Freedom!"

I may not be able to uphold the superiority of freedom over other values in a philosophical debate. I don't really care. I know when I woke up the morning after my arrival in Toronto, free to walk anywhere, without guards, without restrictions, free to explore the streets of a city I did not yet know, there was nothing greater, no thrill more exciting, than the realization that I was free. The sheer delight of it all! To shop in a drug store, to watch children going to school, to cross a busy road—everything was new, exciting, exhilarating. I got a new suit. Mr. Moshe Primer, a dedicated supporter of Rabbi Price's yeshiva and the owner of a dry-goods store on College Street, had connections with the garment trade, so he was able to clothe the new yeshiva students who had nothing but their camp wardrobe. Everything was new and thrilling and redemptive, an exciting metamorphosis.

Actually, I was not as free as I felt. The yeshiva students whom Rabbi Price had liberated from the internment camp were not accorded the normal landed immigrant status and we were only granted temporary admission. We had to report to police at certain intervals. But these restrictions did not spoil the ecstasy of freedom.

The euphoria did not last. According to the Book of Exodus the children of Israel, liberated from Egyptian slavery, walked three days in freedom before they started complaining. Forty-two days later, they rebelled against their liberator, Moses. "Would we were again at the flesh pots of Egypt!" With the wisdom of hindsight, some fifty years later, it is easy to diagnose my distemper as the peculiar kind of homesickness to which I am prone. Again I reacted to change by idealizing the past, and comparing it to the present, though in my case it had nothing to do with flesh pots.

I felt blue. I was unhappy. Was it the long Canadian winter? Spring comes late to Toronto; March is a difficult month. We expect to see signs of spring, especially those of us who come from western Europe, but the cold hangs on. Skies are drab and we feel frustrated by procrastinating nature. Even the snow looks stale and old and dreary. I felt dried out spiritually and emotionally. There was no splendour, no passion, no excitement; neither despair nor joy. Had I been drained and dried by the drab desperation of internment?

My discontent was partly due to my dissatisfaction with the yeshiva, a reprise of my initial maladjustment in Würzburg and, later, in London. I hankered for the Lithuanian style of Talmud study with its subtle analyses and rational probing. While Rabbi Price's *pilpul* approach demonstrated his mental acuity and brilliance, it did not impress me as a serious way of trying to discover the meaning of a text. However, after a while, I learned to appreciate the benefits of Rabbi Price's approach to the teaching of Talmud. Though the Lithuanian quest for depth is intellectually attractive, it is easily over-done. The student studies smaller amounts in order to understand the text more deeply; yet quantity is indispensable for a student. In the end, unfortunately, the ephemeral definitions and speculative analyses of the Lithuanian method are no less contrived than the fantasy flights of *pilpul*. In time, I created my own synthesis. I also realized how enriching it had been to have been exposed not only to a variety of methods of study, but also to a variety of philosophies of Torah and styles of Jewish life. And that realization came even before I entered university where another culture shock was awaiting me.

Another cause of the wintry distemper, so soon after my initial ecstasy, had to do with vanity, which is certainly one of my many weaknesses. I have an excessive need for approbation and recognition. I did not feel accepted in Toronto. On the totem pole of the social order, refugees ranked near the bottom. Perhaps it had not been different in England, but in London the yeshiva was a self-contained insular entity that had only superficial and occasional contacts with the British Jewish community. Yeshiva students rarely met with people outside the yeshiva, other than friends and relatives who were refugees like themselves. In Toronto it was different. None of us had local friends or relatives; but there were many Jewish people with whom we interacted: local yeshiva students and alumni, their parents and families, and many well-meaning supporters.

Rabbi Price, as head of the yeshiva, had no intention of curtailing social contact between the newly arrived ex-internees, of whom the rabbi was very proud, and their peers in the community.

It seemed to me that the established Jewish citizens looked down on us. Sure, they were happy that they had saved us from internment camp, for which we ought to be grateful. Their feeling for us was one of pity mixed with a bit of contempt. Some individuals also regarded us with a little suspicion, for how could we corroborate the stories we told our new neighbours and hosts about our own past and background? The magnitude of the Holocaust—and thus the significance and singularity of absorbing some survivors—had not yet dawned on the good citizens. Despite the general concern and fear for the Jews of Europe, the reality of the catastrophe taking place on the Nazi continent had not yet penetrated the consciousness of most Canadian Jews.

The elders of the community—many of them good, generous, and friendly individuals—considered us to be "greenies"—as they had been when they came from Europe decades before: ignorant newcomers in an unfamiliar foreign environment. That most of the "yeshiva boys" were well-educated, from refined, respected families, that we spoke better English than most of the locals, who were Yiddish-speakers, that we had a better understanding of the contemporary world than many long-term members of Toronto Jewry, went unnoticed. A prejudice against German Jews was also apparent to me. The fact that we were pitiable refugees, dependent for freedom and sustenance on Jews of eastern-European origin, was our just comeuppance for the stinging slights and derogation that Polish and Russian Jews had suffered at the hands of German Jews when they had migrated to German cities in the early part of the twentieth century. I cannot deny that this happened, but I felt no personal guilt for which I ought to atone by accepting a socially inferior status.

Perhaps I was reluctant or too bashful to open myself to new friends and take the initiative to enter new circles of hospitable families that had welcomed many of my colleagues. Besides, my social maladjustment, though I remember it acutely, can only have been of short duration.

I received a psychological boost when I was chosen by Rabbi Price to address, as a representative of the yeshiva, a public rally at the Victory Theatre on Spadina Avenue. The event, co-sponsored by the yeshiva, was in response to the alarming reports that had begun to trickle in from Europe. Naturally, my task was to highlight the importance of the yeshiva at a time when we could no longer count on European Jewry to safeguard the tradition of Torah for the future generations.

The Victory Theatre was full. I have no recollection of the content of my speech other than that I spoke in the declamatory oratorical style that I had been taught in German schools and that used to be favoured by Yiddish public speakers. I guess my style, poise, and the surprise of a recently arrived yeshiva student speaking in fluent English were more important than the content of my message. I received tremendous applause and basked in the sunshine of admiration. Members of the yeshiva circle took notice of me. I believe my climb out of depression began that evening.

I carried on as best I could. I thought of my parents and Margot, who had vanished in the darkness of Europe. I thought of my friends who had also disappeared. How lucky I had been! I corresponded with those who were alive and accessible. I heard from Susi Speier-Holstein in England. I was in touch with other friends from Würzburg. Contacts with my old friends gave me great strength and comfort. I missed my close friend Betty Stern and re-read many times the letter her girl friend had written to notify me of her death and to comfort me.

On the other hand, I was encouraged by my brother's relative proximity. He was stationed at Camp Wheeler in Georgia, close to Macon, the home of Beckie Michael, whom he had married on January 25, just a few weeks before my release from the internment camp. I was also happy to hear from my Uncle Felix and Aunt Bertha Schild. They were adjusting to life as refugees in New York, but they were worried about their son, Joseph, who was fighting in the Pacific war theatre.

As my first spring in Toronto turned into summer, I felt much more at home and socially secure. I became friendly with a few families who were hospitable to the yeshiva students. I was on my way to achieving the acceptance that I craved and, in my youthful vanity, believed to be my due. However, the spirit that once stirred my thoughts and feelings had not yet returned. I still lived in a shell of solitude. My world was still shades of grey. There was no technicolour.

It was soon going to change.

Chapter *THREE*

Changes

MY DIFFICULTIES IN ADJUSTING to life in Toronto as a student of the yeshiva were paralleled by the problems that Rabbi Price faced in managing the absorption of so huge an influx of new students. At first, the new students were billeted in private homes. My hosts were the Gottfried family, who lived on Grace Street, just south of Bloor. Since this location was too far from the yeshiva, and even farther from the Brunswick Talmud Torah where we had our meals, I soon moved to another address on Palmerston Avenue. I was not as fortunate as some of my colleagues, a number of whom were housed with families with children of compatible age. It did not take these students long to form permanent bonds with their host families. Their homes remained social centres for clusters of yeshiva students, even after the students moved out. The Silverberg home, the Wolfson home, the home of the family of the late Rabbi Kelman, just a few doors down Markham Street from the yeshiva, were focal points of hospitality.

Before long, however, it became evident that the dispersal of students' lodgings was detrimental and impractical. It not only wasted time, but inhibited the growth of a cohesive spirit among the members of the student body. To solve the logistical problems, the yeshiva bought a house, at 399 Markham Street, directly across from the academic building. It was a wise move on the part of Rabbi Price. The house, immediately dubbed the White House because of the white pillars and banisters gracing the wide veranda, was spacious and beautiful, and served as dormitory, refectory, and administrative building for the yeshiva.

The advantages of having a dormitory so close to the *bet hamidrash*, the study hall, was immediately evident in terms of efficient use of time. Just as important, however, was the fact that living together brought the individual students into a closer personal relationship. We were free to go out in the evenings, if we had time, or to spend the hours reading and playing chess. Rabbi Price, whose marriage had ended in Europe and who had not yet remarried, often joined us at Shabbat and festival meals. The Pesach seder, conducted by Rabbi Price in our own yeshiva building, was memorable.

But the growth of a more cohesive yeshiva spirit and camaraderie was not entirely due to the new facility. Our group of released internees had shrunk. We had never been a homogeneous group. Pressure from the outside had held us together during internment, but in Toronto, tensions began to surface. Although Rabbi Price was an adherent of the Gerer Hasidic movement, he did not affect a Hasidic style in his dress and deportment. His outward appearance reflected his sojourn in Berlin and he dressed in the style of a German *rabbiner*. He followed Hasidic custom in ritual, but he was a Gerer Hasid mainly in learning and temperament. He was definitely not a *rebbe*. He did not wear a *shtraimel* (a fur-trimmed hat) or sport curled earlocks and in private he was inclined to make fun of those who did. He was too much of a rationalist to foster, or even exemplify, the kind of fervent piety and emotional spirituality associated with Hasidism.

For some members of our group, that was a disappointment. They could not adapt to the yeshiva's style of study and probably did not approve of the modernity of many of their fellow students. Toronto did not offer them the kind of Hasidic environment that they knew existed in Montreal and was more suited to their spiritual needs. I am sure Rabbi Price regretted to lose the Sputz brothers, the Feigelstocks and several others, but he did not try to dissuade them from moving to Montreal. An allegation was circulated some time afterwards that the rabbi had secretly tried to enlist the help of the immigration authorities to prevent such defections, but I believe this allegation was a fabrication made by his enemies.

Similarly, the rabbi did not put any obstacles in the path of students who wanted to pursue secular career goals, although they had been released from internment as yeshiva students. When they left the yeshiva, they left with the rabbi's blessings. He loyally continued to take a benevolent interest in their progress and well-being. Especially remarkable was the fact that Albert Schild and his cousin Henry Wolf remained at the yeshiva while they were full-time students in mathematics and physics at the University of Toronto. They participated in the religious life of the yeshiva—

Albert as the Torah reader for several years—and lived in the yeshiva dormitory until they married. Eventually, both of them were to enjoy highly successful careers in their chosen field in the United States. Rabbi Price was as proud of them as of those who opted for the rabbinate.

I shared a room in our new dormitory with Albert Schild. As I have already mentioned, we first met at the seminary in Würzburg, but our friendship had really been forged in Dachau. I had said good-bye to Albert in Dachau, when I was released, and had not seen him until we met again in internment. We were good companions for each other. Our friendship was marked by mutual respect, and by consideration of our need for privacy as well as companionship. Our shared interests and our common background and experiences made us very compatible roommates.

Both Albert and I enjoyed good music. We bought an old radio set, a long case housing the large number of vacuum tubes. For music lovers not restrained by Shabbat observance, the radio broadcasts from the Metropolitan opera in New York were a weekly treat, but they took place on Shabbat, when switching on an electric device such as radio is not permitted. Albert, the future scientist and mathematician—he also grew to become a truly pious and learned Jew—devised an ingenious scheme to access these broadcasts without violating the Shabbat rules. In the absence of commercial Shabbat clocks, Albert hitched two alarm clocks—each with only a twelve-hour range—to the on/off toggle switch of our radio. The first clock was to trigger the alarm switch of the second clock, which was set to turn on the radio on Saturday afternoon. It worked perfectly on the second Shabbat—on the first, the radio awoke us in the middle of the night!

Albert and I remained roommates until I moved out of the yeshiva to be married, in December 1944.

Only two houses and the width of Ulster Street separated the home of the Kelman family from the yeshiva. Its proximity and, even more, the hospitality of its residents made it a favourite place for the students to visit whenever we wanted to temporarily escape from the institutional ambiance of the yeshiva to the warmth of a real family home.

The Kelmans were also fairly recent immigrants. They had arrived from Vienna in 1930, years before the *Anschluss* turned Austria into a part of the Nazi Reich. Thus, they had sincere empathy for the newcomers. Yeshiva students were always welcome in their home and found the members of the family to be understanding, friendly, and gracious. Unfortunately, the family had also been touched by tragedy: Rabbi Tzvi Juda Kelman, father and husband, who had served as rabbi in the community, had died at an early age in 1936. Rebbetzin Kelman was a wonderful, well-educated, and thoughtful person, a model of Jewish piety and hospitality, and her aged father shared the family home. It was a lively place. There were three sons and three daughters, all more or less in the age range of the new yeshiva students. All three sons were to become distinguished rabbis. The eldest, Adolph—who for obvious reasons preferred to use his Hebrew name Abraham—had already been ordained by Rabbi Price and, as I mentioned, I eventually succeeded him as the rabbi of his congregation. The second son, Wolfe, at the time serving in the Royal Canadian Air Force, later played a leading role in the Conservative movement as executive director of the Rabbinical Assembly; the third son, Joseph, a few years younger than I, grew up to be a beloved colleague and friend serving a great Toronto synagogue.

One Saturday night in the spring of 1942, a few months after my arrival, the end of Shabbat found me in a melancholy mood. I neither felt like studying nor reading, so I left the dormitory and ambled over to the Kelmans. There was a piano in the living room. I enjoyed playing the piano, though my formal piano training had been minimal. For years I had watched my talented brother play and I had learned enough to improvise popular songs and melodies with enough skill to make them sound good—as long as I transposed everything into the key of C. I began to express my mood that evening by playing some sentimental Hebrew songs and a few popular numbers such as "Indian Love Call." Celia, the oldest of the Kelman daughters, was in the kitchen entertaining a number of her girl friends. The girls saw me arrive at the house and they heard me play, but they were too bashful or coy to join me in the living room. All except one. A tall girl, with lovely long hair, came into the living room, leaned her elbow on the top of the piano and, though she did not say very much, obviously enjoyed listening and watching. I do not remember our conversation, though I am sure we exchanged some words, but I was sufficiently impressed to ask Wolfe Kelman about her when I saw him on the street a few days later. "Oh, Laura Saxe?" he replied. "She's very nice, but I believe she has a boyfriend."

Nevertheless, I hoped I would see her again. And see her again I did. One day, as I crossed Markham Street from our dormitory to the academic building, Laura was walking down the street with another girl. I was bold enough to stop and say hello. Laura explained that she was on her way home from school, the Central Commerce Collegiate. Happy to have met her again, I made a mental note of the time of day.

Obviously, with all the letters I was writing to friends and relatives, I often had to buy postage stamps at the post office in a drug store on College Street, south of the yeshiva. So I had a rational alibi for frequent trips down Markham Street, if someone was nosy enough to ask. And even when I had no stamps to buy, I might still have to go to the mail box to mail my letters. If I timed myself judiciously, my trip to the mail box or the post office coincided with Laura walking past, if she chose that way as her route home. I could still pretend that we were meeting purely by chance, of course, and walk down the street together with her. We got to know each other a little better that way during the following weeks. I was wondering whether she still had a boyfriend. But how could I ask?

While my timidity hampered my progress on the field of romance, no impediments slowed the advance of my studies. I was doing well. My study partner was Joel Litke, who had been one of the more advanced scholars at the yeshiva in London. I derived immense benefit from studying with a more experienced student and I tried hard to keep up with him. Despite our reverence and appreciation for Rabbi Price as a scholar, and as our teacher and benefactor, Joel and I preserved a measure of independence and objectivity. We paid a courtesy visit to Rabbi Price's political antagonist, Rabbi Jacob Kamenetsky. We wanted to show that our respect for an outstanding Torah scholar of the Lithuanian school transcended politics. Our courtesy call was intended to make a statement that, although we were loyal disciples of Rabbi Price, we had not lost our admiration for a noted scholar from the school whose approach to Talmud had guided our studies in London. Rabbi Kamenetsky received us graciously and showed a friendly interest in our background, our studies, and our future hopes. Although Rabbi Price neither criticized nor commended us for our visit, I am sure he understood our message.

Joel Litke and I belonged to the highest class in the yeshiva, and enjoyed a close personal relationship with Rabbi Price, who taught our Talmud class every day. Actually, Rabbi Price, on his level, studied along with us. While he resolved our difficulties, we shared questions and listened to his observations and comments on the text that occasionally grew into elaborate discourses.

The rabbi had every reason to be satisfied and proud. Acting independently, without the support of the official community structure, he had been able to obtain the release of all these religious students. He had ventured right into the lion's den, the Department of Immigration in Ottawa, where he had successfully confronted F. C. Blair, the director of the department, who had steadfastly resisted the entry of Jewish immigrants. Rabbi Price appealed to Mr. Blair's devout Christian sentiments in pleading for the admission of young Jewish scholars. Impressed by Rabbi Price, whose appearance and bearing conjured up the image of a Biblical patriarch or prophet, Blair yielded.

Although the leaders of the Canadian Jewish Congress have disputed Rabbi Price's version of the events, as I have already mentioned, it was clearly the rabbi's recollection that the official Jewish establishment had not shared his enthusiasm for making the release of yeshiva students a priority. Jewish communal leaders were cautious, mindful of the precarious position of the Jewish minority in a society still rife with anti-Semitism. They did not want to appear as the champions of foreigners who were held in camps because of their alleged connections with the enemy, Germany. They were on safer ground when pressing for the release of engineers, farmers, and skilled workers who might be helpful to the Canadian war effort. What could young students of Torah contribute? Perhaps the rabbi gloated a little, having succeeded against the odds, without the support or endorsement of the official Jewish community. His yeshiva had truly become a place of serious scholarship.

The rabbi conceived the idea of a learned journal to be published by the yeshiva and he wanted me to assist him in preparing the first issue, which appeared in September 1942. I contributed an article on *Teshuvah*—the theological concept of return or repentance. My article was pretty heavy going. It was a deep philosophical treatise based on my Musar ideology. When I occasionally read it again, I chuckle with satisfaction and smile at the ponderous language and sentence structure that reflect my German linguistic origins. Rabbi Price had asked his friend, the well-known Jewish writer and journalist David Rome, to edit my article. I remember Mr. Rome's comment that came with his flood of editorial pencil marks: "I am black, but beautiful," he quoted from the *Song of Songs*. He praised the content of my article, but had to work very hard to translate my elevated vocabulary and convoluted sentences into language that an ordinary person would be able to read.

Rabbi Price's own article, which bears traces of my efforts to translate it into English from the Rabbi's Yiddish, was an interesting homily on the release of the Torah students from captivity and on the great blessings that their sacred studies would bring to the community.

Unfortunately, only two additional issues of the journal appeared in the following years. I have a contribution in both of them. I worked on the first issue during the late spring. To see my name and my thoughts in print, only six months after my arrival, must also have helped to raise my spirits.

In the background, there was still Laura and our frequent meetings on Markham Street. Was it folly to think of her?

Chapter *FOUR*

Niagara Falls

MY WEEKS WERE FULL and time was slow. Spring yielded to summer. The war raged. Japan stretched its tentacles across the Pacific islands. The Axis was near the zenith of its power. On the Russian front, the Germans continued to advance. America was mobilizing its potential. Dreadful apprehensions haunted me. I choked on the news in the press or on radio.

Suddenly, excitement struck. Kurt had a few weeks leave from the United States army. He and his new wife, Beckie, whom I knew only from letters, pictures, and newspaper clippings, were on their way to visit me. By car! How exciting! With the help of Mr. Margolis, the yeshiva secretary, I made all necessary arrangements for my brother's visit. We would have so much to talk about. What did he think had happened to our parents and Margot? How is the war going, now that America is a belligerent? How is life in the United States? I was anxious to meet Beckie, whom Kurt had always described in glowing terms.

Then, unexpectedly a telephone call came for me from Niagara Falls, New York. Trouble. Although Kurt was a soldier travelling in a United States army uniform, he still had to show documents to cross the border into Canada. He was not yet an American citizen, even though the army had drafted him, and therefore he was not eligible to enter Canada. Naturally, my status as a released internee, still technically a German citizen, barred me from entry to the United States, even as a visitor. However, as a humanitarian gesture, the Canadian border officials agreed to let me meet my brother in the Canadian customs post, right on the Rainbow Bridge. "Come tomorrow, as soon as you can!" I was frantic. I cannot recall whether I got to Niagara Falls by train, by bus, or by a combination of both. Before I left, some of my Toronto yeshiva friends urged me to call on the Luwish family in Niagara Falls, an observant Jewish family who would welcome a visitor, especially a yeshiva student, into their home for a kosher meal or any other assistance that was needed.

My new sister-in-law, Beckie, as a native-born American carrying the required documentation, had no trouble crossing the border into Canada. She picked me up at the station and took me to the Rainbow Bridge. High above the Niagara River, at the border between Canada and the United States, Kurt and I had an emotional reunion. We had not seen each other since I left Germany on January 26, 1939. Three years and a few months is not a terribly long time, but to us it had seemed like an eternity. So much happened to both of us and so much had happened to the world. The uncertain fate of our parents, our sister, and other relatives heightened the intensity of our meeting. Added to this was the frustration that, after driving all the way from Georgia, Kurt was allowed only this one brief opportunity to spend time with me. He had so much wanted to come to Toronto and exercise the responsibility of an older brother by ascertaining that, after the vicissitudes of internment, I was now being properly cared for in my new home. When our allotted time was over, Kurt returned to their hotel on the New York side, while Beckie and I spent a little more time together in Niagara Falls, Ontario. Then she drove me to the home of the Luwish family and we said good-bye.

Mrs. Luwish and her older daughter, Claire, who was about twenty years old, were at home and insisted that I not only have dinner with them but stay overnight so that I could see Niagara Falls properly. As a recently arrived refugee, I deserved a break, they suggested. Mr. Luwish was away on business, but would return soon. Claire, a fine-looking young lady, took me for a walk to the falls. She was a gracious person who spoke fluent English with an eastern-European accent. She told me that she was engaged to a young man in Toronto, Naftali Green, whose father was a loyal follower of Rabbi Price. She also said that her younger sister, Sally, would soon be home from work and would join us on our walk. Sally would look after me for the rest of my stay and I would like her very much, she assured me.

The Luwish family had come to Canada just shortly before the war. They were *Galitzianer* from Kolomeia, an area that had vacillated politically and culturally between Poland, Austria, and Germany. The Luwish parents spoke the kind of German-Yiddish typical of Galicia. Mr. Luwish made a living from rural trade and had done reasonably well for a new immigrant. They were down-to-earth, hospitable, and traditionally religious people.

Claire had not promised too much. Sally caught up soon with us, parked the 1926 Ford that she drove with amazing expertise—for many years I would tease her by referring to the car as a 1924 model while she adamantly maintained that it was a 1928—and then walked up to us and offered me her hand. I was floored—to use the colloquial expression. I thought she was the most beautiful girl that I had ever seen.

Sally was friendly, sweet, and coquettish, and volunteered to be my guide and companion in Niagara Falls. She spoke English without the trace of an accent and appeared to be intelligent, informed, and thoughtful. Surprising for her age of about eighteen years, she was also mature; she understood the problems facing a newcomer like myself, appreciated my background, and—to make me even more comfortable—she occasionally switched to an impeccable German, which had been the language of instruction in the school she had attended before coming to Canada. Before we had a chance to get to know each other, Sally set out the parameters of our friendship: she told me that she was pledged, if not formally engaged, to another young man from Toronto, who was serving in the Canadian army and was now stationed near Winnipeg. His name was Nat Garnick, and she loved him and planned to marry him after the war. I guess she knew how attractive she was and did not want to cause complications.

Sally was able to take some time off from work to keep me company over the next few days. She easily persuaded me to extend my visit, first by one more day, and then over Shabbat, so that we could travel back to Toronto together. We would be going by boat; at the time, a popular marine link connected Toronto and Port Dalhousie. Sally was going to visit her fiancée's family and wanted me to meet her future sister-in-law, Ruth Garnick, who—Sally had decided— would be a great friend for me.

The next few days were paradise. The weather was warm and sunny. Sally served me breakfast on the porch and we walked together through the beautiful parks and gardens bordering the Niagara river. She knew the area well and was eager to show me her favourite places, except one which, she said, was a secret spot for her and Nat exclusively. We talked and talked; she wanted to hear all about my parents, my family, and my background. She had a remarkable intuitive understanding for my feelings as a new person in Toronto; she reassured me that my life was just beginning to unfold and that I was a really great guy. Sally talked about her family, her childhood in Europe, her life in Niagara Falls, and her friends. She had a very good voice and enjoyed entertaining me with her songs. I just loved her rendition of "The White Cliffs of Dover," the beautiful wartime song looking ahead to the time "when the lights go on again, all over the world." I asked her to sing for me again and again.

I was ripe for the encounter. I could feel myself stepping out from the shadows and into the sunshine. After the masculine worlds of internment camps and yeshivas, I welcomed feminine gentleness and warmth. Sally touched my soul. The inner drought, the inability to feel deeply, the grayness of my world that had bothered me since my release, was finally over. The crust melted. I felt alive again. I fully believe that Sally understood what she was doing for me. I knew our attraction was a mutual one; she, too, enjoyed my company, my musings and philosophizing, my reminiscences and hopes. She found me interesting, sometimes amusing, and stimulating. She was relaxed, carefree, her natural self. She trusted me. She wanted me as a friend.

I remember our return to Toronto very clearly. The sun was shining as we sat in adjoining deck chairs on the steamship. Floating on Lake Ontario, we felt disconnected from the real world as if we were sailing on a private ocean. We talked and were silent together. We were happy and melancholy, knowing our illusion would soon dissolve. The Toronto skyline hove into sight. Ruth Garnick was waiting dockside.

Sally, who moved to Toronto shortly afterwards, introduced me to the Garnick family, hearty, plain, hospitable people, with a large number of relatives. Mr. and Mrs. Max Garnick lived above their furniture store on Queen Street West. Like most soldiers' parents, they were worried about their son in the army. Actually, they were the first non-Orthodox family that I had met in Toronto.

Ruth Garnick was a beautiful and vivacious person. She had a fine musical talent. Not only did she sing very well, but she had also written and recorded a number of songs that were occasionally heard on the radio. She was open, friendly, and fun-loving, so that her company was always very pleasant. From her mother, a feisty business-woman, she had inherited a streak of practicality and good common sense. Ruth and I soon became friends and her family welcomed me very cordially. Her father, a down-to-earth, hard-working business-man, was skeptical of my plans to become a rabbi: how terrible to have a hundred bosses! He would have gladly offered me a job in his furniture business.

I joined Ruth, Sally, and other friends quite often on Sunday outings or at the Garnick home, where we had pleasant get-togeth-ers and lively parties. I kept Ruth company a few times when she babysat for her relatives. We have remained friends throughout the years. Once Ruth and I made a date to meet in Queen's Park, if the weather was right. The day turned out to be a little drizzly and bleak. Ever the enthusiastic optimist, I showed up at the appointed place and time and, a little damp, waited vainly for Ruth, who had sensibly assumed that the weather had postponed our date.

I have always remained grateful to Sally for having "restored" me. The lustre of our special friendship did not tarnish with the pas-sage of time.

❖

After they married, Nat and Sally appeared to have a glorious life together—happy, prosperous, and sharing many values and interests. His furniture business did not keep Nat from involving himself deeply in the theatre and he produced many plays and musicals in which Sally frequently played and sang starring roles.

Unfortunately, their marriage fell apart in the 1980s and Sally was very unhappy. The lively, glamorous, and carefree young woman who always seemed to skip through life had her problems, her demons, and foibles. Then her health failed—her sister Claire had died of cancer a few years earlier. Now Sally battled a malig-nancy with every means possible and impossible. I tried to be a true friend to her, visiting often, taking her for walks as long as she was able to walk, and comforting her in her despair when she knew death was near. I helped her buy a burial plot near her parents' graves. I sat at her hospital bed during the last stages of her struggle. She promised that if it was possible to communicate from the other world, she would be in touch with me. I dream of her once in a while. She always looks as she did in death, pale and ethereal. Then I dispel the morbid mood by looking at two beautiful portraits of Sally as a young girl. She had instructed her children to give these two portraits to me after her death.

Chapter *FIVE*

Laura

I WAS A COWARD. I did not have the courage to ask her the question. I dreaded that she might refuse, that she might answer, "Sorry, but I really don't want to go out with you."

My "accidental" meetings with Laura Saxe on her way home from Commerce—short for Central Commercial Collegiate—had become more frequent. I felt attracted to the fine-looking girl, tall, athletic as she walked, with dark blonde hair falling to her shoulders in gentle waves, one of them decorating her shapely forehead. She was a religious girl, with a good Jewish education, lighthearted, and seemingly pleased with our casual rendezvous. But would she want to go out with me?

Why was I so afraid of being rejected? By the end of the summer 1942, I should have felt much more self-confident. The circumstances of my life were definitely improving. I was well adjusted to the yeshiva. I corresponded with friends and relatives. I often visited the Garnick home on Queen Street. My fears and uncertainties derived from the world situation, not from any feelings of inadequacy or inferiority—from my worries about my parents and my sister and about the course of the war. Even in the news from the battlefronts, we were starting to see signs that the long string of defeats and reverses might be coming to an end. Was the balance of victories and losses beginning to shift in our favour? Or was it wishful thinking?

Finally, one afternoon in October, after I had accompanied Rabbi Price to the funeral of a yeshiva supporter, I asked Laura the question that I had so often rehearsed in my mind, but had not had the courage to utter: "Would you like to meet me this coming Shabbat afternoon? We could go together to the Royal Ontario Museum." Wonder of wonders! She said yes. She seemed happy that I had asked her. Our date was set for Saturday, October 17.

Laura's home was on Dundas Street, just west of Bathurst. It was a beautiful Shabbat afternoon. I walked down Bathurst Street from

College Street, and there was Laura coming to meet me, right on time, as we had arranged. There was no admission charge to the Royal Ontario Museum—the ROM—at that time, so we could go on the Shabbat. I think both of us were relaxed. Laura talked about school and her friends, while I talked about my family and my worries, about the yeshiva, and about all the other thoughts that occupied my mind. After viewing the museum exhibits, neither of us wanted to go home. So we turned north, and walked and walked— and walked. It seems fantastic that we reached the intersection of Eglinton and Yonge before we turned south again on a meandering route home. We must have walked more than seven miles! Had Laura always cherished a suppressed love for walking and exploring neighbourhoods—or did she enjoy my company so much? I didn't know; but when I brought her home many hours later and invited her to see a movie with me in a few days, she said yes without hesitation.

So it began. We no longer relied on chance meetings on Markham Street, but made dates. Most were walking excursions. We had no qualms about walking from Laura's home all the way to High Park, which became one of our favourite destinations. Once— I remember it distinctly, though it seems impossible—we walked along the lakeshore past High Park, then on the far side of Grenadier Pond, to Bloor Street and back to Laura's home. I became an expert on streetcar routes and on the park lands of Toronto. Nor did we neglect some of the finer forms of recreation. I took Laura to see one of my favourite operas, Verdi's *Il Trovatore*, at Massey Hall. If we met in the evening, I might accompany Laura to the library, and possibly help her with school work—she had a little trouble with French and composition—or we might take a walk on city streets. Often we returned past midnight, definitely too late for a yeshiva student.

Laura asked me to write a page in her autograph book. My entry, dated December 28, 1942, and adorned with a Hebrew verse on its four corners, reflects a little sadness and resignation. Would I eventually lose this friend, too? It also reflects the state of my English.

> Even when the road of life is stony, leading over
> rough ground, through wild deep ravines, and is
> wrapped in the dark shadows of thick forests—
> there will always be some bright patches of

sunlight interspersed with it.
And to a good companion on such a sunlit stretch,
I dedicate this page as a souvenir—
for who knows when the crossroad will turn up?

I introduced Laura to the Garnick family. On Sunday afternoons, we sometimes joined Sally, Ruth, Nat, if he was in Toronto, and other friends, or spend time within the growing social circle of yeshiva students and their female friends.

Laura and I were in love. Her parents were not enthusiastic. Philip and Eva Saxe were fine, hard-working people, observant, religious Jews. They had come from Poland to Montreal, where they had done well in the millinery business. Laura's mother was artistically skilled and her father was very handy with tools of all kinds. He had very much wanted to live in *Eretz Yisrael*, the Land of Israel, or Palestine, as it was then known. So, when Laura was still a toddler, her parents had taken her and her older brother, Eli, to Palestine, where the family hoped to settle. However, the young children were never able to adjust to the climate.

Forced to return to Canada, Philip Saxe had chosen to settle in Toronto since he felt too embarrassed by the failure of his attempt at aliyah to return to his former community. During the next few years, Laura's father made two more journeys to Palestine to liquidate some holdings, including orchards on Allenby Street in Tel Aviv! When I met Laura, they had opened a grocery store on Dundas Street, near Bathurst, with living quarters behind and above the store. They had acquired a little residential real estate and were generous supporters of the Eitz Chaim Talmud Torah, which Laura had attended. They had even donated a *Sefer Torah* to this institution. Mr. Saxe spent most of his time studying the Talmud or other sacred books.

Laura's parents had serious reservations about me. Who was this young man from Germany who monopolized their daughter's time? How could they be sure about him? Did he have family? Who were they? He had been in Dachau—had the Nazis performed medical experiments on him? They had better hopes for their daughter.

Yet Laura was not to be dissuaded. All she wanted was to make me happy, she said, and she meant it. So her parents tolerated our relationship. After all, I was a yeshiva student and Rabbi Price thought very highly of me. On the other hand, could they trust Rabbi Price? Mr. Saxe was an adherent of Rabbi Kamenetsky...

During this time, my routine at the yeshiva was occasionally enhanced by interesting and challenging activities in the community. For a few weeks, I substituted for a teacher at the Hebrew school of the Beach Hebrew Institute, a synagogue in the east end of Toronto. I spent two weeks in Hamilton filling in for a teacher at the Talmud Torah. Some very poetic and romantic letters to Laura show how much I missed her during this period of separation.

I once made an appearance on the *Jewish Hour*, which was broadcast weekly on CHML Hamilton. I accompanied Rabbi Price to the studio in Hamilton and he spoke in Yiddish while I added some remarks in English. It was the first time I had travelled on the new Queen Elizabeth Way, Canada's first superhighway, although wartime restrictions limited the speed to 40 miles an hour.

Another highlight of my pre-rabbinic career was a religious service I conducted for Jewish soldiers at Camp Borden, a Canadian army base near Barrie, Ontario. Considering that my previous contact with Canadian soldiers had been as a prisoner, you may empathize with my feeling of closure and vindication. The shame of having been imprisoned as an enemy alien had become irrelevant—just picture me being driven by a uniformed lady driver in a fine army vehicle!

A small synagogue on Oxford Street applied to the yeshiva for a Torah reader for the Sabbath morning services. My training in Köln-Mülheim had equipped me to accept the position. The financial compensation for my weekly preparations was minimal, but I learned how a small congregation works, how it relies on benefactors and participants. I also developed a taste for the whiskey that was served, in large glasses, at the kiddush, the convivial collation that follows the Shabbat prayers.

Kurt and Beckie, my brother and my sister-in-law, were not permanently dissuaded by their futile attempt to visit me in 1942; they did not give up. In April 1943, they drove up from Georgia again to visit me. By this time, my brother had become an American citizen and had no trouble at the border. Their visit to Toronto included a wonderful Pesach seder that the yeshiva allowed us to celebrate together in my room. I introduced Laura to Kurt and Beckie. Together we spent a memorable evening at the home of the Garnick family. Kurt played the piano magnificently; Ruth Garnick, who had already performed professionally and recorded a number of her own songs, entertained us with her beautiful voice, and Beckie enthralled everyone with her fabulous southern accent.

Their next visit would be for my wedding!

Chapter *SIX*

The University of Toronto

RABBI PRICE HAD A NEW IDEA: he encouraged his students who were planning to enter the rabbinate to pursue a university education along with their studies for ordination. Perhaps he was impressed, more than he allowed himself to admit, by American seminaries, at which the combination of academic and rabbinic training had become the norm. Rabbi Abraham Kelman, whom the rabbi had ordained before I arrived in Toronto, had enrolled in the University of Toronto after his ordination. A higher education and an academic degree seemed important for a rabbi in a modern congregation whose members were bound to include university graduates.

I needed little persuasion. I did not regret in the least that I had dedicated the past five years to the study of Torah. On the contrary, the study of Torah had been fulfilling and had given my life meaning. But I also felt a strong desire for the kind of academic learning that I would have pursued in Germany if my life had been "normal." My roommate Albert and his cousin Henry had entered the University of Toronto in the fall of 1942 to study mathematics and physics. I was a little envious when they talked about university life.

Thus, in the summer of 1943, I applied for admission to the University of Toronto, together with a number of other yeshiva students, all former internment camp inmates. The group included Albert Pappenheim and Joel Litke, who were eventually ordained with me, and Joseph Faust and Ernest Meyer, who had different plans for their future.

The tuition fee for the first year of an honours course in the Faculty of Arts at University College was $200. That first year, it was provided by the yeshiva. I was able to pay the fee for subsequent years myself, even though the fees were raised to $300.

Fortunately, a copy of my German *Abitur*—the high school matriculation—was all I needed for admission to the university. The document was among the articles I had sent to me from England soon after my arrival in Toronto. Rabbi Price had established a friendly relationship with Professor Samuel Beatty, Dean of the Faculty of Arts—he was appointed chancellor of the university in 1953—whose benevolent concern smoothed problems that might have arisen in our admission procedures.

We chose the four-year honours course in oriental languages, offered by the Department of Oriental Studies, and leading to a Bachelor of Arts degree. In the academic terminology of the period, which emulated the model of British universities, oriental did not refer to the Far East, but to the area the West now calls the Middle East or Near East. The Department of Oriental Studies had an excellent faculty, including such renowned scholars as James Theophile Meek and William R. Taylor. However, except for one solitary course in Mishna offered to fourth-year students, post-Biblical Judaism barely existed as an academic discipline and was not highly appreciated by most of the members of the department.

The yeshiva group, despite quaint religious scruples that seemed to puzzle the faculty members, were warmly welcomed and received a great deal of special attention. Our professors, although impressed by our surprising command of English, evinced great sympathy and concern for us and were anxious to alleviate any difficulties, including language problems, that we might encounter in adjusting to the university. I became very friendly with some of my teachers.

As yeshiva students, we were granted one important concession: in view of our familiarity with Hebrew, we did not have to take the otherwise mandatory course of first-year Hebrew; we started with the second year. This seemed reasonable, as all of us could understand Biblical Hebrew texts. Nevertheless, it was not easy because we were strangers to a great deal of the grammatical terminology and to the concepts of Hebrew morphology and syntax at the university level. The greatest benefit of starting Hebrew at the second-year level was that it enabled us to eventually take both of the fourth-year Hebrew courses offered in alternate years by Professor William Taylor, who was then the head of the department and later became principal of University College. Thus, in my third and fourth years, I took his justly renowned final-year course in Biblical poetry, as well as his course in Wisdom literature. Professor Taylor was a great teacher and these courses gave me a profound understanding of Biblical literature. I was also privileged to study Hebrew language, and Bible and Near Eastern history with Professor Meek.

If I had to nominate the best years of my life, that distinction would go to the years I spent at the University of Toronto—my years as an undergraduate, as a graduate student, and as a junior member of the faculty. I was in my element. I loved my studies—the lectures, the new knowledge, the research, the essays, and the spirit of inquiry, the growth of understanding, the atmosphere of the academic world and its learned journals, the exciting realm of the library stacks, and even the tests and examinations, in which I usually excelled. I studied Arabic and Aramaic, Bible and post-biblical texts, languages and archaeology with Professors Stuart McCollough, Fred Winnett, and Ron Williams—the latter an outstanding linguist and Egyptologist—in addition to my studies with Professors Taylor and Meek. Courses in philosophy, English literature, and psychology rounded out my university curriculum.

Since the number of honour students in the department was relatively small, many of my courses were really seminars, allowing for a close relationship between faculty and students. I felt I was truly a member of a learning community. I worked very hard, but with great success. After the final examinations of each year, students were graded in categories such as First Class Honours or Second Class Honours, and then ranked individually within each class. In each of my four years, I stood first in First Class Honours, despite the close competition of Albert Pappenheim, who always stood second in First Class Honours. For my efforts in the second year, I won the Lyle Silver Medal for studies in oriental languages.

My workload was substantially increased when Rabbi Price appointed Albert Pappenheim and me to the yeshiva teaching staff. For the next five years, I taught one of the higher classes at the yeshiva, all boys, on Sunday mornings and four afternoons each week. I now earned a salary and, for the first time in my life, was financially independent.

I remained at the university beyond my four undergraduate years. After I received a Bachelor of Arts degree in 1947—also the year of my ordination as rabbi—I combined my rabbinical position at the Adath Israel Congregation with a two-year graduate program leading to a Master's degree in semitics. I was appointed reader and assistant lecturer in the department, as well. I taught courses in Hebrew, Arabic, and Hebrew history, set and marked final exams, read essays by students, and substituted for professors on sabbatical. As part of the university community, I also continued my own studies. I successfully submitted my first learned article to the prestigious Biblical journal *Vetus Testamentum*.[1]

Finally, the growth of my congregation and Professor Taylor's insistence, as head of the department, that the time had come for me to decide whether I was going to be a congregational rabbi or an academic, forced me to make a decisive career choice. The synagogue won. Naturally, I have often wondered whether I made the right choice. I know I could have been successful in the academic world. However, I sensed the isolation from "real" life that confines professors of ancient literature and history to the proverbial ivory tower. In my congregation, small as still it was, I could make an impact on people, on a community, on lives. So I made an existential commitment. I have no remorse, except that sometimes I do wonder with a bit of sadness what might have been waiting for me on the path not chosen.

Still, university had opened new vistas for me and had a liberating effect on my thinking. I learned to understand and appreciate Biblical texts through the textual and historical criticism that were part of the academic approach to Scripture. Confronting the so-called higher criticism may have been uncomfortable for an Orthodox yeshiva student, but it led to valuable new insights and to a greater appreciation of our sacred texts. I learned critical thinking and acquired a new set of concepts to apply to the Bible and to other fields of study. Indeed, I believe that my effectiveness in the rabbinate as a conduit of ideas owes a great deal to my university training. Besides, it completed my attainment of writing and speaking skills in the English language.

At the same time, however, I had to wrestle with the contradictions in my system of thought and belief. There was an obvious clash between modern Biblical and historical scholarship on one side, and the accepted theological axioms which ruled the faith of the yeshiva, on the other. This conflict was not easily resolved, nor did it cease

[1]*Vetus Testamentum* Vol. IV, No. 3 (1954)

after I left university. In the course of time, it led to a restructuring of my personal theology. I probably would not have embraced Conservative Judaism as the framework of my Jewish ideology had it not been for the insights I received at the university.

I have also often wondered whether Rabbi Price knew what we were studying at the university. He probably assumed that our university studies were a valuable supplement to our yeshiva curriculum. I am sure he had heard of higher criticism and textual criticism, but he probably assumed that these subjects were secondary to our acquisition of the academic credibility that he associated with some of his learned friends on the faculty of the Jewish Theological Seminary, such as Professor Saul Lieberman, whose methods and scholarship impressed him. I believe it was because Rabbi Price appreciated modern methods of research that he diligently consulted variant manuscripts while working on his commentaries on, and critical editions of, several classical rabbinical works, such as the *Sefer Hasidim* and the *Sefer Mitzvot Gedolot*.

After morning prayers and breakfast in the yeshiva, I hurried to the university, either walking along College Street or taking the streetcar if I was in a rush. In the afternoon, I returned to the yeshiva to study with Rabbi Price. We concentrated on the tractate Shabbat. When the time came to start preparing for ordination, we studied the tractate *Hullin* to acquire the background knowledge of the sources for the dietary laws. Traditionally, a candidate for the rabbinate has to master the laws of Kashruth in order to qualify. The next step in our preparation was, therefore, the study of the *Yoreh De'ah*,[2] the part of the *Shulchan Aruch* that deals with the dietary laws and other ritual regulations with which the rabbi has to be familiar in order to resolve questions of Jewish law. Later in the afternoon, I taught my class in the yeshiva for three hours. I used the remainder of the day to do my work for the university, and for the private Hebrew lessons that I gave up as soon as I could.

I was quite busy. To my regret, I was unable to take part in any extracurricular activities at the university, or in the social whirl of campus life. I missed the opportunity to become acquainted with students outside our department. During peak periods of the aca-

---

[2]This section of the *Shulchan Aruch*, the Standard Code of Jewish Law, is a traditional prerequisite for rabbinic ordination.

demic year, such as the weeks before and during annual examinations, we even had to curtail yeshiva studies. Then, during the long academic vacations, we concentrated again on study at the yeshiva.

Despite my busy schedule, however, I found time for Laura and my other friends. I remember a wonderful surprise birthday party for Albert Schild and me. Not only do we share the same last name, but Albert's birthday is only six days before mine. Laura and several of her girl friends were the hostesses and the party was held at the Naimans' on Major Street. By this time, my relationship with Laura had progressed. We were not formally engaged but, as we used to say in those days, we were "going steady." Another highlight of our courtship was a trip to Niagara Falls.

Some of Laura's friends invited us to join a new Zionist club for young people. We liked the members and enjoyed the ambiance of the club rooms in the Zionist building at 651 Spadina Avenue. Dr. Mark Zimmerman, our mentor, was a dentist by profession and a man of varied interests and hobbies. He was truly inspired by a passionate love for Zionism and the Jewish people, and made a great impact on my political thinking as a Jew. Dr. Zimmerman remained our dentist for many years, until he retired from his profession.

At first, the club had no name. I suggested the name Club Tarna, a Hebrew-sounding word made up by the numeral 651—the house number on Spadina Avenue—in Hebrew letters. My suggestion was warmly received and the name was adopted. Laura and I made some new friends at Club Tarna and the club premises gave us a place to go to when we did not feel like walking. It gave me also some experience in the running of an organization. I did not realize at the time that it was a valuable preparation for an aspect of the practical rabbinate. However, Club Tarna was a secular Zionist club. Laura was an alumna of the B'nei Akivah movement, the youth organization of religious Mizrachi Zionism, and I also felt more at home in the Mizrachi ideology. I had left behind my ancient allegiance to the non-Zionist Agudat Israel long ago.

Eventually, some friends and I founded Yeshurun, a Zionist social, religious, and cultural organization for young men within the framework of Hapoel Hamizrachi, the activist branch of the religious Zionist family. I served as its president for several years after our marriage. Yeshurun was a wonderful environment for us and created lasting bonds of friendship.

I finished my first year of university in the spring of 1944. The fortunes of war in Europe and in the Pacific had turned in our favour. A victorious end was in sight. Laura and I were thinking of marriage. Sally and Nat Garnick had married in March. My salary as a teacher at the yeshiva was $25 a week, and soon rose to $27.50. Private lessons provided a little extra income. And Laura had left school and started a job as a secretary. Even Laura's parents were showing signs of impatience. They asked, "How long can you walk around in High Park?"

Chapter *SEVEN*

Our Wedding

W<small>E SET THE DATE</small>: D<small>ECEMBER</small> 31, 1944. We found the place: the Kiever Shule on Denison Square, a picturesque old synagogue. It was to be an afternoon wedding, the ceremony to be followed by a sweet-table reception. But as Laura and I were walking down Markham Street—we may have been looking at a flat to rent—she turned to me and said, "You know, you have never proposed to me!"

She was right. There had been no specific point in our relationship when we had formally resolved to marry. We took it for granted. We had told each other many times that we belonged together. No doubt, we were becoming impatient. I wanted to build my new life together with Laura. Laura wanted to make me happy. Eventually, obedient to our own desires and to the gentle urging of her parents, through the pressures that came from knowing what was right and proper, we had begun to plan our life. But I had never "popped the question." How could I, ever the romantic, omit the formal proposal from the script of our romance as it was about to culminate in marriage after nearly two years. Wedding arrangements were already being made! So I had to propose retroactively. On the spot—although without getting down on my knees—I stopped, faced Laura, and solemnly asked her: "Do you want to marry me?" She said yes.

Actually, in hindsight, it was not such an appropriate time to get married. The war in Europe had just taken a decisive turn. The Allies had finally invaded the continent, an event we had long been waiting for. Ever since the apparently irresistible German advance into the Soviet Union had been stopped and—miracle of miracles!—had actually been reversed, the Allied nations had been waiting for the opening of the second front. The Soviets had been pleading for an Allied invasion of western Europe to relieve the pressure on the forces of the USSR.

Finally, in June 1944, the hour had struck. The Allies, though suffering horrible losses on the beaches of Normandy, finally secured and expanded their bridgehead and started their advance. Perhaps, we thought, in a few months, we would know whether the terrible rumours of a genocide of Jews were true. Why marry now, when the war might soon be over and peace change our lives? Perhaps my parents and sister had survived. But we did not really want to wait any longer. Although hopes for victory over the Germans had grown to near-certainty, we could not assume that this victory would come quickly. The war in the Pacific was still drawn out and bitter, despite dramatic American victories.

So we made preparations, just as the Allies were about to face their last fierce test in the Battle of the Bulge, the desperate German counterattack in the Ardennes Forest. The Allied forces on the continent were in grave peril, but I was optimistic. I believed the Germans would not be able to turn the tide in the west after their huge losses in the east. I had faith in an Allied victory, even if it was delayed.

It was not easy making all the necessary preparations for the wedding. Laura was working; I was busy with university and the yeshiva. I had also taken a giant step toward my rabbinical vocation: I was the acting rabbi on the High Holidays at the Berkeley Street Synagogue, a rather large synagogue in East Toronto, where a substantial Jewish population lived in the area around Parliament Street. My teacher's salary was essential to our plans. Above all, we had to find a place to live and wartime conditions had created a housing shortage. Our search led to a two-room flat, consisting of a kitchen and a bedroom, at 205 Markham Street, just around the corner from Laura's parents and close enough to the yeshiva. The rent was just right: $25 a month, a quarter of my monthly salary, exactly what a young couple was supposed to spend on accommodations. Our landlords were an elderly couple who lived on the ground floor of the undivided house. Their livelihood depended on the rental income provided by tenants on the upper floor, of which we would occupy a part. The bathroom—there was only one in the house— was shared by all and, it turns out, not all the bathroom users were human. Before the Jewish holidays, a large carp was kept alive in the bathtub so as to provide fresh gefilte fish for the landlady.

Busy as Laura and I were, we had to take time off to get our marriage licence at city hall in downtown Toronto and December 12 was set aside. Older Torontonians will recognize the significance of the date: December 12, 1944. By daybreak, the most severe snowstorm ever recorded in Toronto had paralyzed the city. Public transportation and traffic was forced to a standstill. Streets were impassable. Most offices and businesses could not open. Of course, it was impossible to get to city hall. People were marooned in their homes. A little later in the morning I waded through almost hip-high drifts to College Street, where the last streetcars had levelled the snow on the tracks a little before giving up, allowing pedestrians to follow a trail on the main streets. The university library was open, although it was nearly empty except for some dogged footsloggers like myself and a few intrepid souls who made their way down Yonge Street on skis.

Undaunted, Laura and I went to city hall a few days later, when the city had regained a kind of wintry normalcy. We paid our five-dollar fee and got our licence. The process was not without obstacles, however. I was, of course, still technically a German citizen. According to the laws in force at the time, Laura would lose her Canadian citizenship if she married an alien, even though she was born in Canada. Since she was not yet eighteen, her parents had to give consent to her loss of citizenship before the marriage licence could be issued. It was a humiliating embarrassment for me. It also demonstrated the second-class status of women, who could lose their birthright through marriage.

We continued our preparations for our new life together. We bought a kitchen set and bedroom furniture. And an ice-box! What else did we require in our humble home? Yet what a deep change in my life it would be! For the first time in an eternity, I would live in a home again.

On our wedding invitations, my parents, along with Laura's, were named as hosts. I desperately hoped that, although they would not be at our wedding, they would be able to share our happiness when the war was over. In the meantime, Kurt would represent them at our nuptials. Neither Laura nor I had many relatives attending, because wartime conditions made travel difficult. I was happy, therefore, when Kurt and Beckie came up from Georgia, Kurt still resplendent in his United States army uniform. I had missed their wedding two years ago while I was interned in the Canadian refugee camp, but they were here for my marriage to Laura.

Our wedding date had been chosen for several practical reasons. The university would be in recess, Laura would be able to take time off, and it was easier for Kurt to get leave near the end of December. In due course, I would receive another benefit. Canadian tax regulations deemed a taxpayer to be entitled to a married exemption for the entire year as long as he had that status on December 31. The yeshiva had deducted tax payments from my salary, but the marriage exemption now brought my income below the minimum for income tax. I received a full refund of all the tax that had been withheld: $70!

A few days before the wedding, we took pictures in formal cutaways and gowns at the Gilbert studio on College Street. Kurt and Beckie are in the photos, as well as my best man, Albert Schild, my yeshiva roommate, and the maid-of honour, Rhoda Kay, one of Laura's girl friends who married my friend Albert Pappenheim soon after. I was called to the Torah as groom on the Shabbat before the wedding. A drink at the kiddush had affected Kurt's balance a little as we made our way from the yeshiva to Laura's home, where we were to have lunch. The snow was still piled up high on the sidewalks, with a narrow passageway for pedestrians between two high walls of snow. Kurt bumped against the snowy sides a few times as we walked. "I am a disgrace to the United States army!" he lamented.

Cantor Weiss, father of Rabbi Samson Raphael Weiss, the rabbi and spiritual mentor of the Würzburg Teachers' Seminary, came from Ottawa to officiate as cantor at the ceremony. My Würzburg connection was still very significant for me. Rabbi Price was the rabbinical officiant, joined by Rabbi Abraham Kelman, at whose home Laura and I had met, and Rabbi Shlomo Langer, the rabbi of the Kiever Synagogue. It was a happy celebration. Yeshiva students and members of the yeshiva community attended, together with our many personal friends. Several of my university professors were also among our guests.

After a very brief honeymoon—just long enough to attend a New Year's Day showing of the film *The Nutcracker Suite*—Laura and I took up residence in our apartment. The next day, it was back to work for both of us. Fortunately, Laura's mother was generous. Each day after work, Laura would pick up our dinner that Mrs. Saxe had prepared. On most days, Laura only had to make breakfast and prepare sandwiches for me to take to the university. I usually ate my sandwiches in the Hart House coffee shop or the University College common room, sometimes in the company of Ben Friedberg, later

Rabbi Friedberg, and Sarah Edell. Sarah, who later married Rabbi Samuel Schafler, became a good friend. She was also the first teacher I hired for our religious school after I became the rabbi of Adath Israel Congregation.

Married life was a great adventure, even in our modest circumstances. A residence of our own, a home, be it ever so humble and small! It was ours! I worked hard. My second-year course at the university was demanding; Arabic created a new challenge. At the yeshiva, I continued preparing myself for the rabbinate. I taught my class at the yeshiva, and gave private lessons one evening every week. In case I was not busy enough, I had also successfully applied for a part-time job in the field of journalism. I always enjoyed writing and now I was the Toronto social correspondent for the *Canadian Jewish Chronicle*, published in Montreal. Each week I sent in a collection of social notes covering weddings, bar mitzvahs, fundraising parties, and other social events.

After a busy week, Shabbat was a redeeming pause. Instead of spending our free hours on Friday evening and Shabbat afternoon alone together, as Laura and I had been in the habit of doing before we were married, we now either welcomed our friends in our home or visited others. We had become part of a very pleasant circle, consisting of yeshiva students and other young men and women. Some had belonged to Laura's group of friends who had shared their Jewish education or membership in Hashomer Hadati, the Mizrachi youth organization.

Our social circle was rearranging its shape as many of our friends followed our example and got married. New constellations of friendship began to form. Among our closest in the ensuing years were Dr. Morris ("Moe") Weinberg and his wife, Rose, née Naiman, Joe and Shirley Silverberg, Ben and Ruth Laker, Max and Helen Fishbein, and Nat and Sally Garnick. In their company, we traversed the first milestones of marriage—the birth of our children, the launching of our professional or business careers, and our integration into community. For many years, each week began at the end of Shabbat with a phone call to the Silverbergs. We often spent Sunday afternoons in their company, Laura and I with our children, while Shirley and Joe had to wait ten years before Shirley conceived.

Our wedding anniversary, as it coincided with New Year's Eve, was a convenient occasion for a lively celebration. For many years, we enjoyed an annual party with the Silverbergs, the Lakers, the Fishbeins, the Garnicks, and other occasional guests. It was always an evening of imaginative fun and slapstick humour. We really let our hair down and had a fabulous time. Then, the Fishbeins made aliyah to Israel. Our circle started to fray and we drifted apart. Members of my synagogue became our close friends. But beautiful memories linger of these precious friendships that, unlike other friendships of the past, no cruel fate would tear apart. These friends sweetened the years during which I, the accidental immigrant, the yeshiva student, the stateless refugee, became a householder, a member of the community, a Torontonian, a firmly rooted Canadian.

Chapter *EIGHT*

The Lights Go On Again

*I*N SHARP CONTRAST TO THE TRANQUILITY of our domestic scene—
a young couple getting adjusted to married life—world events
rushed forward at a ferocious pace, to constantly changing rhythms
of overlapping beats—flashes of hope eclipsed by peals of fear, signals of triumph expunged by eerie silences. The war in Europe had
entered its final stage—that much was now sure. The Battle of the
Bulge, which had threatened to nullify the victories of the Allied
invasion forces for many anxious days had ended with another, albeit
costly and painful, victory for the American, British, and Canadian
forces. We followed the events with heightened tension and grating
impatience.

The battlefronts were moving into familiar territory: the
advances of the Allied forces were measured by the familiar names of
German towns; Soviet forces clawed back areas where Jewish communities had once flourished. I was enthralled by the names of towns
captured in the west. Cologne fell. On March 7, 1945, the Rhine
bridge at Remagen was captured by the Americans before the
Germans were able to blow it up, enabling the Americans to establish their first bridgehead on the eastern bank of the river. Remagen
evoked memories of ship excursions on the Rhine with my parents…

Where were my parents? Where was my sister? Had they survived? Who would have believed that, in the last months and weeks
of the war in Europe, the Germans would pursue the annihilation of
the Jews with unabated fury, killing as many Jews as they could,
even after all hope for winning the war had evaporated.

Another signal event overshadowed our private lives: President
Roosevelt died on April 23, 1945.

Now the war in Europe was almost over. German armies were
surrendering.

On May 4, German forces surrendered to British Field Marshal Montgomery in northern Germany.

On May 7, all German military forces surrendered to General Eisenhower, the supreme Allied Commander in Europe.

I had finished writing my final Arabic examination at the university. From the confinement of the examination hall, I emerged into the brightness of the day. At the newsstand, the banner headline of the *Toronto Daily Star* trumpeted the news: "GERMANY SURRENDERS!" I felt an electric charge racing through me, an explosion of triumphant joy, of ecstasy. We won! The Nazi beast was slain. Victory! Revenge! The foe who had almost ruined my life, had deprived me of parents, friends, and family, and had made me an exile, was finally defeated. After all the years of despair, defeat, despondency, fear— redemption at last. The arrogant Nazis, the hateful Germans, had been forced to surrender unconditionally. Their defeat was absolute; our victory complete. How sweet revenge would be!

Weeks of confusion and anxiety followed. There was no way yet of finding missing individuals on the continent. The news came through of horrible death camps, of starving, emaciated survivors; of camps set up to gather the dislocated remnants. Fragmentary reports began to indicate that genocidal slaughter had been perpetrated, dimensions of murder too horrible to believe. The reality that was now revealed, little by little, dwarfed our worst fears that had been nourished in past by the occasional reports and rumours trickling through the wartime fog. We groped for a word; there was no vocabulary for such a catastrophe. The meaning of a Greek word of Biblical provenance denoting total consumption by fire was strained to describe the unprecedented: Holocaust.

Hasty attempts were made to reconnect Jewish survivors to the world, to reunite family members, to find relatives in other countries. After a few weeks, we began to hear about the survivors that had been found. When would we—Kurt in Macon, Georgia, and I in Toronto—hear news from our parents, from Margot? Or were they all gone, vanished, lost forever, in the ruins of European Jewry.

Then came the miracle, a telegram from my brother, dated May 30, 1945, at 9:51 am: "MARGOT SAFE IN SWEDEN PHONE US TONIGHT. LOVE KURT."

That morning, Kurt had received a telegram from the director of a refugee camp in Sweden. It was addressed to Kurt Schild, care of the Michael family—Beckie's parents. In one of the last letters that Kurt had been able to send to our parents and Margot in Cologne, Kurt had mentioned Beckie Michael, the girl he had met and about whom he was serious. To write from a United States army camp to our family, whose mail was certainly censored by the Nazis, might expose our parents and sister to extra danger. So Kurt had given them the Michael's home as a return address. Margot had committed that address to memory, holding fast to it through three and a half years of deportation, ghetto, labour camps, and cruel forced marches ahead of the retreating German army. A few days before the end of the war, the Swedish Red Cross had been able to evacuate a few busloads of young Jewish survivors from a death camp in northern Germany and take them to Sweden. There they were housed, fed, and restored to humanity in a refugee camp that Margot would later describe as unbelievably luxurious. As soon as it was possible, Margot had asked the camp director to try to contact Kurt at the remembered address. If he had not married Beckie, Margot reckoned, Beckie or her family might still be able to contact him somehow. But she need not have worried. The Michaels phoned Kurt at Camp Wheeler to give him the electrifying news. "SAVED IN SWEDEN CABLE YOUR ADDRESS," read the telegram.

Kurt replied immediately and sent Margot some money. In her second wire, this time sent to Kurt's home address, Margot first asked, "WHERE IS ERWIN?" Then followed the bad news: Father had died December 21, 1943; Mother's fate and whereabouts were unknown. The last words of the telegram an urgent appeal to let her come to the United States. The news of my father's death reached me on June 4. In our flat at 205 Markham Street, I sat shiva for my father for an hour or so, as prescribed if news of a death comes more than thirty days after its occurrence.

Kurt immediately started to initiate immigration procedures for Margot. It was not easy, although Kurt was able to enlist the help of two Georgia senators and a congressman. Kurt's funds were very limited; he was still in the army. I was not able to contribute very much. But Kurt was determined and fought for our sister. "LEAVING FOR WASHINGTON TOMORROW TO ARRANGE IMMIGRATION DONT WORRY," he cabled her.

Margot's letters following over the next few months told us more about her fate and that of our parents.

Shortly after Kurt had left Germany in April 1940—he was one of the last Jews to leave Germany legally—our parents and Margot were evicted from their home in Cologne-Mülheim and forced to live in a "Jews' house" in Cologne. Since the United States was not yet a belligerent, Kurt was able to maintain postal contact with them. Then came Pearl Harbour, on December 7, 1941, and communications stopped. Margot and our parents were deported to Riga, Latvia, where they lived in one of the most terrible ghettoes. Margot was separated from our parents in the fall of 1943 and survived a number of labour camps. Thus, she was not present when our father perished, but received the news through an intermediary. Mother was sent to another labour camp, from which no survivors returned. There was little hope that she could have survived. Indeed, we were never able to find any trace of her.

Margot was among a group of women who were marched under brutal conditions to the central area of Germany that had remained under Nazi control. Although German authority was falling apart, Margot and her remaining companions might have been liquidated if Swedish intervention had not saved them. Now, there was nothing that Margot wanted more than to join her brothers. Knowing that Kurt was doing everything possible to speed her immigration, she tried to be patient. Living conditions in her refugee camp, she wrote, were excellent. The Swedes did everything possible for the comfort and well-being of the survivors they had rescued. We wrote Margot often and her letters flowed to us and to other relatives and friends as she relished her opportunity to enter our world again.

Gradually, we were able to piece together the scraps of information about our relatives and friends—who was alive and who had died. Among the dead were all the members of the Mohl and Speier-Holstein families who had remained in Germany. Jojo, Heinz, Walter, Hannah, and Martha had been murdered with their parents. My dear friends Ruth and Edith Speier-Holstein...all were gone, with their father, the doctor. There was no one left to bring from Europe. The Simons family had been more fortunate. The parents—the rabbi and his wife—were dead, but their children Martha and Ruth were alive, and my friend Ernst, married meanwhile to Ans, had been liberated from Bergen-Belsen. He had been near death, but recovered. Of my uncles and aunts who had remained in Europe, only Willi and Else Neugarten of Amsterdam survived.

Fortunately, all my uncles and aunts had children who had been able to flee in time.

Despite Kurt's devoted efforts, the application for Margot's admission to the United States proceeded very slowly, straining not only our patience, but also Kurt's financial resources. I could help but little. With the war in the Pacific turning in favour of the Allies, Kurt was discharged from the army and started civilian life in Macon.

At long last, on December 19, 1945, on a cold Shabbat, Kurt stood at dockside in Boston, waiting for the arrival of the ocean liner carrying our precious sister to America where she was to begin a new life at the age of twenty-three. Kurt had to wait a little longer because Margot insisted on waiting for Shabbat to end before disembarking.

The lights had gone on again in Europe. Peace! A destroyed continent was beginning to rebuild, but for Jews, there was nothing left to rebuild. The Jewish world of Europe had vanished. Most of the survivors were in camps, having no homes to which they could return. They had become "displaced persons."

The Jewish people had celebrated a hollow victory. Their new struggle—the struggle for a Jewish state in Palestine—had only begun.

Chapter *NINE*

The Exciting Years

IT WAS NO SURPRISE, BUT EXCITING, nonetheless. Laura was pregnant. When she returned from her medical appointment with the good news, I thought right away of my parents. It was early in 1945; the war was still on and we had not yet heard the news of my parents' death. I had become an uncle a year earlier, when Beckie Schild had given birth to Michael. Now I was about to become a father. And my parents would be instant grandparents, if and when we found them after the war. Alas, my parents would never share the joy of children with us.

For Laura, 18, and me, 24—a young couple, just getting used to living together—pregnancy was a bit scary and awesome. New rules, new symptoms, new responsibilities.

Laura's parents had closed their grocery store a few months after our marriage. They no longer had any reason to remain on Dundas Street, where they lived behind and above their store. They owned a duplex—a house divided into two separate dwellings—on elegant Brunswick Avenue. They had intended to move into the upper duplex apartment, the larger of the two, and arrange for us to live in the lower one, an ideal arrangement in view of Laura's pregnancy. Both apartments, however, were tenant-occupied. Because of the shortage of housing during wartime, there were provincial or municipal regulations for the protection of tenants and it was nearly impossible for a property owner to require a tenant to vacate a rented dwelling unless the tenants wanted to move out. Finally, in July 1945, my parents-in-law got possession of the upper duplex and moved in. They continued their effort to obtain possession of the lower apartment as well.

It was no longer convenient for Laura to pick up dinner at her mother's. The city was hot, and our small flat especially so. To escape from the city and the heat, Laura and I rented a room in a house on Hanlan's Point, part of the Toronto Islands. Toronto is blessed with a complex of islands which protect the harbour and lakefront of the inner city. The islands, delightful for walking and biking, are separated by picturesque lagoons, suitable for boating and other water sports. A ferry service operated by the Toronto Transportation Commission connects the islands to the city. In 1945, the islands, while in a much less developed state than today, were a popular excursion destination that could be reached for the cost of a TTC ticket.

Laura and I joined our friends Henry and Rae Wolf and a number of other young families who had rented rooms in a spacious cottage on Hanlan's Point. We were right on the sandy beach, only a few minutes walk from the ferry docks. We enjoyed a very pleasant stay, relaxing and having fun. It was ideal for Laura and Rae, both of whom were pregnant. Although I grieved for my parents and worried about my sister waiting in Sweden for an American visa, I was less tense than I had been in years and opened my heart to the future, visible in Laura's distended belly. After my vacation ended and I started teaching my class again—yeshiva vacations were short—I could still commute and spend the greater part of each day on the island. On Thursdays, I also visited my mother-in-law and took the Shabbat food she had prepared for us out to the cottage.

Once more the West rejoiced. Two nuclear bombs that exploded over the Japanese cities, Hiroshima and Nagasaki, had ended the war in the Pacific. It was August 1945. World War II was over. My cousin Joe Schild, an American soldier in the Pacific, was safe, although it took several months before Joe and his comrades could come home. His parents were grateful, and so was I.

The summer was over. The High Holidays came. For a second year I preached in the Berkeley Street Synagogue. To prepare and preach sermons for a fairly large congregation was a daunting challenge. Laura had come to term after a normal pregnancy. She had given up her secretarial job a few weeks before. We were waiting. Laura was due. On October 17, celebrating the third anniversary of our first date, we made a visit to High Park, where we had often wandered during our courtship. Laura and I ran down a few gentle hills, hoping that the exercise would hasten the baby's arrival.

It worked. The next day, her labour set in, and her mother took her to Mount Sinai Hospital, then located on Yorkville Avenue. I was at one of my classes at the university when I became a father on October 18, 1945. It was one of the most profound changes in my life. In those days, fathers were considered quite unnecessary in the delivery room and were, in fact, excluded from it. Without my attendance, Dr. Samuel Norris delivered a healthy baby boy, weighing seven pounds and sporting a full head of hair. I visited the hospital within the first few hours of our son's life. Laura was fine and the baby was beautiful. The same day, I kept an appointment for a routine medical examination at the University Health Service. For the first time a slight congenital heart murmur—"well compensated"—was diagnosed. I could not believe it and attributed the abnormality to the excitement of becoming a father.

The conflicts of fatherhood were instantaneous. The academic year—my third—was only a month old when our son was born. I had to squeeze hospital visits into my busy schedule of study and teaching. Fortunately, Laura had enough company. One day Sally and her sister-in-law, Ruth Nefsky, came, both visibly pregnant. The medical custom of the time was to keep new mothers in the hospital for at least a week, so the *bris* took place in the hospital. A modern, large-scale circumcision ceremony was unknown then; the hospital authorities severely restricted attendance. Chazan Wladowsky, one of the old-timers in the community, was the *mohel*.

Laura and I had decided that our children would receive Hebrew names that could be used as English names as well. We did not agree with the general practice of giving a child one name in Hebrew and an unrelated name in English. We liked the name Daniel for our son, but also I wanted him to bear my father's name, Naftali in Hebrew, Herman in German. So we named our son Naftali Daniel in Hebrew, and registered him as Herman Daniel. But we always called him Daniel.

It was difficult to manage our lives as parents with a very young baby in our small flat on Markham Street. We were greatly relieved when Laura's parents finally got possession of the lower duplex on Brunswick Avenue and we were able to move into the luxury of a ground floor apartment with a large veranda on an avenue shaded by huge chestnut trees. Our apartment consisted of a large living room in front, two bedrooms, and a kitchen. Behind the kitchen, a so-called "summer kitchen"—an unheated enclosed space for storage—added more space. The telephone found its place on a little table which stood in a nook half-way down the long hallway leading from the front door to the kitchen.

Having Laura's parents in the upstairs apartment was a great convenience in keeping house and raising our infant son. For a while, we let the front room to a roomer, so that we could enjoy a little extra income from space that we did not yet really require.

A few years later, after Judith was born on October 8, 1947, and Naomi on May 15, 1952, we exchanged apartments with my mother-in-law. My father-in-law had died on May 29, 1950. We moved upstairs to the spaciousness of six rooms on two floors. As rabbi of the growing Adath Israel Congregation, I needed the additional space and comfort. But in 1946, we were happy with the four rooms on the ground floor.

Our first out-of-town visitor was cousin Joe Schild from New York. Cousin Joe, weary from the battles in the Pacific, had at last come home. While trying to adjust to civilian life again, he decided to visit us. We were happy to welcome him in Toronto.

My only cousin on my father's side, Joe was indeed more than a war hero for us. He had saved his parents and my brother from Germany. Joe was still a bachelor. He loved to play with Daniel, who was just about six months old and seemed to get pleasure out of scratching Joe's face with his fingernails. Joe did not mind. He was enthralled that he could hold a member of the new generation of Schilds in his arms.

Now that the war was over, the legal difficulties that had prevented me from applying for citizenship in Canada were finally removed. Laura, who had temporarily lost her status as citizen because of her marriage to an alien, had successfully reclaimed her citizenship after only a few months; I had to remain in a legal limbo for much longer. After a long wait, the released internees had been granted landed immigrant status by the magnanimous immigration authorities, but we could not apply for citizenship until the war was over. At last, on December 2, 1946, I was naturalized as a British subject in the Dominion of Canada. I became a citizen of the country I had grown to love. Canadian citizenship did not actually exist yet, so naturalization meant becoming a British subject. I was proud to swear allegiance to the king. Nevertheless, I was even prouder when, some years later, Canada shook off the bonds of obsolete colonialism and established Canadian citizenship.

Without naturalization, travel outside Canada had been impossible. I would have liked to visit my Uncle Felix and Aunt Bertha, Joe's parents, in New York. Alas, Uncle Felix, my father's only surviving brother, died of a heart ailment in March 1947, before I could make the trip to visit him. He did not live to see his son's wedding to Norma in June of the same year, nor, a few months later, Margot's wedding in their home.

After staying a few months with Kurt and Beckie in Macon, and sharing their delight in their little sons, Michael and Eddie, Margot decided to move to New York, where she would be able to live the strictly Orthodox life that she had chosen. In Macon, that was quite difficult. New York was home to many thousands of refugees from Germany and offered a better social environment for her. After all, she was now twenty-three years old. Uncle Felix and Aunt Bertha invited her to stay with them. Margot enjoyed her new environment, and was soon introduced to Joseph Schuster. His parents and their four sons, a highly respected Orthodox family from Germany, had settled a few years earlier in Washington Heights, a part of Upper Manhattan that was home to a large number of German Jewish refugees. They clustered around the Adass Jeschurun Synagogue, successor to the renowned Orthodox congregation in Frankfurt-am-Main.

Chapter *TEN*

The Homestretch

As 1946 PROGRESSED, it became clear in which direction I was moving. My final undergraduate year was to begin in the fall, and in the yeshiva, I was preparing for rabbinic ordination. My preparation for the rabbinate was not confined to the yeshiva. I relinquished the position of Torah reader at the yeshiva—I had moved from my earlier Torah-reading position at the Men of Slipia Synagogue—for a more ambitious job at the Goel Tzedec Synagogue, more commonly known as the University Avenue Synagogue because of its location on one of the grandest thoroughfares in Toronto.

The University Avenue Synagogue was the largest and most grandiose of the traditional synagogues in Toronto. It was this congregation that, in later years, joined with the prestigious McCaul Street Synagogue—officially known as Beth Hamidrash Hagadol—to form the Beth Tzedec Congregation, one of the largest on the continent. Goel Tzedec invited me to lead its Junior Congregation. However, no sooner had I started my job, than Rabbi Samuel Sachs, the very popular rabbi of the synagogue, was incapacitated with the throat ailment that ultimately led to his retirement. At first, it was expected that he would recover. In the meantime, instead of looking after the Junior Congregation, it became my duty to lead the service in the main synagogue and to preach the sermons when required. I must have done quite well. I remember receiving compliments from Mr. Edward Gelber, a congregational leader who played an important part in the community as well as in the business and cultural sphere of the city. He recommended that, after obtaining ordination from Rabbi Price's yeshiva, I pursue a rabbinical degree at the Jewish Theological Seminary in New York. No doubt his advice was very sound, but practical considerations did not allow such a detour.

In the spring of 1946, the pulpit of the First Romanian Hebrew Congregation Adath Israel became vacant. The incumbent,

Rabbi Abraham Kelman, had accepted a new position at a larger congregation, the Dovercourt Street Synagogue, officially named the Beis Yehudah Congregation. Rabbi Kelman, at whose home I had met my future wife, had also been a graduate of Rabbi Price's yeshiva. He had led the Adath Israel Congregation successfully for several years and was ready to move on to a more promising post.[1] In the eyes of the Romanian Jews, who suspected all others of trying to take advantage of the Romanian minority, he had learned to be a rabbi at their expense and, naturally, was now ready for something better. So the synagogue elders went back to Rabbi Price and requested a new rabbi. Rabbi Price recommended me. I was not quite ready to receive *semicha*, the rabbinic ordination—that would not happen till 1947—but, by the time Rabbi Kelman left, my ordination would not be far off.

A *probe*—Yiddish for an audition or try-out—was arranged. I would preach on the two days of Shavuot in June, in Yiddish on the first day, and in English on the second. Now it was serious. Rabbi Price helped me a little to prepare, especially the Yiddish sermon. I was confident. I knew what I wanted to say and how to say it. Indeed, I felt I had spoken well. The members had received me in a very friendly manner and had been very complimentary. Months went by. I had expected to hear from the congregation, but no contact ensued. The position was still open. Rabbi Kelman left before the High Holidays in the fall of 1946, but no successor had been appointed. I had been rejected, I assumed. Yet one day, I received a request from the congregation to officiate at a funeral for one of its members. Why should I accept? Laura asked. "If they don't want you for the living, why should you look after the dead?" I do not remember whether I conducted the funeral service, but I heard no further. My hopes sank. Were other candidates hard to find, or were they worse than I? Or did the congregational officers, in retrospect, like my trial sermons? The congregational minutes that I searched about thirty years later were amusing, but not very informative.

[1] Before long, however, the Beis Yehuda Congregation declined, as did most downtown synagogues. Rabbi Abaraham Kelman moved on to a distinguished career in New York City, while Beis Yehuda Congregation was eventually absorbed by the new suburban Beth Emeth Congregation, led by Rabbi Joseph Kelman, Rabbi Abraham Kelman's younger brother.

However, in the spring of 1947, the congregation contacted me again. They were considering me for the position.

I was invited to come before the executive for an interview and for a discussion of the terms of my prospective employment. I was certainly awed, but not intimidated. The members of the executive—all venerable elders to me at twenty-seven—explained what duties were expected of me. I would supervise the religious Sunday school, conduct the Shabbat and festival services, and look after the pastoral needs of the congregants. My trial sermons had been well received, they said. I would preach in Yiddish most of the time, but in English when there was a bar mitzvah or on the festivals when *yizkor*—a memorial service—brought out the younger, English-speaking members of the congregation. The lay leaders of the congregation were evidently resigned to the fact that on an ordinary Sabbath or festival the congregation would consist of members of the immigrant generation who spoke and understood Yiddish rather than English. The younger generation would only be attracted by the magnet of a bar mitzvah celebration or the remembrance ritual for departed parents.

Although this sad situation was accepted as inalterable, the hope for change nevertheless coloured the crucial question put to me a little later in my interview. "Are you sure, Rabbi Schild, that you will be able to attract our youth and the younger members of the congregation?" How could I be sure? From my experiences at the university, from my experiences in my own social circle, I had learned that I was pretty good at attracting other people and communicating ideas to them. Did I know whether those skills would be sufficient? I was sure, however, that I had to answer the question affirmatively if I wanted the position. Yes, I felt sure, I said. I know how young people feel and react. I will attract them to the synagogue. I will introduce programs that will interest the younger generation.

My answer was reassuring. All that remained to be settled was my salary. Unfortunately, this being my first, and so far, only interview, I could not negotiate from a position of strength. I asked—as Rabbi Price had instructed me—for the princely sum of $2,000 per annum. That would come to $40 a week, not too bad in conjunction with my salary as yeshiva teacher, which was about $30 weekly. "Two thousand dollars!" That was too much, the congregational representatives said. Fifteen hundred dollars, they countered. I looked disappointed. Mr. Joseph Donnenfield, the president, took me aside. "Look, young man," he said. "What do you really know about being a rabbi? You are just out of the yeshiva! You still have everything to learn. Accept fifteen hundred dollars, and the congregation will not expect so much of you! It will be better for you!" Eventually, we compromised. My first-year salary would be $1,500, but the synagogue would have an option on my services for a second year at $2,000. That concluded the session. A few days later a letter signed by the officers arrived to confirm the agreement. I was hired.

I could scarcely believe my good fortune. I was overjoyed, elated. Laura shared my excitement when I came home after the meeting. The synagogue was only a few blocks away from our home on Brunswick Avenue. Yet we felt also a pinch of anxiety, as we looked forward to a new kind of life: responsibility for a synagogue, meeting new people whose friendship and respect we had to earn. We were so much younger than most of the members of the congregation! Would they accept us, take us seriously? Looking ahead, I felt the pangs of *eimata d'tzibura*, the Talmudic term for the reverential fear that sweeps the heart of one who faces the public in a serious encounter.

My education was now essentially complete. In a few weeks, I would receive my BA from the university. Rabbi Price had already written my Letter of Ordination, although the traditional ordination festivity was not scheduled for a few months yet. I was married and the father of one child, with another on the way; I needed to make a living. Naturally, a position in Toronto was the ultimate. Unlike most young rabbis, I did not need to move out of town. I would have the opportunity to continue studying at the University of Toronto. My friend and colleague Albert Pappenheim was not quite so fortunate. He secured a position as rabbi in St. Catherines, Ontario, a smaller community, away from Toronto. Later, he left St. Catherines for Louisville, Kentucky, before returning to Toronto as founding rabbi of the Beth David Synagogue.

I had come a long way from the little boy born in Köln-Mülheim twenty-seven years before. No one could have foreseen the turns in the path of my life. Who could have predicted that this young boy so proficient in the use of the German language and so enamoured of its literature would make it his life work to communicate Jewish values and ideas in English and, for a while, also in Yiddish, in a land practically unknown to his parents? It was only much later, years after I had extricated myself from the uncertainties of Jewish fate, that I could, in retrospect, discover how the pieces of my life's mosaic were meant to fit together in a meaningful configuration.

Chapter *TEN*

295

Chapter *ELEVEN*

Life Begins Again

THE SPRING OF 1947 WAS A BUSY TIME. Final examinations at the university, held in May, were especially challenging, since I was completing my undergraduate studies. Ordination by Rabbi Price was not granted easily. We had to cover extensive sections of Jewish ritual law in the *Yoreh De'ah*, as well as their Talmudic foundations. The dos and don'ts of the rabbinate are not all found in books, however, especially not the demands made on the rabbi by a congregation in the 1940s. Rabbi Abraham Kelman gave me a crash course in "practical rabbinics," and initiated me into the idiosyncrasies of the Romanian Congregation.

In early June, Margot made her first visit to Toronto. We had an emotional reunion. How much had happened to both of us since our parting on January 26, 1939, at the railway station in Cologne! Only after the full dimension of the Holocaust was revealed had we realized how miraculous her survival was. She did not come alone. She was engaged now, and her fiancé, Joseph Schuster, accompanied her to Toronto. They came in time to attend my graduation ceremonies at the University of Toronto, to watch as I received my Bachelor of Arts degree.

Following my graduation, there was a hiatus. Suddenly, everything was suspended. Our son, Daniel, would soon turn two years old, Laura was expecting our second child, and I was a rabbi-in-waiting. My work would officially start on September 1, 1947. About the same time, I would resume studies at the University of Toronto School of Graduate Studies, to obtain my master's degree. My pupils at the yeshiva were on vacation. Thus, the summer of 1947 came as a last interval of relative tranquility. I was a citizen, free to travel with my Canadian passport! This was the pause I had been waiting for. I decided that it was my turn to visit Beckie and Kurt in their home in Macon, since they had been to Toronto several times to visit us.

Laura's obstetrician would not allow her to travel. Physicians were much more conservative at that time. So we made arrangements for Laura and Daniel to vacation during my absence in Belle Ewart, a popular resort village on Lake Simcoe. They would share a cottage with our friends Henry and Ray Wolf and their son, who was the same age as Daniel. The two toddlers always got along fine.

It was my first journey out of Canada. I went by train. It was very exciting to visit at long last the "Land of the Free." It had been our Promised Land, the country where our family had hoped desperately to find a new home when one was so sorely needed. Only Kurt had achieved the realization of this hope, and then Margot, after the harrowing experiences of Holocaust and war.

The names of the cities alone were electrifying and romantic, almost mythological, places. Detroit. Toledo. Cincinnati, where I changed trains. Atlanta, where Kurt and Beckie picked me up with their car. They were mythological places from my reading about the New World. I had read the tragic story of the civil war. "From Atlanta to the sea" was the refrain of a song I still knew by heart. And now to see Kurt and his two sons, to meet real Southerners and note their different lifestyle—what an adventure! And to ride in Kurt's car!

I returned to Canada in time to spend a few days in Belle Ewart. We enjoyed the country, as people referred to the lake-side refuge where they escaped the summer heat of a not-yet-air-conditioned city. We would spend a few summers there over the following years.

In September I made another trip to the United States. Margot was getting married on September 3, and Kurt and I stood by her side under the *chuppah*. A few years earlier, we had clung desperately to the frail hope that we might see her again, and now she was a beautiful, pious bride about to become part of a truly wonderful and admirable family. How fortunate she—and we—had been. It was a solemn moment, pregnant with deep emotions.

The visit had to be brief. I had to be back in my synagogue. Yet I managed to see a little of New York and to visit my relatives, the Kracko family, and my father's aunt, Sophie Schild, who had survived the Theresienstadt camp. Naturally I saw also Aunt Bertha and cousin Joseph Schild.

Some time later I visited New York again. The occasion was a visit to New York by my Uncle Willi and Aunt Else from Amsterdam. With the younger of their two children, Hank, they had survived the war in Holland, hidden in a cellar by Christian employees. Unfortunately, their beautiful daughter, Hannerl, already married, had been rounded up with the majority of Dutch Jews, sent to Auschwitz, and murdered with her husband.

Willi and Else Neugarten had been able to re-establish their ladies wear manufacturing plant in Amsterdam after the war, and were doing very well. They now wanted to export some of their products to the United States and were in New York to open a sales office that would be managed by their son, Hank. Naturally I was very anxious to see them. They had been hospitable to me during my brief stay in Holland in 1939. We had a nice visit. Their business venture, however, did not succeed. After a few years, Hank returned to Amsterdam.

My sister's wedding in New York on September 3 delayed the starting date of my rabbinical duties. I preached my first sermon on Shabbat, September 13, 1947, only two days before Rosh Hashanah. It was a desperate time of crisis for the Jewish people. More than two years had passed since the end of the war in Europe. The Holocaust was over; the killing had stopped, except for a number of Holocaust survivors who were killed in Poland while trying to return to their former homes. European countries were being rebuilt. Yet no solution, except immigration to America on a very limited scale, was offered to the homeless Jews who had survived the Holocaust. Still considered displaced persons in the countries where they found themselves at the end of the war, the Holocaust survivors had one uppermost wish: to go to Palestine and exchange their wasted lives in the displaced persons' camps for the opportunity to participate in the building of a Jewish society in their homeland.

Britain, the mandatory power in control of Palestine had drastically curtailed Jewish immigration. Its navy, patrolling the Mediterranean Sea, was determined to foil attempts at "illegal" immigration. Camps on Cyprus had been opened to detain would-be immigrants intercepted by the British naval forces. The agony of the remnants of European Jewry and the angry frustration of fellow Jews who shared their pain had risen to a fever pitch. Jewish leadership in the free world tried to mobilize support for increased Jewish immigration and for the Zionist vision of a Jewish state. In September 1947, pressure and resistance had built up to an explosive degree. World attention was focused on the ship *Exodus* that was being prepared in an Italian port to break the British blockade and land Holocaust survivors in Palestine.

Here I now stood, in front of my own congregation for the first time, trying to give vent to our anguished emotions and act as a leader called to rally my community. Only eight years before I had escaped from continental Europe. My emotions ran high. I felt empathy for the survivors and was furious not only with our antagonists, but also with Jews who could be indifferent to the ongoing struggle. I am sure that the intensity of my feeling exceeded my immature preaching skills.

I stood at the pulpit of the small but beautiful sanctuary of the First Romanian Hebrew Congregation Adath Israel on September 13, 1947. I quoted a verse from Isaiah, chapter 62, the prophetic reading of that day, "For Zion's sake I will not be silent, and for Jerusalem I will not be still." From that moment on, I dedicated my service as rabbi to the recovery of the Jewish people. The congregation of which I was taking charge had to be committed to, and had to become part of, the revival, the restoration, and the vindication of the House of Israel.

Not many months later, the State of Israel came into being. Its creation and the turbulence of the first fifty years of its history remained tightly intertwined with my work as rabbi.

A month later, on the first Simchat Torah that I celebrated with Adath Israel, Laura gave birth to our second child, our first daughter, Judith.

Our daughter Naomi was born in May, 1952.

Epilogue

I Live; Therefore, I Wrote

I AM WRITING THE EPILOGUE to my memoir on the eve of Rosh Hashanah 5760, the beginning of the year during which—please God!—I will celebrate my eightieth birthday. As the great sage Hillel said, "If not now, when?"

My brother and sister are no longer alive.[1] My brother always wanted to write about not only the terrible years, but also about the good years of his youth: what made the good years so good and how did they turn so terrible? Like me, he wanted to be understood, and understanding a person requires some knowledge of his or her background. He never did write, dying too soon, at age sixty-seven, two years after he retired. My sister, once she was in America, rarely spoke of her harrowing experiences, her ordeal in the Riga ghetto, in cruel work camps, and on the death march during the last weeks of the war. She aspired for her family, and herself, a harmonious, benevolent, deeply religious Jewish life. I can only guess that she did not want the horrible past that she herself could never forget to intrude on her family and her new life.

What I have written was never intended as a Holocaust memoir; I do not claim the title of Holocaust survivor. My suffering was minimal compared to the suffering of those who survived death camps and murderous marches. Although my biography includes a bitter taste of Dachau, it is not a Holocaust memoir.

Nor did I intend to write a history of my time; I am not a historian. I have merely tried to describe events and circumstances as I saw and experienced them; how they affected my life, how I and my contemporaries interpreted their meaning and adjusted to them. I hope, however, that historians may be able to use my version of the events that had such a radical impact on my life as source material for their research.

---

[1] Kurt died in Hollywood, Florida, on June 20, 1979; Margot in New York City on January 22, 1991.

Writing the story of the first twenty-seven years of my life has aroused a dormant past and connected it to the present. Blurry shadows were sculpted into sharper images by their conversion into a text. Forgotten episodes staged an eerie reappearance. Have I desecrated the graves in which past events moulder in their restless sleep while they turn into nutrients for our subconscious—into the unreachable DNA of our souls that we pass on to our descendants?

Why do I not wish to continue my memoir beyond 1947?

I wrote in obedience to a mighty imperative. I have seen my children grow into adults with a matter-of-fact naturalness that was never mine. I watch my grandchildren defining their worlds according to their inclinations and their own choices. I celebrate happily the joys of life's passages with my nieces, nephews, and cousins, all sprung from the same roots as I and, in so doing, I marvel at the normalcy of their lives.

When a friend asked me why my life story finishes with my appointment as rabbi of my congregation, I replied: "Because there was no life after that!" Of course, that was a jest. There was a great deal of fascinating life for me in the second half of the century and in the exhilarating adventure of guiding the Romanian Congregation of less than 200 families as it grew into a veritable community of 1,900 families. But it was normal life; my experiences were similar to those of many colleagues in the rabbinate and of people generally, who have the good fortune of combining meaningful, creative, and fulfilling professional careers with the raising of a family and a rewarding personal life.

By contrast, the first twenty-seven years of my life were not normal, if judged by contemporary norms. They were extraordinary, unusual, unpredictable, and capricious. They were lived in a different world, a planet unknown to my children and most of their peers. Millions who had to share experiences similar to mine had their lives snuffed out; the experience itself precluded them from bearing witness to it. I lived—therefore, I wrote.

I have told my story because it is different, even unique in a certain way. When I started to write it, it was meant for those who know and love me—my descendants, relatives, and friends; those whose lives are so "normal" and natural.

Then it dawned on me that I must also write for others who, though their lives were similarly disrupted and fragmented, could not or would not write. I am thinking of immigrants of an earlier era whose adjustment to the new country may have been much more difficult than mine, or Holocaust survivors who arrived bearing the heavy baggage of their frightful experiences. If they read my story, it may become easier for them to accept the reality of memories that have troubled them. My story may help them justify their former lives and release them from the false shame, from the discomfort of feeling that the past requires an apology. It may help them, I hope, to reassemble the fragments of their lives and make them whole.

Finally, I believe that the very elements that make my story different also make it interesting, meaningful, and, perhaps, even inspirational, for others. I am accustomed to speak professionally with the goal of modifying people's thinking and behaviour. I call that kind of speech a sermon. I realized that the story of my young life is a sermon, too, and that I would like to address it to younger men and women beyond my personal circle and my generation.

I want them to know how precious their own lives are.

I have told the sweet and the bitter, the good and the bad, the trivial and the tragic. I hope I have told it with patience and reverence; I know I have told it with much love.

Postscript

*I*F MY INAUGURATION AS RABBI of Adath Israel Congregation in 1947 was so incisive a moment in my life—a new beginning, in fact—that I chose it as the end of my memoir, then my retirement forty-two years later and my assumption of the largely honourary post of Rabbi Emeritus should have marked an equally significant break in my life.

It did not. Retirement has not changed my life. It was the occasion for an exuberant celebration, thanksgiving, and anticipation. I slipped easily into my new role, because there was one. There was no void, only a liberating transformation, a delightful metamorphosis.

It was easy because of the graciousness of my successor, Rabbi Steven Saltzman, and the loyal affection of my congregation. I spend time almost every day in my synagogue study. My study on the second floor of the Rabbi Erwin Schild Wing of the synagogue—it was a new wing when it was named in my honour on my twenty-fifth anniversary as rabbi of Adath Israel—is even nicer than the one I had while serving as Senior Rabbi. I enjoy the continuing support of my secretary, assistant, manager, critic and, most importantly, loyal friend, Beatrice Solomon, who has worked with me for the last forty-eight years. I have ample opportunity to contribute, both in the synagogue and in the community.

In addition, I have time to travel, without any restrictions other than those imposed by myself and Laura. We try to make good use of that freedom.

I also have more time to write, to study, and to lecture. My book *World through My Window,* a collection of sermons, was published three years into my retirement. The present memoir has occupied part of my creative time over several years. Material for another book of sermons is coming together.

Lecture tours in Germany have become almost annual events for me. A faithful community of listeners and students waits to welcome me.

It is no wonder that the first ten years since my "retirement" have flown by.

During the writing of my memoir, I sensed very deeply the presence of my parents. I felt as if they were looking over my shoulder.

It was as if they were testing me to find out whether I remembered. After all, I spent only eighteen years with them, and sixty-one years have passed since our last good-bye. All the same, they would have been disappointed, had I forgotten everything.

I felt as if they wanted to know what happened to me; how my life unfolded after they received the last letter from me that I wrote in London in 1939. They could not have had more than a vague notion of my subsequent whereabouts and circumstances. I often had the feeling that I was writing my story for them.

Before I close the computer on my reportage, I would like to assure my parents that their genetic heritage seems safe. Although they fell victim of attempted genocide, their family survives.

Laura and I have contributed three children: Daniel, Judith, and Naomi. A fourth child, Esther, was born with a heart defect and died at the age of three months.

Our children have enriched us with eleven grandchildren. Of these, five are married. Great-grandchildren are growing up, and—God willing—their number will increase.

My brother, Kurt, and my sister-in-law, Beckie, have a generous share in the proliferation of our clan. They had four wonderful sons: Michael, Edwin, Leroy, and David. Unfortunately, Leroy died in his early twenties of bone cancer; Michael died at age fifty-three, two years ago. There are nine grandchildren and six great-grandchildren to continue the line.

My sister, Margot, the Holocaust survivor, very fittingly contributed the largest share of my parents' descendants. Margot and Joseph Schuster had three daughters, Hetti, Jeanette, and Beruria, and one son, Herbert. Some of their twenty-five grandchildren and their two great-grandchildren were born after Margot died.

I am glad to say that not only their biological progeny, but also the spiritual heritage of our parents continues to increase and to be enhanced. My parents' values of education, character, responsibility, stability, good citizenship and community service are being maintained by their descendants. Loyalty to Judaism, devotion to Torah, synagogue, and the Jewish way of life, and traditional Jewish piety flourish among my parents' posterity and bring new lustre to their memory. However, a small number of their descendants in the third and fourth generation are not Jewish. And although a few of their marriages have ended in divorce, their descendants do cherish family values.

My parents would applaud our firm connections to our more distant relatives: the families of my parents' sisters and brothers. Although many of my cousins are no longer alive, we have warm relations with their children and even their grandchildren. Thus our loving family network is spread far. We are in regular contact, by mail, phone, e-mail, and visits, with relatives in Montreal, New York, New Jersey, Illinois, Florida, Texas, Britain, Dominican Republic, the Netherlands, Germany, and Israel.

Inevitably, as time passes and new generations are added to our family's ancestral chain, there will be a loss of cohesiveness. Third- and fourth-degree cousins will lose contact. I hope that my memoir, read by future descendants of the Schild and Neugarten families, will inform them of their common ancestral roots. I also pray that the knowledge of their origins will encourage them to live with dignity and pride, and to walk with God in the world of men and women.

Index